ISLAM
AND
INDIAN CULTURE

Mohammad Shujaat

ANMOL PUBLICATIONS PVT. LTD.
NEW DELHI - 110 002 (INDIA)

ANMOL PUBLICATIONS PVT. LTD.
4374/4B, Ansari Road, Daryaganj
New Delhi - 110 002
Ph.: 23261597, 23278000
Visit us at: www.anmolpublications.com

Islam and Indian Culture

First Published, 2004

ISBN 81-261-1891-1

PRINTED IN INDIA

Published by J.L. Kumar for Anmol Publications Pvt. Ltd., New Delhi - 110 002 and Printed at Mehra Offset Press, Delhi.

Contents

Preface *ix*

1. **Introduction** **1**

2. **Historical Background** **15**

Old Traditions
Age-old Experiences
Muslims under Hindu Rulers
Hindus under Muslim Rulers
Sufi and Bhakti Movements
Public View
Two Nation Theory
The Prospects
Secular Traditions

3. **Distortion of History** **45**

Liberal Muslim Rulers
Political Strategy of Muslim Rulers
Overall Prosperity
Fall of Muslim Authority

4. **Impact of Islam** **127**

The Backdrop
Caliph's Idealism
Spread of Islamic Culture
Practical Religion
Equal Rights for Women
No Right by Birth
Rise of the Downtrodden
Respect for Hindu Culture
Political Influence
No Hereditary Rights

Sphere of Religion
An Organised Way of Life

5. Islam's Influence **147**

The Legacy of Hinduism
Other Religions
Aryans of the Vedic Age
Doctrines of Jainism

6. Development of Literature and Art **183**

Promotion of Indian Literature
Muslim Poet in Hindi
Influence of Sufism
Great People and Events
Iranian Influence
Art and Architecture
Musical Arts
Hinduism and Islam Together
Union of Two Faiths
A New Form of Art

7. Mahatma Gandhi's Contribution **213**

Mahatma's Philosophy
Constitution of India
Rise of Secularism
Constitutional Principle

8. A New Life for Dalits **243**

Muslim Mystics
Rights for Downtrodden
Backward People in Mainstream
Dalits Mustering Courage
Awareness for Political Rights
Special Status
The Outcastes
The Safeguards

9. **Evil from the West** 285

Legal Niceties
Interests of the English
Ethos of a Race
British Domination
Historical Materialism
European Concept
Teachings of Islam : The Answer

10. **Conclusion** 309

Bibliography 313

Index 317

Preface

India is proud of its millennia old civilization. It has a long, rich history of culture, literature and philosophy. Islam, on the other hand is relatively a newer faith, only one and a half millennium old. But, Islam, as a philosophy, religion and way of life came on the world scenario as a strong force. The first generation Muslims in their strides swept over ancient civilizations, like those of Egypt, Iraq and Iran.

Almost half of the contemporary world came into the fold of Islam, abandoning the indegenous cultures and adapting a new civilization, evolved and developed by the followers of Islam. But, Islam and Muslims underwent a new experience in India. Unlike other nations, Indians were not totally swept away. Instead they embraced the new powerful culture liberally, absorbed all the good in it and in turn also influenced it to a great extent.

The fusion of two civilizations and the interaction between two cultures, culminated into a unique confluence of two powerful streams and the outcome was a new compound culture—later to be known as 'Ganga Jamuni Culture'—the cosmopolitan culture, first of its kind in world history.

The experiment was reciprocal. Islam gave a lot to India and received in turn, an equal share. For instance, Islamic mysticism in India, is totally different from any spiritual order, elsewhere. Here, it was highly impacted by the Bhakti movement. Similarly, the new mixed culture produced rich literature, a new language and introduced new forms of art and architecture—termed as Indo-Muslim.

This book covers all the above aspects. It discusses very liberally and academically the influence of Islam on India and simultaneously enlightens its readers, on how an ancient Indian civilization moulded Muslims, before absorbing them in its social and cultural fabric.

The editor has accomplished a challenging task in presenting a small but comprehensive and exclusive work on a vast subject. He is hopeful to be acknowledged and recognised for this humble effort.

—Editor

One

Introduction

Although Islam came to India after it had played out its progressive role, and its leadership had been wrested from the learned and cultured Arabs, the revolutionary principles of the days of its origin and ascendency were still inscribed on its flag ; and a critical study of history might reveal that the Muslim conquest of India was facilitated by similar native factors as in the case of Persia and the Christian countries. No great people, with a long history and old civilisation, can ever succumb easily to a foreign invasion, unless the invaders command the sympathy and acquiescence, if not active support, of the masses of the conquered people. Brahmanical orthodoxy having overwhelmed the Buddhist revolution, India of the eleventh and twelfth centuries must have been infested with multitudes of persecuted heretics who would eagerly welcome the message of Islam.

Mohammad Ibn Kassim conquered Sindh with the active assistance of the Jats and other agricultural communities oppressed by the Brahmin rulers. Having conquered the country, he followed the policy of the early Arab conquerors. "He employed the Brahmins in pacifying the country by taking them into confidence. He allowed them to repair their temples and to follow their own religion as before and placed the collection of revenue in their hands, and employed them in continuing the traditional system of local administration. When even the Brahmins, some of them at any rate, were prepared to go over to the side of the mlechha conquerors, the social conditions of the country could not be very normal. Evidently, society was in such a disintegrated and chaotic state as to make the position even of the most privileged class insecure. That is usually the result of counter revolution. A revolution may be defeated by a combination of forces ; but that does not enable the triumphant forces of reaction to remove the causes of social disintegration which brought about the revolution. In India, the Buddhist revolution was not defeated; it was miscarried owing to its internal weakness. Social forces were not sufficiently mature to carry the revolution to victory. Consequently, after the downfall of Buddhism, the country found itself in a worse state of economic ruin, political oppression, intellectual anarchy and spiritual chaos. Practically, the entire society was involved in that tragic process of decay and decomposition. That is why not only the oppressed masses readily rallied under the banner of Islam which offered them social equality if not political equality ; even the upper classes offered their services to the foreign aggressor out of selfish motives. That shows that, while the masses were in a state of despair, the upper classes were thoroughly demoralised.

As regards the spread of Islam in India, an ardent admirer of ancient Hindu culture like Havell, who cannot be suspected of any sympathy or even fairness to the Muslims, gives the following highly interesting testimony : "Those who did so (embraced Islam) acquired all the rights of a Mussalman citizen in the law courts, where the Quran and not Aryan law and custom decided dispute in all cases. This method of proselytism was very effective among the lower castes of Hindus, specially among those who suffered from the severity of Brahminical law with regard to the 'impure' classes."

This is certainly not a very complimentary remark wrung from a firm believer in the perfection of Brahminical law. In any case, it is clear that at the time of Mohammedan conquest, there lived in India multitudes of people who had little reason to be faithful to Hindu laws and the traditions of Brahmin orthodoxy, and were ready to forsake that heritage for the more equitable laws of Islam which offered them protection against the tyranny of triumphant Hindu reaction.

In another place, Havell chooses to deprecate the spiritual values of the teachings of the Arabian Prophet, but at the same time makes a very significant statement regarding the spread of those teachings in India. " It was not the philosophy of Islam, but its sociological programme, which won so many converts for it in India." Of course, for the masses philosophy has no appeal. They are always attracted by a " sociological programme" which offers them something better than the given conditions of their life. And a bad philosophy, that is to say, a reactionary outlook of life, cannot be associated with a sociological programme which secures the support of the downtrodden masses. If the sociological programme of Islam found support of the Indian masses, it was because the philosophy behind that programme was better than the Hindu philosophy which had been responsible for the social chaos from which Islam showed a way out for the masses of the Indian people. By the above statement, Havell admits that even in the thirteenth and fourteenth centuries, when Islam was winning adherence in India, it had not altogether played out its social-revolutionary role, and that it was by virtue of its social-revolutionary character that it struck so deep a root in India. That is to say, even in its days of degeneration and decay, Islam represented spiritual, ideological and social progress in relation to Hindu conservatism.

Havell is a famous eulogist of Indo-European culture which he considers to be the noblest product of the creative genius of man. On the other hand, he has bitter antipathy for the Muslims. His opinion cannot be dismissed as biased against the Hindus. As a matter of fact, his bias is entirely on the side of the Hindus. So, if even a historian like him found distasteful things happening in India -in the past, conditions were very deplorable indeed. He writes : " But the victorious progress of Islam in India is not to be accounted for by external reasons. It was mainly due to the political degeneration of Aryavarta which set in after the death of Harsha ..... The social programme of the Prophet ..... gave every true believer an equal spiritual status ..... made Islam a political and social synthesis and gave it an imperial mission. Islam was a rule of life sufficient for the happiness of average humanity content to take the world as it is ..... Islam reached the zenith of its political strength at the critical period when the conflict between Buddhist philosophy and that of orthodox Brahminism was a potent cause of political dissension in northern India."

King Harshavardhan died in the middle of the seventh century. Thus, the political disintegration of India was a process parallel to the rise of Islam. The death of a king, however great, does not mark the turning point of history. The process had been going on for many centuries. The Buddhist revolution arrested it for a time, only to be aggravated, accentuated and accelerated on its defeat. Indeed, the monastic degeneration of Buddhism and its disintegrating influence on the entire Indian society greatly helped the Muslim conquest just as Christian monasticism had done elsewhere.

Commenting on Mahmud of Ghazni's invasions, Havell further writes: "The almost invariable success of his arms added immensely to his prestige and brought Islam many adherents among the uncultured warrior classes of the North Western Provinces to whom fighting was a religion and victory in the field the highest proof of inspiration." Mahmud's exploits could not but deal a staggering blow to the faith in the divinity of the shrines where the Indians had brought their offerings from times immemorial. Consequently, the religious feeling which found expression in the worship at the shrines, and the faith in their presiding deities were rudely shocked and inevitably shaken. In such circumstances, "religious feelings and spiritual instincts" induced the masses to transfer their devotion from the gods of demonstrated impotence to the more mighty one, the belief in, and worship for whom, incidentally, was rewarded so magnificently. For ages, millions had believed in the supernatural power of the gods worshipped at the famous temples of Thaneswar, Muttra, Somnath, etc. The priests of those temples had amassed fabulous riches at the expense of the believing multitude by virtue of their pretensions to the ability of invoking the protection of the powerful divinities. Suddenly, the whole venerable structure of belief and tradition collapsed like a .house of cards under the cruel blow of the invading infidel. When Mahmud's hordes approached, the priests told the people that the invaders would be devoured by the fiery wrath of the gods. The people confidently expected a miracle which failed to happen. Indeed, it was performed by the God of the invader. Being based upon miracle, faith necessarily is transferred to the most miraculous. Judged by all the traditional standards of religion, those who embraced Islam at that crisis were the most religious.

A critical investigation of the internal as well as the external causes of the Muslim conquest of India is of practical value today. It will remove the prejudice that makes the orthodox Hindu look upon his Muslim neighbour as an inferior being. Freed from preconceived ideas, the Hindus will lie in a position to appreciate the constructive consequences of the Muslim conquest of India. That will enable them to live down the hatred of the conquered for the conquerors. Unless a radical change of attitude is brought about by a sober sense of history, the communal question will never be solved. The Hindus will never be able to look upon the Muslims as integral parts of the Indian nation until they come to appreciate the contribution they made towards the emergence of Indian society out of the chaos caused by the breakdown of the antique civilisation. Besides, a proper understanding of history derived from a correct understanding of 'the successful advent of the Muslims in India, will enable us to ascertain and stamp out the deeper causes of our present misfortune.

On the other hand, few Muslims of our days may be conscious of the glorious role played on the stage of history by the faith they profess. Many may disown and repudiate the rationalism and scepticism of the Arabs as deviations from the teachings of the Koran. But Islam occupies a memorable place in history thanks to its original unorthodoxy and irreligiously made evident by the Arab philosophers, than to the later growth of a reactionary priesthood or to the barbarous fanaticism of the Tartar converts. Islam had played out its progressive role before it penetrated India. Its Rag was planted on the banks of the Indus and the Ganges not by revolutionary Saracen heroes, but by Persians demoralised by luxury and the barbarians of Central Asia who had embraced

Islam. Both had subverted the Arab Empire that magnificent monument to the memory of Mohammad. Still, it was welcomed as a message of hope and freedom by the multitudinous victims of the Brahminical reaction which had overthrown the Buddhist revolution and had consequently thrown the Indian society in a state of chaos. Neither the Persians nor the Moghul conquerors of India were entirely devoid of the traditional nobility, toleration and liberalism of the Saracen heroes. The very fact that comparatively small bands of predatory invaders from distant lands could make themselves the rulers of a vast country for such a long time, and their alien faith found millions of converts, proves that they did satisfy certain objective requirements of the Indian society. Even when much of its original revolutionary fervour had been overwhelmed by reaction, Islam still exercised certain revolutionary influence on the Hindu society. The Mohammedan power was consolidated in India not so much by the valour of the invaders' arms as owing to the propagation of the Islamic faith and the progressive significance of Islamic laws.

Even the fiercely fanatical anti-Muslim Havel grudgingly admits : " The effect of the Mussalman political creed upon Hindu social life was two fold : It increased the rigour of the caste system and aroused a revolt against it. The alluring prospect which it held out to the lower strata of Hindu society was as tempting as it was to the Beduins of the desert ..... (It) made the Sudra a free man and potentially a Lord of the Brahmins. Like the Renaissance of Europe, it stirred up the intellectual waters, produced many strong men, and some men of striking originality of genius. Like the Renaissance also, it was essentially a city cult; it made the nomads leave his tent and the Sudra abandon his village. It developed a type of humanity full of joie de vivre."

To the above highly illuminating statement. It may only be added that the rise of reformers like Kabir, Nanak, Tukaram, Chaitanya, etc, who evidenced a popular revolt against Brahminical orthodoxy, was to a great extent promoted by the social effects of Mohammedan conquest.

In view of this realistic reading of history, Hindu superciliousness towards the religion and culture of the Muslims is absurd. It insults history and injures the political future of our country. Learning from the Muslims, Europe became the leader of modern civilisation. Even today, her best sons are not ashamed of the past indebtedness. Unfortunately, India could not fully benefit by the heritage of Islamic culture, because she did not deserve the distinction. Now, in the throes of a belated Renaissance, Indians, both Hindus and Muslims, could profitably draw inspiration from that memorable chapter of human history. Knowledge of Islam's contribution to human culture and proper appreciation of the historical value of that contribution would shock the Hindus out of their arrogant self-satisfaction, and cure the narrow mindedness of the Muslims of our day by bringing them face to face with the true spirit of the faith they profess.

India during the seventh and eighth centuries A.D. was still a fabulous land, vast, rich and powerful. The Islamic conquest of Persia brought the Zoroastrain sect fleeing to India for sanctuary. The bond between India and Persia was an ancient one, not only racially but also politically. It must be remembered that during the time of Darius I, Shah of Persia, a part of Sind was one of the twenty *satrapies* of the Persian empire. The Magi, the Persian priestly class, were widely respected and many of them had settled down in Western India; the ancestry of a class of sun-worshipping Brahmins can be traced to the Magi of Persia. It is not surprising, therefore, that the Zoroastrians when in distress, looked to this country as a refuge. Even Hazrat Imam Hussain of revered memory, on the eve of the Battle of Kerbala, had sought retreat to India on emigration to avoid bloodshed. There existed cultural and commercial link between India and Arabia in the pre-Islamic era. The Arabs were intrepid sailors and they came to India to barter Arabian steeds for Indian goods, and purchase sea-faring boats of Indian make for which India remained famous form to the beginning of 19th century. India had a fairly widespread colony in Central Asia along the Oxus region down to the borders of Persia. It is testified by Hiuen Tsang, the Chinese traveller, that Khorasan was studded with Buddhist monasteries and Hindu temples and it was more or less a Hindu city as he passed through the region in 643 A.D. on his way back to China. A kind of Buddhism was the universal religion of the nomadic tribes between the shores of the Caspian Sea and the Wall of China. All these monasteries and temples now lie buried under the sands of Takatmakan desert. With the Islamic conquest of Persia, no doubt, the scenario changed, but the fact to be noted is that the Pathans or Pakhtoons are purely an Aryan tribe, and all their clans like the Afridis and Yusufzai are of Indian origin, However, even after Islam had firmly established itself in the region, the Buddhistic and Hindu influence lingered for a long time. Then, again, the Abbasid Caliphs had emerged as great patrons of learning and encouraged free enquiry. While Plato, Aristotle, and other Greek philosophers were studied (in Arabic, translations from Syriac in which the Nestorian Christians had translated them from original Greek in fifth century A.D.) Hindu scholars were invited to teach and hold discussions with their Muslim counterparts in Mesopotamia, Junde Shapur, Damascus and Baghdad which had grown as seats of learning of international standing. Both Indian sciences and the mystical lore of Yoga were taught and discussed. The Paramukhs of the Nava Vihara of Transoxiana became prime ministers, Baramkas, of the Abbasid Caliphs and they invited Hindu physicians, astronomers, and scientists to Baghdad and encouraged the translation of Sanskrit treatises into Arabic. Further, Arabic scholars and scientists were encouraged to go to India to garner the wisdom of the east. Thus, Abu Ma'shar came to Benares and studied astronomy there for ten years.

There was, therefore, no in-built hostility between Islamic world of Arabia and Mesopotamia, the cradle of Islamic civilization, and Hindu thought and culture of India which the Abbasid rulers systematically tried to understand and foster. The Caliphs, however, had shed the simple and austere Arab style of life and were permeated with Iranian culture, having adopted the manner and etiquette of the Iranian court. The first four Caliphs, the Righteous Caliphs, were, in fact, leaders in spiritual matters as well as in secular functions; they were Imams of Muslim brotherhood, Amir-ul-Mominin as well as of the Muslim state.

But this ideal state, the state in which the church was the state and the state the church, lasted hardly for thirty years which was the golden period of Islamic brotherhood. The Umaiyyads who followed began to function merely as heads of state; the Imamat went by default. The Abbasids, with a vast empire to govern took to kingly ways and courtly manners and surrounded themselves with pomp and pageantry and Khilafat became more an emblem of power than of service.

This had a farreaching effect on Iran. Their language, rich and sonorous, with traditions dating from antiquity and a culture in certain ways superior to and different from that of nomadic Arabia and pastoral Mesopotamia, gave to the Iranians the distinct personality in the comity of Islamic brotherhood which has persisted till today. The Iranians had accepted Muslim faith, but had not broken away from their past which remained alive in their memories, and continued to shape their way of life. Their contribution to the development of Arabic literature and Muslim theology and philosophy, was perhaps more than of the Arabs themselves and they never considered themselves camp-followers of the Arabs with whom Islamic faith had originated; they always remembered their pre-Islamic glorious past which gave them individuality and an identity of their own. Islam had thus eliminated ethnic or territorial bounds and ushered in an international society.

The expansion of Islam in Central Asia brought more and more tribes into its fold. Foremost amongst them were the Turks of Central Asia, who, though professing a kind of loose Buddhism since the days of Kanishka, had, nevertheless, a strong affinity, both racial and linguistic, with Iran, which exercised a kind of cultural sway over them. Unfortunately, India had never made any effort to woo them, as a central agency, unlike Iran, no longer existed in India. The Shahiya dynasty of Udabanda, a dynasty of sixty generations of rulers since the seventh century, ruling over Kabul and part of the Punjab was in the nature of a frontier sentinel of India, but it had neither the magnetic grandeur, nor the sweeping attraction of Iran to exercise a pull over the Turkish tribals even though the Turks professed largely the same religion as the Shahaiyas. The Palas, the Rashtrakutas, the Pratiharas, the Cholas, and the Chauhans, though magnificent in their own way, were engaged on the main land in bloody wars and petty quarrels among themselves to show their *parakram*, and were too busy to take note of the storm that was gathering on the western frontier land mass of India in the beginning of the second millenium of the Christian era. The nomadic tribes of Central Asia after their conversion to Islam were being knit together into a collective brotherhood and with their war-like lifestyle and their economic need for new resources and new pastures had, of necessity, to look to fabulous India for expansion, conquest and immigration. Forgetting their past Indian link completely, of which they were perhaps never an organic part, they sought to be Iranised culturally. The myths and fables of Iran became their myths and fables, the exploits of Iran their inspiration and the failures of Iran their tragedy. They became Muslim by faith but Iranian in spirit.

The Ghaznavids, who established their Sultanate in Ghazni, and specially, Sultan Mahmud, initiated the trends of Iranian renaissance in Central Asia. Though of Turanian origin, Sultan Mahmud sought revival of the Persian language, fostered Persian literature and resuscitated the glories of ancient Iran. *Shahnama* by Firdausi, one of the greatest Persian poets, was composed at his command and the exploits of *Darius and Khosrus, Sohrab and Rustam* were recalled with pride. It was not Khalid, the Islamic commander, conqueror of Persia for Islam, who was their typical hero; the romantic Sohrab and Rustam of ancient Iran were the heroes. Sultan Mahmud subdued the hostile Turks and routed the hordes under Elkhan and Sejuqs. His numerous raids into India, the sacking of the Somnath temple in Gujarat, his establishing supremacy in the north-west India in the Punjab, raiding Mathura and seizing Kanauj coincided with the sacking of Patliputra by the Cholas of the South. The Cholas had developed into a great maritime power and fought almost a hundred years war with the Shailendras of Java for supremacy on the Indian Ocean. Rajendra Chola overran Orissa, Southern Kosala (modern Madhya Pradesh), Western-Eastern Bengal, and appeared before Patliputra by way of the Ganges and humbled Mahipal, the Pala king. These events occurred between 1021 and 1025 A.D., while the sack of Kanauj and of Somnath by Mahamud Ghazni took place in 1028 A.D. The beginning of the eleventh century thus saw the whole Gangetic valley ravaged and bleeding, pillaged both from the east as well as the west. Though these forays were not in the nature of any permanent conquest, the resultant violence were terrible. While Sultan Mahmud destroyed the western rampart of the country erected by the Shahaya kings, the Cholas dealt a death-blow to the Magadhan supremacy in the east. The sun of Magadhan splendour shining for more than a thousand years had finally set. Patliputra, from where imperial edicts were sent to the far corners of India and to distant lands was reduced to a ghost of her former self. Magadh thereafter almost ceased to count in the politics of the country and was taken over by adventurer-princes from province of Karnat who along with their retinue settled in Bihar, Mithila and Nepal in large numbers.

The whole of the Gangetic valley from Patliputra to the banks of the Indus now became unprotected, so much so, that though the Kalchuris, Gahadvals and Chauhans tried to fill in the vacuum, they were unable to protect the countryside from occasional raiders from the west. The Kalchuri king, Gangey, who was a devout Saiva, took over the holy city of Banares from the Palas, but was unable to protect it from being plundered by Ahmad Alptgin, the Governor of Punjab under the Ghazanavis, who could come unmolested all the way from the Punjab to Banares. After plundering the city for almost a day, his forces could go back safely along with the loot. Similarly, the Pala king, Neyapal, was unable to protect Gaya from raids by Karna, son of the Kalchuri prince, Gangey, who retreated only after intervention of Atish Dipankar, the great Buddhist monk of international fame. Authority in this entire region had collapsed completely, and north India had ceased to be governed effectively, whether by the remnants of the Pala kings, or by their successor Sena princes from the south or by Kalchuris from the Madhyadesh, or by Gahadvala or Chauhan princes. It is thus on record that for about 200 years, this state of affairs continued, the country sinking fast, politically, and spiritually. The institutional systems were in disarray, corruption was creeping and eating into the vitals of social and religious life, and the grit which makes the life of a nation was getting sapped. The Gangetic valley, or say, Hindustan, as the invaders from the west termed it, was now a prize to be claimed by anyone who was old, enterprising and resourceful.

It would thus appear that the Sultanate at Delhi established in 1206 A.D. after the defeat of the Chauhan king, Prithviraj, did not arise in the name of Islam or for the sake of Islam, as Persia or Egypt or Syria which had been won in the early days of Islamic expansion. The Delhi Sultanate was a result of fortunes of war undertaken for territorial aggrandizement by Muhammad Ghori. The fact that Islamic divines came along with the invading hordes, together with nobles, adventurers, and other camp followers does not make the conquest Islamic in the sense of a rising religious militarism achieving triumph over native religions of the invaded country. Islam could not have come to conquer India in order to convert the Indian people as this was not possible in a land of diverse faiths and numerous religious inclinations. That the raider from across the land in the person of Sultan Mahmud of Ghazni was a Muslim and had looted the temple of Somnath was in conformity with the practice of war prevailing in the world in medieval times. The Hindu mind could not conceive it at that time as an attack on their religion. Thus, no antipathy against Islam as a religion was generated in Indian mind following the assault on Somnath temple: this is a historical fact to be reckoned with. Later on, in the very city of Somnath, King Arjun of Gujarat had not only permitted a mosque to be built by Muslim traders from Ormuz, an Arabian port on Persian Gulf, but also made endowments for its upkeep. He had further ordained that any surplus after meeting the expenses of the mosque had to be made over to the holy cities of Mecca and Medina. An instance like this would show that the later-day interpretation of Mahmud's onslaught on the temple was nurtured with the stereo-type perception, developed particularly after the advent of the British, of Hindus and Muslims as the two warring groups of India.

There remained a constant contact, commercial and cultural, between Muslim foreigners and the indigenous Hindus. It was through such cultural contacts that Islam could spread itself in India. Islam lead a peaceful penetration in India. While an insignificant number of people could have been proselytized due to courtly or official influence, the vast masses of Muslims of Indian origin had accepted Islam voluntarily. This is not different from the way the Indian upper middle class was adopting western life-style when the country came to be ruled by the British in order to come closer to foreigners who were in authority. This is a story which requires some detailed discussion.

Two

Historical Background

A great deal of ambiguity and some amount of misconception, prevails about what exactly is meant by 'secularism', as also 'communalism'. According to the dictionary, 'secularism' would mean exclusion or rejection of religion, something close to atheism. Why did this English word acquire such a meaning? For this, there are historical reasons. In the European societies, down to the 18th century, there was only one choice, either to accept religious faith (as practised by the ruler) as the controlling power over all areas of human activity, that is social, cultural and political, or be irreligious and godless. Adhering to a religion, without allowing it such controlling power, was incomprehensible to the Western mind. Thus, Protestants, Catholics, Puritans, Calvinists, Huguenots, Anglicans and several others were treated like unlawful assemblies subject to persecution, if the ruler happened to belong to another denomination, even though, these were branches of the same religion. Even pioneers in science, such as Galileo, were not spared, if they made a scientific statement which was different from what was written in a religious book. During the five year rule of Mary Tudor of England (1553-1558) about 250 Protestants were burnt alive. Religion was so integrated with political life that the British King Henry VIII (1509-1547) proceeded to create a Church of his own, which came to be known as the Church of England. On the other hand, in ancient India in the Hindu and Buddhist Kingdoms and during the medieval period in the Muslim States, in India and elsewhere, state policy was not overtopped with religion and political power and ecclesiastical authority were not allowed to combine. In Hindu and Islamic societies, profession of one religion and simultaneous recognition of other religions was possible and permissible.

'Secularism' in the Indian context is antonym, or opposite, of 'communalism'. But what exactly is communalism? I would say that communalism amounts to setting up boundaries around social, cultural and political life coterminous with a given religious faith. Thus, all people professing religion 'X' would be assumed to be having not only the same religious interests, but also the same social, cultural and political interests. Consequently, all these interests of community 'X' may not only be different from but also hostile to the same interests of community 'Y'. Having thus bound a community, hand and foot, with multiple chains of religious, social, cultural and political interests, the communal mind ends up creating a tight collectivity which would survive on tension, anger and hatred against other collectivities.

Old Traditions

Indian society, however, since the very beginning, was able to set traditions under which an integrated social, cultural and political life was possible in a multi-religious, multi-ethnic and multi-lingual framework. Why was it possible for this to happen in India? The answer lies in the scriptural doctrines of both our major religions, Hinduism and Islam. Both these religions are monotheistic; that is, they establish the oneness of God and as a result of this, all religions are seen as just various routes for reaching the same destination. The plural character of human society is thus accepted and recognised. As early as about 1000 years before Christ - what we call the later Vedic period - the Aryans had moved away from the worship of natural forces - that is animism - and arrived at the conception of a single divine power. The doctrine of God's unity blossomed in full form during the Epic period. In the *Bhagwad Gita*, God - who is named Krishna - says:

> That is leave all religions and come to me (18:66). These thoughts are translated by Mahatma Gandhi in eloquent language : On Me fix thy mind, to Me bring thy devotion, to Me offer the sacrifice, to Me make thy obeisance, to Me indeed thou shall come.....

The same message is contained in a capsule form in Islam. There is no God but God. Hinduism, which is erroneously presented as polytheistic by Western scholars, admits of no compromise on the singleness of the Divine Being. In *Bhagwad Gita*, God, that is Krishna, issues a warning : Those who worship the gods go to the gods, those who worship Me come unto Me. Mahatma Gandhi has commented "if there were many independent deities who could act on their own, there would be no God." With faith in the oneness of God, the diversity of religions melts down into a social phenomenon. This is explicit in the Holy Quran. Consider the powerful lines in Aayat 13 of Sura 49.

> O mankind : we created you from a single (part) of a male and a female, and made you into Nations and tribes, that we may know each other not that we may despise (each other) ....

Here, diversity of mankind is held to be part of God's own design and, therefore, is not intended to be a cause of hostility but a cause of mutual understanding. In a secular view of life, there is diminishing utility of religiosity, that is exaggeration of religious forms and symbols, and a rising utility of man's proper conduct and righteousness. The meaning of religion, to a secular mind, would approximate to ethical values. This is brought out in the same Aayat in the Holy Quran.

> .... verily the most honoured of you in the sight of Allah is he who is the most righteous of you ....

These thoughts are eloquently voiced also in Aayats 111 and 112 of Sura-e-Baqarah.

> And they say 'None shall enter Paradise unless he be a Jew or a Christian', those are their vain desires. Say, 'Produce your proof if ye are truthful.' May-whoever submits his whole self to Allah and is a doer of good - he will get his reward with the Lord. On such shall be no fear nor shall they grieve.

Similarly, in the *Bhagwad Gita*, right conduct and fulfilment of one's duty is enshrined as the essential religion. In fact, the meaning of the Sanskrit word 'dharma' is not the same as of the English word 'religion'. Indeed, there is no Sanskrit equivalent of the word 'religion'. In the celebrated lines ... (4:7) God promises to arrive whenever righteousness is on the decline, in order to help good people and punish the evil doers. Religious philosophy of this kind raises religion to ethical heights and can serve to create a social environment in which all right minded people can co-exist irrespective of their specific religious persuasions.

Age-old Experiences

Coming now to the history of Indian society, we notice its assimilative character since the Vedic period itself. The Vedic Hindu culture was a synthesis of the pristine Aryan and the indigenous Dravidian cultures, which produced, as Prof. Abid Husain has put it, "a new common religion". This happened despite bitter conflict between the incoming Aryans and the native Dravidians of India. As always, these conflicts were by no means cultural or religious. Buddhism emerged, about 600 years before Christ, as a missionary and proselytizing religion, unlike Hinduism, that is, it was given to converting people into its fold. And Buddhism found a powerful royal patron in Asoka the Great, who used state power to spread the religion far and wide. It is still remarkable that there is little evidence of persecution of the non-Buddhist population, Hindus or Jains, during more than 40 years of Asoka's rule (273-232 B.C.). He is known to have dedicated some of the caves in Barabar hills, near Gaya, to Ajivikas, one of the sects of Jainisms. Despite being an active propagator of the Buddhist faith, Asoka declared in his Rock Edict XII.

> "If a person extols, his own sect, and despises other sects with a view to glorifying his (own) sect, owing merely to his attachment to it, he injures his own sect very severely, by acting in that way"

The Chinese traveller, Hieun Tsang, was in India for eight years (635-643) about middle of the 7th Century, and he found Hinduism and Buddhism co-existing on almost equal terms; the number of Buddhist monks and monasteries being similar to the number of Hindu priests and temples. He does not report any violent conflict between the two communities. King Harshvardhana (606-647), during a festival arranged by him, was found to be worshipping Buddha and different Hindu gods, one after the other. Hinduism and Buddhism were engaged in intense rivalry for predominant position in Indian society, and Buddhism finally lost in the race. However, it is interesting that by the time the struggle ended, Hinduism had adopted Gautam Buddha as the ninth avtar of God, in the same series as Rama and Krishna.

Imposing its own cultural or religious ideas and symbols on others has been totally alien to the Hindu tradition. The eclecticism of Hindu philosophy is best expressed in the words of its greatest exponent, Swami Vivekananda, who said. "I accept all religions that were in the past, and worship with them all. I worship God with every one of them." The French thinker and biographer of Vivekananda, Romain Rolland writes that for Vivekananda "uniformity .... spelt death. He rejoiced in the immense diversity of religions and ideas". The Prophet of Islam, Muhammad (Peace Be Upon Him) had similarly accepted the validity of other `messengers' who had appeared before his time. Kindly see Aayat 148 of Sura no.2 and Aayat 48 of Sura no.5 of Holy Quran where the diversity of faiths is declared to be an essential phenomenon in human society. Aayat 136 of Sura no.2 names other prophets who had appeared before Muhammad and declares : We make no difference between one and another of them. Similarly, Aayat 285 in the same Sura says loud and clear : we make no distinction between one and another of His messengers. As the major Indian religions, Hinduism and Islam, accepted pluralism as part of social existence, it is not surprising that the Indian society developed on secure, secular foundations.

Muslims under Hindu Rulers

The so-called 'Muslim' period of Indian history is deemed to begin in 713 A.D. with the conquest of Sind by Arabs under Muhammad bin Qasim. However, Arab settlers were becoming part of Indian society even before they were Islamized, as a result of the continuing trade and commerce between the Western Coast of India and countries in West Asia. After the advent of Islam, Muslims started to settle down in good number on the Malabar Coast, in Gujarat, and in adjoining territories. The Hindu rajas in these kingdoms extended to them necessary facilities and protection. They were allowed freedom not only to practice their religion but also to propagate it amongst the local people. In the 10th and 11th centuries, Muslim immigrants were being treated with respect by the Hindu rulers in the Gujarat region. A contemporary Muslim chronicler, Masudi, writes that, in the kingdom of Gujarat "Islam is respected and protected; in all parts rise chapels and splendid mosques where Muslims say their five daily prayers...." In the Malabar region, again, the Muslim settlers were treated with honour and consideration. Dr. Tara Chand writes that the honourable epithet *mapilla* was used for them; this word means "a great child" and it also means "bridegroom". They were allowed to ride in planquins alongside the Zamorin, that is the king, and were seated along with Nambutiri Brahmins. In the 10th century, these regions were traversed by Ibn Batuta, the Arab traveller from North Africa, who found the Muslims to be living there in a flourishing state. The Hindu rulers of Vijaynagar, during 16th and 17th centuries, assisted the setting up of various *imambaras* in their kingdom.

Hindus under Muslim Rulers

There is enough evidence to show that the character of the Muslim rule in India, from the 8th to 18th century, was non-theocratic and secular. This was evidenced at the very beginning when Muhammad bin Qasim, after completing the occupation of Sind, decided not to alter the social norms and customs or interfere with the religious activities of the Hindus and Buddhists. He restored the Brahmins to their previous position in administration and allowed their customary privileges to continue which included a 3 per cent share of the revenues. Under the Islamic law, the status of zimmis, that is 'protected' people had so far been accorded only to the 'people of the book', the *ahl-al-kitab*, that is the Jews and the Christians. The law was now extended so as to include Hindus and Buddhists, who became entitled to state protection. The seeds of cultural synthesis were sown at this stage. The Arabic script was adopted for the Sindhi language. The modern numerical system, which was a product of collaboration between Indian and Arab mathematicians, developed at this time, carrying the name 'Arabic numerals' in Europe and 'Indian numerals' in the Arab countries."

The Turko-Afghan rulers of the Delhi Sultanate, during the period 13th to 15th century, generally tried to keep state policy separate from religion and give opportunity to Hindus to participate in administration and pursue their religious activities. The historian, Ziauddin Barni writes that Allauddin Khilji "came to the conclusion that polity and government are one thing and the rules and decrees of Islamic , law are another." Babur, the founder of the Mughal empire, in his testament to his son, Humayun, said

> O my son! The kingdom of India is full of different religions. Praised be God, that he bestowed upon thee its sovereignty. It is incumbent on thee to wipe all religious prejudice off the tablet of thy heart and administer justice according to the ways of every religion.

Using state power to convert people to Islam was not on the agenda of the Muslim rulers. The greatest Hindu leader of modern times, that is Swami Vivekananda, had something to say on the question of forcible conversion during Muslim rule. In one of his speeches he said, "why amongst the poor of India so many are

Mohammedans? It is nonsense to say that they were converted by the sword; it was to gain liberty from the Zamindars and the priests."

The nature of the military conflicts during this period is generally misrepresented. The battles between Akbar and Maharana Pratap, and Aurangzeb and Shivaji, were not communal in nature. All this was by no means a struggle between Hinduism and Islam. The causes were wholly political, and these armies had a mixed composition on both sides. The Muslim rulers had confidence in the loyalty of their Hindu generals, who were not looked upon with suspicion on account of their religion. Man Singh was a leading commander in Akbar's battle against Maharana Pratap and Hakim Sur, an Afghan general was one of the trusted officers in Maharana Pratap's army. Sher Shah sent his troops to chase Humayun under the command of Bramjit Gaur, and Aurangzeb selected Raja Jai Singh to assist his son, Prince Muazzam, in the expedition against Shivaji.

Sufi and Bhakti Movements

The syncretic and secular attitude maintained by rulers as well as common people (during the period 9th to 17th century) is evidenced in the upsurge of religious and spiritual movements led by Hindu saints and poets and by Sufi mystics. I would consider the so called Muslim period to be the most glorious period for the Hindu religion, for it was during this period that Hindu religion got released from the shackles of the priestly elite and was brought to the mass base in society. It was during this period that devotion to Rama and Krishna was brought to the doors of ordinary, poor and common people in the far-flung villages of India, through the vibrant poetry of Tulsidas, Surdas and many others, written in popular vernacular languages.

Co-existence with Islam was decidedly one of the important factors bringing about these moral and spiritual movements. A new emphasis on certain principles in these movements is easily traceable to Islamic influence. An uncompromising assertion of the unity of God, and of the equality of all men, cutting out the caste barriers of Hindu society, were two major themes in the teaching of these saints. These two happen to be the cardinal principles of Islam. Beginning with Ramanuj in Tamilnadu region in 11th century, preachers like Namdeva and Tukaram in Maharashtra and Ramanand and Kabir in north India, presented Hindu religion in a new light. Guru Nanak (1469-1539) is believed to have travelled to Persia and Arabia, and was, in any case, in close contact with Sufi saints in India. According to Dr. Tara Chand, "Nanak took the Prophet of Islam as his model, and his teaching was naturally deeply coloured by this fact."

These spiritual currents fused splendidly with the stream of preaching by the Sufis. The attachment of common masses of people to the Sufi saints was of very personal nature, which made awareness of the Divine Being a cart of their emotional experience. In fact, mystic experience is embedded in the Holy Quran itself, and as was pointed out by Shah Waliullah (1702-1763), the eminent Islamic thinker of the 18th century, mysticism may be treated to have begun with the Prophet himself. Sufi thought had developed as a tradition parallel to orthodox Sunni theology continuously since the 9th century, in Iran and in Arab territories. Nearly fourteen orders, or silsilas, had emerged; several of these developed to great eminence on Indian soil. Moinuddin Chishti (1142-1236), Qutubuddin Bakhtiyar Kaki (died 1235), Shaikh Fariduddin, commonly called Baba Farid (died 1265), Nizamuddin Auliya (died 1356) and Mir Gesu Daraz (died 1422) had large following in different parts of India. In Bihar, Shaikh Sharafuddin Yahya Maneri (died 1381) of Maner, very close to Patna, commanded respect of all communities. The cultural synthesis inspired by saints and sufis was best expressed in the colourful personality of Amir Khusro (died 1325). Prince, poet, musician and Sufi, his verses and his aphorisms became part of the vocabulary in common households, both Hindu and Muslim. He experimented with poetry written half in Persian and half in Brajbhasha.

Devotion to the Sufi saints provided solace to people in their daily life; belief in their spiritual powers sustained them through suffering and distress. Religion during this period was thus brought down from the high pedestal controlled by priests and mullahs and made part of life for common people.

Public View

Thus, Indian people over the long period of history came to develop a non-communal outlook. It is not surprising, therefore, that common Hindus or common Muslims are not communal by nature and in their daily life they treat one another with neighbourly consideration. Communalism has generally been the characteristic behaviour of the so-called upper classes. The elite groups advance their class interests through pursuits of political power and social dominance, in which they find sectarianism greatly useful. By skilful propaganda and rabble rousing rhetoric, they succeed in playing on religious sentiments of less educated people, and using them like fodder for the canon, they ascend the social and political ladder. Sir Sayyid Ahmad Khan made a prophetic statement when he said that Hindus and Muslims in India would like to live and work together, but this would not happen "on account of the so called educated people."

Even while the Mughal State was on a fast decline, the social synthesis achieved during the period appeared to be durable. The dominant picture of the eighteenth century is not that of the Hindus and the Muslims forming exclusive and antagonistic groups but their co-operating in cultural life and social affairs. Over a thousand year period, there is hardly any record of violent clashes between Hindus and Muslims in the towns or villages. The first sporadic incidents of the kind did not occur until the 19th century. If it is true that the two communities suffered always with pent-up hostility against one another, this should have exploded during times when administration was in a state of collapse, as during 1857 rebellion, or during the Quit India movement of 1942. In such periods of near anarchy, the people never lost sight of their common enemy — the British rulers —

and among themselves they maintained total peace and order. Such inter-community cohesion in India has been part of day-to-day existence; this has been beautifully termed by Riffat Hassan as "the dialogue of life", which has never ceased. The perception of a prolonged Hindu-Muslim divide through the ages arises from the traditional historiography which has ignored the role of the people in social development and exaggerated the role of the kings, the invaders, the ruling coterie and other dominant classes. In January this year, 12 students of Ramjas College, Delhi, made a trip to Pakistan. This was after the war-like engagement in the previous year between India and Pakistan in Kargil, leaving a trail of bitterness, and the hair-raising hijack drama involving lives of 160 Indians for which Pakistan was blamed by Indian leaders. These students did not find any trace of the fall-out of such hostility at the people's level in Pakistan. They were touched by the friendliness of students, teachers, intellectuals, shopkeepers and pedestrians. "We were leaving with rich associations, and memories of all those who spontaneously reached out to us, and made our short trip on a shoe-string budget so special."

Two Nation Theory

The creation of Pakistan is viewed by several scholars as an outcome of what they term as Muslim separatism. The doctrine is sometimes stretched so as to make it a part of the Islamic ideology. Nothing can be farther from truth. First of all, it has to be noted that the Pakistan demand did not arise from the Muslim masses of India. The demand was promoted by the Muslim League in late thirties when its following amongst Indian Muslims was negligible. The Muslim League leadership had remained almost unseen by the Muslim masses; it was composed almost entirely of big landlords, nawabs, rajas, talukdars and some professional lawyers. The League's following was so meagre until 1937 that during the elections that year, they could win only 108 out of the total of 482 seats reserved for Muslims in the Provincial Assemblies, that is, a little over 22% only. Muslim League, however, still claimed to represent the Muslim community and made a bid for partnership in the formation of Ministries, in UP and elsewhere. The Indian

National Congress spurned the overtures of the League on the legalistic ground that their electoral performance had been poor. Now, even though the Muslim League had not met with success at the polling booths, the fact remained that the Congress leadership, Mahatma Gandhi included, had itself accepted the League as a body representing the Muslim community for long and had been collaborating with it as such, by allowing the annual sessions of the two organisations to be held at the same place, in a sequence, with common membership. As far back as 1917, when their representative capacity had been even less then what it was shown to be in 1937, the Indian National Congress had signed the Lucknow Pact with the All India Muslim League. This had the active support of Lokmanya Tilak, known to be a leader of conservative Hindus in India. The Congress leadership over time had thus bestowed on the Muslim League coterie a sanctimonious representative character, "legitimising the role of self-appointed guardians of the faith" and closing their own channels of access to the Muslim masses.

After 1937, however, intoxicated with the huge voting support of Muslims at the elections, the Congress leaders acted like politicians about to become Ministers, rather than like statesman being able to see things in perspective, and on a wider horizon. Choudhary Khaliquzzaman in his book *Pathway to Pakistan* and Rajmohan Gandhi, in his recent work, *Understanding the Muslim Mind* have shown how the split occurred between Muslim League and Indian National Congress at this time. This was the signal which opened the doors of Pakistan. Rajmohan Gandhi does not condone Mahatma Gandhi's failure to intervene with the Congress leadership at this juncture. Gandhi's close associate, Pyarelal, refers to this as "a tactical error of the first magnitude ... made against Gandhi's best judgement." Seasoned leaders like Jawaharlal Nehru failed to consider the disastrous effect which religious slogan mongering could create. History is witness to the playing of the religious card for political ends again and again by both Hindu communalists and Muslim communalists. The same happened when Jinnah, this time, decided to take leave of secular politics which had been his hall-mark and create a mass hysteria for a separate `nation', using, like a brilliant lawyer, all possible arguments, including the name of Islam. Jinnah's outlook, all through, had been well known to be nationalistic and non-communal. Gopal Krishna Gokhale had referred to him as "the best ambassador of Hindu-Muslim unity." And in 1925, speaking in the Central Assembly, Jinnah had declared, "I am a nationalist first, a nationalist second and a nationalist last." He now turned his political thought upside down, pronouncing that "the difference between Hindus and Muslims is deep-seated and ineradicable." Bringing religion to the centre of political action, he called upon the Muslim community as "Servants of Islam" to perform the "sacred duty" of achieving the creation of Pakistan in order to save Islam. He led a vigorous mass contact programme all over India. The Indian National Congress too planned a similar programme, to go to the mass base of Muslim community. This was doomed to failure. First, the Congress leadership, right since 1917, had bequeathed to the League the right to speak for the Muslim community and now, they were already distanced from the masses by becoming part of Government. Only three years after these elections, Jinnah in 1940 got the Pakistan Resolution passed at the Lahore session of the Muslim League with an action programme for achieving a new state.

That the Pakistan demand had no real connection with Islam was demonstrated by Jinnah himself, when, as Pakistan became a reality, he promptly abandoned the communal politics he had adopted for a temporary period, and reverted to this normal, natural outlook on nationhood and statehood. Keeping religion and politics separate, he declared, at the first meeting of the Pakistan Constituent Assembly on 11th August: " .... In course of time all these angularities of the majority and the minority communities will vanish ... Hindus will cease to be Hindus and Muslims will cease to be Muslims, not in the religious sense, because that is the personal faith of each individual, but in the political sense as citizens of the state." According to Choudhary Khaliquzzaman, Jinnah with this speech, "bade goodbye to his two-nation theory." Indeed what Jinnah said was the same as had been pleaded by Maulana

Hussain Ahmad Madni with Sir Mohammad lqbal. "Two nation theory was un-Islamic", asserted Madni, and he called for *muttahid qaumiyat* that is a "composite nationhood". This indeed was the true message of Islam, being in the spirit of the secular politics sustained by Prophet Muhammad himself (Peace Be Upon Him) in the celebrated Constitution of Medina, in 622 A.D. The Islamic concept of nationhood had been lucidly expressed by Sir Sayyid Ahmad Khan when he said, "Remember that the words Hindu and Muslim are only meant for religious distinction, otherwise all persons .... Who reside in this country are belonging to the one and the same nation." Prof. Mushirul Hasan in his seminal work *Nationalism and Communal Politics in India* shows in some detail how Pakistan did not originate in Islam, or in Muslim separatism and was "more of an aberration, a historical accident, caused by a complex configuration of forces at a particular juncture."

The Prospects

What, now, is the challenge for contemporary India? The challenge lies in maintaining intact the centuries old secular fabric of Indian society, and preventing any damage to it. Cultural and religious chauvinism and divisive doctrine will spell disaster for the country. History has shown that a nation is strong, not because of military power, but because of social cohesion where every individual is able to put in his best towards national advancement. The Indian-ness of India is far too valuable a treasure to be squandered away. Mahatma Gandhi had given an early warning, when writing in the *Young India* on 30th April, 1931, he said : "Indian culture is ... Indian. It is neither Hindu, Islamic or any other wholly. It is a fusion of all ... and everyone who calls himself an Indian is bound to treasure that culture, be its trustee and resist any attack upon it."

This heritage is celebrated, for example, when three great Muslim artists, Shakeel Badayuni, Naushad and Mohammad Rafi join together to produce a beautiful bhajan when Pandit Jasraj sings and when Ustad Barey Ghulam Ali Khan sings......

Secular Traditions

Half a century ago, the founding fathers of the Indian Constitution had erected its societal fabric on the plinth of what can be compendiously described by two key-words - pluralism and secularism. The pyramidal structure of the Constitution was firmly built over this unshakable foundation so as to preserve the multifarious pluralism prevailing in India since times immemorial. The long-standing religious, cultural, racial, ethnic and linguistic complexities of the Indian society - overwhelming and overlapping as these were - required a Constitution that would protect the multi-faceted pluralism of the newly freed Nation. And, the Constitution adopted in January 1950 did provide the required protective mechanism and safety valves. Based on the doctrine of Unity in Diversity and Equal Protection Laws, the Constitution spoke, at the very outset, of a "Solemn Resolution" of the People of India to balance the "dignity of the individual" with the "unity of the Nation" and to secure to all among themselves "equality of status and of opportunity" as also "liberty of thought, expression, belief, faith and worship." This was a clear prefatory declaration of pluralism and secularism together being the twin pillars of the magnificent Constitutional structure. Dictates of these foundational principles were spelt out at length in several other provisions of the newly adopted Statute. In its Chapter on Fundamental Rights, Articles 14 to18 provided for the right to equality of persons, banning discrimination of all sorts based on religion, caste and race, etc. Articles 19 to 24, then, put forth personal freedom and liberties of all the citizens irrespective of their religious and other social affiliations; Articles 25 to 28 detailed the right to freedom of religion in all its facets for both individual citizens and the numerous communities and sub-communities of India; and Articles 29 and 30 referred to the Minorities based on religion and language and declared their cultural and educational rights. In the chapter on Directive Principles of State Policy, Article 46 talked of the "Weaker Sections" of the people and required the State to "promote with special care" their educational and economic interests. Each of these provisions existed in the text of the

Constitution as originally enacted. All this in itself was a clear recognition of the existence of various religions, castes and races in the country and a declaration of their absolute equality in the eyes of the State. Then, in 1976 were introduced two major amendments. While the Preamble to the Constitution now formally declared India to be a Secular State, the newly added Article 51-A referred to the "religious, linguistic, regional and sectional diversities of the people of India" and imposed on them a Fundamental Duty to "value and preserve the rich heritage of our composite culture." Two years later, another amendment of the Constitution introduced Article 38(2), referring to individuals and groups of people among the Indians and calling for the elimination of inequalities among both in status, facilities and opportunities. Read together, all these original and add Constitutional provisions relating to the societal structure of India and the rights and duties of individuals and groups of citizens clearly and firmly pointed out to only one direction - that of a multi-religious, multi-cultural, multilingual and multi-racial Indian society, of course interwoven into an innate unity by the common thread of National harmony and integrity. By the yardstick adopted by the framers of the Constitution and crystallized into its provisions, the Indian Nation was not to be just a conglomeration of individual inhabitants of this State; it had to comprise of two distinct categories of constituents. The two-tier commonwealth of Indian Nation would include, on one hand, every single citizen of India individually and, on the other hand, the multitude of religious, linguistic, cultural and ethnic groups among its citizens. The Indian Nation was, thus, seen by the framers of the Constitution as an enormous co-parcenary in which the individual citizens were also to be members of their own respective branches taking the form of religious, cultural, linguistic and ethnic groups. And all these groups, like all individuals, were to have the same Fundamental Rights to enjoy and the same Fundamental Duties to discharge. Such, then, was the Equality-based pluralism effectively enshrined in the Constitution and closely inter-linked with its unique concept of secularism.

The ideal of secularism, as thought of and introduced by the founding fathers of the Indian Constitution, was remarkably different from that known to some other parts of the world - represented by the UK, the USA and the late USSR. The Constitution of modern India did not accord any special status to a chosen religion, as is the case in the UK. At the same time it did not erect a "wall of separation between religion and the State", like in the USA. And it surely did not require banishment of religion from the society, as was done in the erstwhile USSR. Had it adopted any of those foreign models of secularism, it would have turned into mere oddities and ugly absurdities many other notable provisions of the Indian Constitution itself. We all know that the Constitution indeed conceded extensive religious freedom to all individuals and full liberty "to manage religious affairs" to every religious denomination or any section thereof, while it also entitled every "section of citizens" to "conserve its distinct language, script or culture." Moreover, certain specific religio-cultural traditions of particular sections of citizens had found protection in the initial version of the Constitution itself -notable among these being the Sikh practice of carrying swords and the Hindu veneration for the cow [Articles 25 (Exp1.II) & 48]. Then, despite its stress on the doctrine of secularism the Constitution, by an amendment introduced in 1956, sanctioned upkeep of Hindu temples in Kerala and Tamil Nadu out of the State funds [Article 290-A]. Notwithstanding the Directive Principle of State Policy for "a uniform civil code throughout the territory of India" [Article 44], two other amendments of the Constitution introduced in 1962 and 1986 accorded to the Naga and the Mizo ethnic groups statutory protection of their "religious and social practices, customary law and procedure and administration of civil and criminal justice involving decisions according to customary law" [Articles 371-A, 371-G]. All these features of the Constitution - whether adopted originally or added later by amendments - reflected the anxiety of its initial makers and subsequent developers to recognize and preserve the rich religio-cultural and socio-ethnic diversity of India. Special religious provisions for chosen communities also gave enough indication that protection had to be accorded also to the essential and established religious traditions of all the other communities as well; any discrimination in this regard would be hit by the Equality Clauses of the Constitution. Secularism by the Indian Constitutional standards was thus not a verdict on irreligion for the Indian State or society; it was only a call for the State's neutrality in religious matters and a pronouncement on the equal status for all the religions in the country. Most certainly, it was not meant to wipe out or curtail the pre-existing religious pluralism of India. A Constitution guaranteeing extensive religious liberties and having so many general and special religious provisions, obviously, could not have been talking either of an absolute secularism of the political myth now prevailing in some countries outside India, or of the religio-cultural Nationalism of the recent wishful thinking of some people in our country. Secularism in the Indian Constitution indeed meant nothing more than an absolute equality of all religions in the eyes of the State. Had it not been so, the history of religion-State relations in this half century of post-Constitution era would have been wholly different from what it has actually been. Throughout these years, the State has indeed played an active role in religious affairs; while religion too has in practice been allowed to play a role in State affairs. This two-way traffic on the road to religion-State relations has in fact not always remained strictly within the Constitutional parameters.

The societal pluralism of India, as fortified by the unique Constitutional concept of secularism, raised the need for the protection and development of all sorts of weaker sections of the Indian citizenry - whether this weakness was based on numbers or on the social, economic or educational status of any particular group. The Constitution, therefore, spoke of Religious and Linguistic Minorities, Scheduled Castes, Scheduled Tribes and Backward Classes, and made for them special provisions of various nature and varying import. Among these various classes of citizens, the Scheduled Castes and Scheduled Tribes were bracketed together and identified by the two separate Constitution Orders initially promulgated in 1950-51 and revised from time to time. Reservation of seats was provided for them in the Central and

State legislatures and in local self governments [Articles 243-D, 243-T, 330, 332, 334]; and special measures were sanctioned for them [Articles 15(4), 46, 335], making room for reservation for them also in the educational institutions and public employment. Proper participation of the Tribes in the administration of the Tribal Areas was also guaranteed by special provisions included in the Constitution. In subsequent years all Scheduled Tribes were assured cultural and juridical autonomy through their total exclusion from the scope of all the modern family and succession laws enacted in 1955-56. And special laws were enacted from time to time for the protection of both the Scheduled Castes and the Tribes against all sorts of harassment and atrocities.

Now look at the religious composition of the two highly privileged classes of the Scheduled Castes and Scheduled Tribes. The Scheduled Castes are by virtue of the relevant Constitutional Order of 1950 and its judicial interpretations, a religion-based class. Initially only a Hindu could, and now only a Hindu or Buddhist or Sikh can, be a Scheduled Caste; any conversion from or re-conversion to these religions results into losing or regaining of the Scheduled Caste status and all its attending benefits. Since Castes are generally identified by their vocations and are favoured with protective discrimination due to their social backwardness, their essential linkage with three chosen faiths is clearly a religious discrimination. The caste system is indeed an Indian social phenomenon and should be kept away from the questions of its origin in Hinduism and de-recognition in Christianity and Islam. This viewpoints has, however, never been accepted by any of the successive governments, and the Scheduled Caste status remains dependent on religion. The Scheduled Tribes, on the other hand, are neither identified with any particular religion nor does any change of religion on their part affect their status in any way. Large sections of the Tribal population of India, residing in various States, follow Christianity and three out of the 28 States are now predominantly Christian. Muslim Tribals are also found in certain parts of the country. Successive Census Reports of India until 1991 have listed over 50 different Tribes under the head "other religions and persuasions" distinct from all the major religions of the country. Not all the Tribals of the country have, however, been declared to be the Scheduled Tribes so as to be admitted to the benefits attached to that class of citizens; and there have been allegations of religious selectivity in this regard. However, some people and their organizations now believe that all the indigenous Tribal faiths are primitive off-shoots of Hinduism and, therefore, conversion of Tribals to Christianity is seen by them as an onslaught on the majority religion and therefore sought to be restricted. Providing necessities of life to the needy with an expectation that enamoured by the providers' humanism they would, embrace their religion is not acceptable to them as selfless service to humanity. Before the advent of Independence Hindu rulers in certain princely States outside British India had enforced anti-conversion laws with a view to controlling proselytization by Christian Missionaries. After Independence demand for a similar central law, though repeatedly made, were never accepted; but three of the 25 States - Madhya Pradesh, Orissa and Arunachal Pradesh - did enact such laws during 1967-1978. Their Constitutional validity was challenged. but was upheld by the Supreme Court. There have been, however, no reported convictions for the violation of any of these laws. A similar law is now under enactment in the Gujarat State Assembly. Attempts have been made, of late, in some parts of the country to formally convert Tribal to Hinduism, calling it re-conversion or 'home-coming'. Like the Scheduled Castes, thus, the Scheduled Tribes are also now being seen and projected as religion-based groups so as to keep the scope of the privileges enjoyed by them to chosen religions. This essential linking of both the Scheduled Castes and the Scheduled Tribes to particular religions to the exclusion of others is, in my opinion, against the letter and spirit of the Constitution.

Now look at the other weaker sections of the Indian citizenry, viz., the Minorities. As regards the linguistic minorities, the Constitution as initially enacted provided a protective mechanism for them, as it indeed did for the Scheduled Castes, Scheduled Tribes and Backward Classes, and also identified 15 select languages of India, now revised to 18. For the religious Minorities, however, the Constitution provided neither any identifying process nor any specific protective mechanism. This was indeed a silence zone in the Statute left to be attended to by the State in response to its obligation to enforce secularism and ensure equality of citizens and communities. Establishment of Minority Welfare Departments in some States and of the central and local Minorities Commissions and Minorities Development and Finance Corporations were the steps taken in this direction.

In the capital of India a Minorities Commission was set up in January and a Scheduled Castes and Tribes Commission in July, both in 1978 and by executive action. Attempts made to accord Constitutional status to both these bodies simultaneously, made twice during 1978-79, had miserably failed due to strong political opposition to the Minorities Commission. This Commission was initially given jurisdiction over both the religious and linguistic Minorities; but the latter were taken out of its ambit in 1988. The Scheduled Castes and the Tribes Commission eventually did get Constitutional status in 1990, while the Minorities Commission had to be content with Parliamentary legislation enacted two years later. For its work the Government identified, by an official notification issued in May 1993, five religious communities, viz., Buddhists, Christians, Muslims, Parsis and Sikhs - thus perpetuating the trend of identifying Minority status, rather the word Minority itself, with particular religions. This, however, goes against the demographic reality of India which is a large federal country having States and Union Territories as its actual constituent Units. The Linguistic Minorities are in any case determined at the State level. The same yardstick should in fact apply to the religious Minorities as well, since three of the National-level Minorities - the Muslims, the Christians and the Sikhs - are indeed State-level Majority in some parts of the country, and there it is the National-level Majority community which is a Minority.

By its 1992 Charter, the Minorities Commission has to evaluate the progress of development of the Minorities, monitor the working of the safeguards provided for them by the Constitution and the laws and recommend steps for their effective implementation, look into their specific complaints of deprivation of the rights and safeguards and conduct studies into problems arising out of discrimination against them and on their socio-economic and educational development. The SC-ST Commission has, under the newly added Constitutional provision, to perform more or less the same functions for the SCs and STs. When the National Human Rights Commission was set up in 1993, the chairpersons of both the Minorities Commission and the Scheduled Castes and Tribes Commission were made its ex-officio members. This was an implied recognition of the fact that the rights of the Minorities and the Scheduled Castes and Tribes are, equally, in fact human rights.

As the things now stand, the NCSCST (National Commission for SC and ST) has however wider powers and far superior logistics and work arrangements than the NCM (National Minorities Commission). Both the Commissions have been submitting annual reports to the Government. Their tabling in Parliament, now a statutory requirement, is often delayed for various reasons. As regards the Minorities Commission, none of its reports have made it to Parliament ever since its elevation to a statutory body eight years ago. The political party now ruling at the Centre and in several States has in the past been dead opposed to the creation and continued existence of the Central and State Minorities Commissions. It strongly opposed in Parliament in 1992 the proposed statutory status for the Central Minorities Commission; and its governments in Maharashtra and Rajasthan virtually abolished the pre-existing State Commissions in 1995 and 1996 respectively. In Uttar Pradesh only last year the State government scuttled the then existing statutory the State Minorities Commission by passing a special Bill to that effect. About the Central Minorities Commission, the declared policy of the ruling party regarding its abolition and merger into the NHRC has, however, not been followed due to political compulsions. When the party came to power in March 1998 the 2nd such Commission, constituted in 1996 by the previous government, was allowed to continue in office; and after the expiry of its tenure in November 1999 a 3rd such Commission has been duly constituted. At the State level, Minorities Commissions now exist in Andhra Pradesh,

Bihar, Delhi, Karnataka, Madhya Pradesh, Rajasthan, Tamil Nadu and West Bengal. The record of the central and the State Minorities Commissions in discharging its obligations for the protection of Minorities has not been uniform. They have acted differently in different periods of their history, depending on the policies of the chair. Ironically, the central Minorities Commission has been for seven long years headed by a staunch opponent of its own existence and purposes.

As regards the Muslim in India, a coherent reading of all the relevant Constitutional provisions makes it abundantly clear that Hinduism, Islam and all other religions have in this country absolutely the same legal status. Nothing that may be available to one religion, one religious community, or one individual, following a particular religion, can be legally denied in India to another religion, religious community or individual, following a different religion. It is this unqualified and unconditional equality of all religions, all religious communities and all individuals following different religions, which is the hallmark of the Indian Constitutional concept of "secularism". And it is here that Islam, like any other religion, finds its legal status in the country. Nothing more - but not an iota less than - what Hinduism and the Hindu community can have does legally belong in India also to Islam and Muslims, as indeed also to all other religions and their followers. This basic legal position emerges from the clear postulates and principles of the Constitution. Any State practice or policy that goes against it has to be regarded as un-Constitutional. Operating within the Constitutional parameters of Law Religion-State relationship, the religion and religio-cultural beliefs and practices should have a respectable place in this country. There is nothing in the theory of the Constitution that may compel a Muslim individually, or the Muslim community as a whole, to disregard the substantive teachings and the basic injunctions of Islam. The Muslims cannot expect this country to be run according to the principles of Islamic Constitutional Law. But the Constitutional Law of this country does enable the Muslims to adhere to Islamic teachings individually and also to manage their religious affairs collectively in accordance with those teachings. The Constitutional Law of India in no way restricts the freedom of Muslims to believe in strict monotheism, in One Unseen God, His Books and Messengers and the Life Hereafter, to adhere to the commands of the Quran and the Sunnah addressed to individuals, to say prayers individually and collectively, to observe the Ramadhan fast, to pay Zakat, to perform Haj, to abstain from all that is absolutely prohibited by Shari'ah, and to regulate family life in accordance with the Shari'ah rules.

The question, however, is what is happening in actual practice? Do all the Minorities and especially the Muslims, in fact benefit from the Constitutional provisions on secularism and Minority rights and enjoy, always and in all situations the freedom to adhere to the injunctions of their religion? Is the Constitution being faithfully followed in this regard? Let me state what I feel about it and have experienced in this matter.

The Constitutional parameters relating to the multi culturalism and religious pluralism of India have of late come under heavy stresses and strains, to the detriment of smaller and numerically weaker religious, linguistic, cultural and ethnic groups. Though there has been no dearth of just, liberal, honest and faithful interpreters, appliers and enforcers of the Constitutional provisions on secularism, a confused - and sometimes unconsciously partisan - thinking has often resulted into denial of what is legitimately due, or into intercommunity discrimination that is jurisprudentially untenable. In respect of the scope of secularism and National Integration, an attitude of selectivity has been adopted not too infrequently by the executive authority in disregard of the Constitutional stress on equality, and occasionally also by the judiciary unmindful of its inequities. Concern for secularity has, thus, not always been uniform. The Constitutional goal of secularism has often been considered more relevant for particular communities than the others, and for the rules of behaviour inside the privacy of homes than in public life and for the political processes in the country. Conflicting attitudes regarding the limits of religious liberty, have been noticed in quite a few situations. Most of these problems have arisen since the

Constitution used the expressions "secularism", "minorities" and the like but did not define them; made special provisions for chosen groups of citizens but did not spell out clearly enough their message that others too could be duly favoured with similar measures by its interpreters and appliers. These are indeed the zones of silence and ambiguity in the Constitution that need attention.

Among the various Minorities of India, the Muslims are an incomparably larger community. Their population now exceeds a 100-million mark, while that of the second largest Minority - the Christians - remains about 20 million; the 16 million Sikhs and 7 million Buddhists standing next in order. The Parsis, having a total population of 76,000 only and confined just to two western States are also recognized as a National-level Minority. Muslims constitute the majority in the Union Territory of Lakshadweep [94.31%] and in the State of Jammu and Kashmir [64%] as per 1981 Census. In three other States their population is much above the National-level average - viz., Assam [28.43%], West Bengal [23.61%] and Kerala [23.32%]. Number-wise, the largest Muslim population is in UP [25 million, followed by West Bengal over 16 million] and Bihar above 13 million]. There are Muslim majority districts in Assam, Kerala, Bihar and West Bengal and high Muslim-concentration districts scattered over six different States. The total Muslim population of India according to the 1991 Census is about 110 million. This is larger than the population of England and France taken together and the largest Muslim population anywhere in the world except Indonesia. Yet the Muslims are a Minority in India often treated alike, and sometimes even worse than, the other much smaller Minorities. This is palpably unfair and iniquitous.

The enormous Muslim population of India is terribly under-represented in all public services both at the national and State levels - while some other Minorities are often over represented. Their numbers in these services have been, and still are, wholly disproportionate everywhere to their population and is some times nil. The provision for "Special Consideration" to be given to the

Minorities in public appointments, found in Indira Gandhi's much talked-about 15 Point Programme for Minority Welfare has remained confined to the text of the law and has never been implemented to any extent. This Programme, adopted in 1983, is in its entirety an outdated and ineffective document. With its stress on the prevention of communal riots which also it has failed to control, it has not played any significant role in protecting the Minorities and promoting their socio-economic development.

The presence of Muslims in the general educational institutions of the country is also much below their population ratio - and is often found nil. Educational backwardness of the Muslims is both the main cause and the inevitable effect of their under-representation in public employment and resource-generating bodies. Especially, among the Muslim women of India the illiteracy rate is deplorable. In the two States with the highest Muslim population, viz., Assam (percentage-wise) and Uttar Pradesh (number-wise), it is 73.4% and 85% respectively. Though under the National Education Policy of 1986 the Muslims were declared to be one of the educationally most backward communities, no special measures have been taken for their educational advancement even during these 14 years.

In a bid to ensure full and unfettered participation of the Minorities in the educational resources of the country, the Constitution had made two very significant provisions both of which are now being distorted and often violated. First, Article 28 of the Constitution clearly prohibited compelling of unwilling pupils to attend chosen religious invocations or instructions in public educational institutions. Yet complete secularization of general education is an ideal which has never been fully achieved in the country; and in recent years the situation in this regard has been noticeably deteriorating. Of late there have been reports from certain parts of the country about alleged plans to introduce select religious practices and teachings in the school schedules and curriculum; and this has adversely affected educational prospects of the Minorities.

Second, Article 30 of the Constitution gave an unfettered right to the Minorities to "establish and administer educational institutions of their choice." In practice no other aspect of the Constitution has been so much undermined as this provision meant to ensure a proper educational development of the Minorities on a par with the Majority community. Legislative Charters of the over a 100 Universities in the country and the Statutes and Ordinances framed thereunder include no specific provisions to enforce Article 30. Education Codes of most States either include no provisions for Minority Educational Institutions, or their provisions on the subject conflict with the clear principle of Article 30. The provisions of Article 350-A and 350-B of the Constitution, relating to Education in and use of the mother tongue, are not fully in force in respect of the Minorities. Especially, those desirous of setting up Urdu medium educational institutions often face tremendous difficulties. Seeking permission to set up a Minority educational institution, or recognition of the Minority status of an existing one, often turns out to be a cry for the moon. Those asking for the implementation of this Constitutionally guaranteed Fundamental Right have to run from pillar to post often without any success.

By the St. Stephen's College verdict handed down in 1990, half of the admission intake in Minority educational institutions was virtually reserved by the Supreme Court for non-Minority candidates, and this was done assertively in the interest of National integration. No such corresponding arrangement was ever thought of for the Minorities in non Minority educational institutions - either those established and run by the Majority community [e.g., the chain of DAV, Sanatan Dharma & Hindu schools and colleges] or those of a general nature run under the State authority. Minority community students are often turned back from general educational institutions on the plea that they should approach a Minority educational institution; and no one insists that they must admit a reasonable number of Minority students also in the interest of National integration. All this is, clearly, not only wholly iniquitous and unjust but also un-Constitutional.

Moreover, the insistence of the State authorities for Scheduled Castes reservation in the admission intake and faculty appointments in Minority educational institutions is greatly hampering a proper educational development of the Minorities - especially the Muslims - although they are, by official admission itself, an educationally backward community. Various State Governments and the University Grants Commission have insisted that the reserved quota for Scheduled Castes admissions have to be adhered to also in all Minority educational institutions. Reservation for Minorities in general educational institutions is, on the other hand, denied on the plea of enforcing secularism. This is against the spirit and objects of Article 30 and also violates the Equality Clauses of the Constitution as it amounts to according benefits of affirmative action in favour of one religion-based class, viz., the Scheduled Castes at the cost of another religion-based class, viz., the educationally backward religious Minorities.

My submissions here lead to the conclusion that the Indian Constitutional concept of secularism is not always properly understood. It has often been misinterpreted to deny to the Minorities, especially the Muslims, what is in fact their due under the Equality Clauses of the Constitution. A lofty Constitutional ideal, which was in fact meant to prevent the hegemony of any particular community, and to ensure an absolute equality of all Indian communities in the process of National development, has often been put into service to achieve purposes diametrically opposed to its objects. The current stresses and strains on the meaning and import of secularism are further strengthening and enlarging this trend. The principle of secularism was not meant and cannot be used to curtail the legitimate rights of the Minorities as recognized by the UN Declaration on the Rights of Minorities 1992, and indeed by the Constitution of India itself if read by unprejudiced eyes and with a sense of justice and equity. Any special laws or measures meant to protect and safeguard the rights and interests of Religious Minorities of the country so as to ensure them factual equality with the rest of the society in respect of social, economic and educational progress will be perfectly valid under the Constitution which contains enough indications to that effect. There is a pressing need to revive and reinforce secularism in its original meaning as envisaged by the Freedom-Fighters and the Constitution-Makers so as to ensure, in its true spirit, an equal socio-economic development and educational advancement of all the communities of India irrespective of their numerical status. This will also be a step in compliance with the Human Rights and Minority Rights Declarations and Conventions of the United Nations to which India is a party, and will thereby enhance our National prestige in the international human fraternity.

Three

Distortion of History

In this vast land of ours have dwelt, since time immemorial, peoples of different races and cultures and into this land entered races from beyond the mountains and the seas. But the old inhabitants and the new comers, after they had struggled and fought, eventually forgot their enmities, made peace and joined in their common endeavour. Each epoch of such a fusion was marked by an efflorescence of culture in which the different elements were so cunningly mixed as to make one whole.

This unity of spirit has ever been conveying to the different groups and communities, which form part of the whole, known as India, the fundamental realization that although the waves upon sea are many and play of winds upon its surface gives rise to varied and even contradictory phenomena like calms and storms, yet the substance of this multiplicity and variety is the unchanging sea.

The socio-economic continuity is the distinguishing feature of Indian history. The harmony found in the many-sided cultures of the people of India stems from this source. Thus, although India has many religions, many languages, many races, its fundamental attitudes towards life have persisted through centuries and millennia. It is a remarkable fact that the socioeconomic structure of India, which originated in the settlements of the Aryans and their assimilation of the pre-Aryan inhabitants of India, continued without any radical change till the nineteenth century.

This unity of her history, her ideals and of her humanity is the living spirit of India. It is greater than any of its particular manifestations in time or in type. It underlines the multiplicity of our creeds and sects, customs and institutions, and art and philosophies. It underlines our historic failures and successes, our struggles and triumphs. It abides in the midst of these changes. It is this spirit which fused the pre-Dravidian, the Dravidian and the Aryan, into that ancient social organism, which found utterance in the sublime philosophies, beautiful crafts, the stirring arts, which make up the first chapter of our history. Rama and Krishna, Mahavira and Buddha, Chandragupta and Ashoka, Valmiki and Vyasa worthily represent the spirit of this culture. The monuments of Sarnath and Sanchi, the paintings of Bagh and Ajanta, the temples of Khajuraho and Bhubaneswar, the dramas of Kalidas and Bhavabhuti constitute the living memory of this glorious age.

The close of this epoch saw the impact of new races-Arabs, Turks and Mughals. The ancient culture of India came into violent conflict with the newcomers, but even before the political struggles had ended, our construction had begun. Islam and Hinduism, which appeared at the start, so antithetical, at last intermingled, each one stirred the profoundest depth of the other and, from their synthesis, grew the religion of Bhakti and Tasawwuf, the religion of love and devotion, which swept the hearts of millions following different religions and sects of India. The currents of Islamic sufism and Hindu Shakti combined into a mighty stream which fertilized old desolate tracts and changed the face of the country. It was in this spirit of India which achieved apparently an impossible task of reconciling the puritanical severity and awe-inspiring transcendence of Islam into the luxuriant fullness and abundance of forms and the intuitive perception of their immanent unity with Hinduism, and created those monuments of architecture and painting, music and poetry and love inspired religion which are the heritage of Indian history during the middle ages.

A harmonious study of Indian History, a study both wide and deep, seem urgently called for now, more than ever before.

The question arises : can we cut up history into little bits, and say : this is ancient history, this is medieval and that is modern history? The central doctrine of the modern scientific study of history, according to the great Oxford Professor Freeman's teaching, is the unity and continuity of history The theory is supported by Dr. B. R. Bhandarkar, who says : "We cannot divide history of India into the three water-tight compartment:, namely the Hindu period, the Mohammeden period and the British period. Nothing can be more absurd In the first place they should be either Hindu, Muhammadan and Christian, or ancient, medieval and modern. The first is a communal division of Indian history and should be banished from all history books for ever. The second classification may be resorted to for convenience of study, especially for the study of culture. But it should be invariably borne in mind that although in the world of thought there may be a temporary division of history for the sake of specialisation, in the world of action history ought to be treated as having a continuous sequence. This, in fact, is the basic idea of history, as any student of historiography will tell us".

Let us consider the facts that are responsible for continuously aggravating disunity, disharmony and disintegration between Indian communities. The underlying primary cause is misunderstanding This misunderstanding takes many forms and expresses itself in numerous ways. It inspires the interpretation of Indian history and makes it possible for extremists on both sides to press the distortion of historical facts and movements into service to uphold their different theories. The distrust affects our judgement of men and their motives and exaggerates every intentional or unintentional neglect into a deliberate piece of oppression, and every petty incident of a quarrel or suppression of a breach of law and order into a calculated piece of atrocity. This suspicion colours the whole outlook upon life; every little difference of customs, manners, modes of speech and dress, ways of living and of vocational pursuits is magnified into profound difference of culture, of economic, social, political and spiritual ideals. Is there any wonder that every clash of personal and of group ambition is regarded as a symptom of deep social cleavage and of communal and cultural disharmony?

The task is not easy, because unfortunately the histories of India which have been taught in our schools and colleges for generations past were originally compiled by European writers. And Indians have not yet succeeded in shaking off the biases inculcated by their European teachers. These so-called histories have produced indelible impressions on the minds of their readers and corrupted the springs of national life. They have laid emphasis on difference, and drawn pictures in which the relations between Hindus and Muslims bear most prominently the marks of violence, conquest, rapine and religious bigotry. They have presented the Muslims as destroyers of Hindu culture and traditions, despoilers of Hindu temples and palaces, and brutal idol-breakers who have offered to their Hindu-victims the terrible alternative of conversion or the sword.

It is hardly surprising that educated men in India, drugged with such poisonous stuff from the most impressionable period of their lives, grow up to suspect and distrust each other. The Hindu has been brought to believe that the Muslim period of Indian history, which extends over eight hundred years and more, is a nightmare. Not only does he feel no pride in it, but when he turns back his mind to find inspiration in the past, he skips over this long interval and draws highly idealized pictures of the golden past which lies beyond. The Muslim, on the other hand, having lost the power built-up by his co-religionists to a Christian nation from the West, and being regarded as a mere intruder by the Hindus, naturally feeds his self-respect upon deeds by which he won conquest and glory and completely ignores the remoter past which moulded his cultural achievement of which he sought to be justly proud. How British historians have used these sentiments would be clear from the following quotation from the well-known compilation, Sir H. M. Elliot's *History of India as told by its Own Historians*. The passage occurs in the general preface to volume I: "We behold kings sunk in sloth or debauchery and emulating the vices of a Caligula or a Commodus. Under such rulers we cannot wonder that the fountains of justice are corrupted: that the state revenues are never collected without violence and outrage; that villages are burnt and their inhabitants mutilated or sold into slavery; that the officials, so far from affording protection, are themselves the chief robbers and usurpers; that parasites and eunuchs revel in the spoils of plundered provinces; and that the poor find no redress against the oppressor's wrong and proud man's contumely. The few glimpses we have, even among the short extracts of this single volume, of Hindus slain for disputing with Muhammedans, of general prohibitions against processions, worship or ablutions, and other intolerant measures, of idols mutilated, of temples razed, of forcible conversions and marriages, of proscriptions and confiscations, of murders, and massacres and of the sensuality and drunkenness of the tyrants who enjoined them, show us that this picture is not overcharged".

A glimpse into official British records will show how the policy of *Divide-et-Impera* was taking shape. The Secretary of State, Wood, in a letter to Lord Elgin said: "We have maintained our power in India by playing-off one part against the other and we must continue to do so. Do all you can, therefore, to prevent all having a common feeling".

George Francis Hamilton, Secretary of State for India, wrote to Curzon, "I think the real danger to our rule in India not now but say 50 years hence is the gradual adoption and extension of Western ideas of agitation, and, if we could break educated Indians into two sections holding widely different views, we should, by such a division, strengthen our position against the subtle and continuous attack which the spread of education must make upon our system of government. We should so plan the educational text books that the differences between community and community are further strengthened".

Cross informed the Governor-General, Dufferin, that: 'This division of religious feeling is greatly to our advantage, and I look for some good as a result of your Committee of Inquiry on Indian Education and on teaching material".

Thus under a definite policy, the Indian history text-books were so falsified and distorted as to give an impression that the medieval period of Indian history was full of atrocities committed by Muslim rulers on their Hindu subjects and the Hindus had to suffer terrible indignities under Muslim rule. And there were no common factors in social, political or economic life.

Liberal Muslim Rulers

Now let us briefly examine the truth of these allegations. Let us see what the contemporary Muslim historians say : Qazi Mughis-ud Din laments: Although in the medieval period the head of the State in India was a Muslim, the State was not Islamic, the State did not follow the injunctions of the holy scriptures- the Quran, the Hadith, or the laws elaborated in the four schools of Sunni jurisprudence. It is a mistake to call medieval state in India, theocratic, for it did not function under the guidance of the Muslim theologians."

Almost everyone of the Muslim monarchs of India from the 13th century onwards expressed his inability and indicated the impossibility of conducting government in accordance with Shariat. Iltutmish, Balban, Allaudin Khalji and Mohammad Tughlaq were among the pre-Mughal sovereigns of India who questioned the suitability of applying Muslim law to India. Zia ud-Din Barni, a historian, in his *Fatawa-i-Jahandari*, says:

"True religion consists in following on the foot-steps of the Prophet. But royal government, on the contrary, can only be carried on by following the policies of Khusro Parvez and great emperors of Iran".

He admits that: "Between the traditions (Sunnat) of the Prophet Muhammad and his mode of life and living, and the customs of the Iranian emperors and their mode of life and living, there is a complete contradiction and total opposition".

But he pointed out that Shariat, which is command of God, could be followed in State matters only in exceptional times. Muhammad succeeded in enforcing Shariat because he was already inspired by God; the first four Khalifas did so because they had been the associates of the Prophet. But prophet hood is a perfection of religion and the kingship is the perfection of world fortune. These two perfections are opposed and contradictory to each others, and their combination is not within the bounds of possibility.

Nizam-ud-Din, observes : "Balban gave precedence to the affairs of the State over religion."

Barni states: "In the matter of punishment and exercise of royal authority he acted without fear of God and whatever he regarded to be in the interest of government, irrespective of whether it was in accord with Shariat or not, he carried into action."

Allaudin Khalji's discussion with Qazi Mughis-ud-Din is well known. His parting reply to the Qazi was: "Whatever I consider to be in the interest of Government, I order. I do not know what the exalted God will do to me on the day of Resurrection"

Prof. M. Habib says: "it is true that Muslim kings, mostly of foreign extraction sat on Indian thrones for some six or seven centuries. But they could only do so because their enthronement was not the enthronement of the Muslim rule. Had it been otherwise they could not have lasted for a single generation".

Now, let me give a few illustrations as to how the historical facts have been distorted.

While I was doing some research, on Tipu Sultan in 1728 at Allahabad, some office-bearers of Anglo-Bengali College Students Union approached me with a request to inaugurate their History Association They had directly come from the college with their text-books. Incidentally, I glanced through their history text-book. I opened the chapter on Tipu Sultan. One of the sentences that struck me deeply was:

"Three thousand Brahmins committed suicide as Tipu wanted to convert them forcibly into the fold of Islam".

The author of the text-book was Mahamahopadhyaya Dr. Har Prashad Shastri, Head of the Department of Sanskrit, Calcutta University. I immediately wrote to Dr. Shastri for the source of his information. After many reminders came the reply that he had taken that fact from the Mysore Gazetteer. The Mysore Gazetteer was not available either at Allahabad or at the Imperial Library, Calcutta. So I wrote to Sir Brijendra Nath Seal, the then Vice-Chancellor of Mysore University, seeking a confirmation of the statement of Dr. Shastri. Sir Brijendra Nath Seal forwarded my letter to Prof. Srikantia, who was then busy editing a new edition of the Mysore Gazetteer.

Prof. Srikantia informed me that the episode of the suicide of 3000 Brahmins is nowhere in the Mysore Gazetteer and he, as student of history of Mysore, was quite certain that no such incident had taken place. He further informed me the Prime Minister of Tipu Sultan was a Brahmin, named Purnea, and his Commander-in-Chief was also a Brahmin, named Krishna Rao. He supplied me with the list of 156 temples to which Tipu Sultan used to pay annual grants. He sent me 30 photostat copies of Tipu Sultan's letters addressed to the Jagadguru Shankaracharya of Sringeri Math with whom Tipu Sultan had very cordial relations. Tipu Sultan, as was customary with the rulers of Mysore, daily visited the temple of Lord Ranganatha located inside the fort of Srirangapatnam before taking his breakfast. Prof. Srikantia suggested that Dr. Shastri might have based his narrations on the so-called *History of Mysore* by Col. Miles, who claimed to have translated his *History of Tipu Sultan* from a Persian manuscript which was said to be in the personal Library of Queen Victoria. On investigation, it was found that there was no such manuscript in the library of Queen Victoria, and that most of the facts in Col. Miles's history book were concocted and false.

Dr. Shastri's book was approved as a course book of history for High Schools in Bengal, Assam, Bihar, Orissa, UP, MP, and Rajasthan. I approached Sir Ashutosh Chaudhary, the then Vice-Chancellor of Calcutta University, and sent him all the correspondence that I had exchanged with Dr. Shastri, with Mysore

University, Vice-Chancellor, Sir Brijendra Nath Seal, and Prof. Srikantia, with the request to take proper action against the offending passages in the text book. Prompt came the reply from Sir Ashutosh Chaudhary, that the history book by Dr. H. P. Shastri has been put out of course.

However, I was amazed to find the same suicide story was still existing in the history text-books which had been prescribed for junior High School in UP for the students of VI, VII and VIII classes in 1972.

In Young India, edited by Mahatma Gandhi, dated January 23, 1930, on page 31 appeared the following item

"Fateh Ali Tipu Sultan of Mysore is represented by foreign historians as a fanatic who oppressed his Hindu subjects and converted them to Islam by force. But he was nothing of the kind. On the other hand, his relations with his Hindu subjects were of a perfectly cordial nature ...The Archaeological Department of Mysore State is in possession of over thirty letters written by Tipu to the Shankaracharya of Shringeri Math. These letters are written in the Kannada characters.. In one of the letters written to the Shankaracharya in 1793 Tipu acknowledges receipt of the Shankaracharya's letter and requests him to perform *tapas* (i.e. to undergo self-purificatory discipline) and to offer prayers for the welfare and prosperity of his own realm as for that of the whole universe. And finally he asks the Shankaracharya to return to Mysore; for, the presence of good men in a country brings down rain and makes for good cultivation and plenty. This letter deserves to be printed in letters of gold in every history of India, and no apology need, therefore, be offered for reproducing Devanagari characters, the original Kannada, which is full of Sanskrit words, some of these being printed here."

"Tipu made lavish gifts of land and other things to Hindu temples, and temples dedicated to Shri Venkataramanna, Shrinivas and Shriranganath located in the vicinity of Tipu's palaces they still bear testimony to his broad-minded toleration, and indicate that the great martyr at any rate-for a real martyr he was in the cause of liberty-was not disturbed in his prayers by the Hindu bells calling people to worship the same Allah whose devotee he was. Tipu died fighting for liberty, treating with contempt the suggestion that he should surrender to the enemy. When Tipu's corpse was recovered from among the heap of unknown soldiers' whose fate he proudly shared, it was found, that even in death his hand had still clutched the sword which was his instrument for the vindication of liberty. Let us remember the following seasonable words of Tipu : 'Better a lion's life for two days than a dog's life for two hundred years and also the lines repeated at the end of each stanza of an elegy composed in his honour: "Ya Allah, it is better to die beneath the clouds of battle raining blood upon our heads than to live a life of shame and degradation."

Similarly, when I was the Chairman of the Allahabad Municipality (1948-53), a case of mutation (Dakhil Kharij) came up for my consideration. It was a dispute over the property dedicated to the temple of Someshwar Nath Mahadev. After the death of the mahant, there were two claimants for the property. One of the claimants filed some documents which were in the possession of the family. The documents were the *farmans* issued by Emperor Aurangzeb. Aurangzeb conferred a Jagir and a cash gift on the temple. I felt puzzled. I thought that .the farmans were fake I was wondering how Aurangzeb, who was known for the demolition of the temples, could confer a Jagir on a temple with the words that the jagir was being conferred for the puja and bhog of the deity? How could Aurangzeb identify himself with idolatry ?

I felt sure that the documents were not genuine. But before coming to any conclusion, I thought it proper to take the opinion of Dr. Sir Tej Bahadur Sapru who was a great scholar of Persian and Arabic. I laid the documents before him and asked for his opinion. After examining the documents, Dr. Sapru said that these farmans of Aurangzeb were genuine. Then he asked his munshi to bring the file of the case of Jangum Badi Shiva Temple of Varanasi, of which several appeals were pending in the Allahabad High Court for the past 15 years. The mahant of the Jangum Badi Shiva temple was also in possession of various other farmans of Aurangzeb granting Jagir to the temple.

It was a new image of Aurangzeb that appeared before me. As advised by Dr. Sapru, I sent letters to the mahants of various important temples of India requesting them to send me photostat copies, if they are in the possession of the farmans of Aurangzeb, granting them jagir for their temples. Another big surprise was in store for me. I received copies of farmans of Aurangzeb from the great temples of Mahakaleshwara, Ujjain, Balaji Temple Chitrakut, Umanand Temple Gauhati and the Jain temple of Shatrunjai and other temples and Gurudwaras scattered over northern India. These farmans were issued from 1065 AH (1659) to 1091 AH (1685).

Though these are only a few instances of Aurangzeb's generous attitude towards Hindus and their temples, they are enough to show that what the historians have written about him, was biased and is only one side of the picture. India is a vast land with thousands of temples scattered all over. If proper research is made, I am confident, many more instance would come to light which will show Aurangzeb's benevolent treatment of non-Muslims.

In the course of my investigations on the farmans of Aurangzeb I came in contact with Shri Gyan Chandra and Dr. P. L. Gupta, the former Curator of Patna Museum they have also been doing research of great historical value on Aurangzeb: It pleased me that there were many other scholar-investigators of truth who were contributing their share in clearing the image of much-maligned Aurangzeb, whom the biased historians have made the symbol of Muslim rule in India. An aggrieved poet has sorrowfully said:

> *[tumhen iedeke sarl dastan men yad hai itna ke Alamglr hindukush tha, zalim tha, sitamgar thai]*

(i.e., of the thousand year Muslim rule in India they remember only this much that Alamgir was a butcher of Hindus, and a tyrannical and cruel monarch).

While accusing Aurangzeb as an anti-Hindu monarch, much has been made of a farman, which is popular by 'the name of Banaras Farman'. This farman belongs to a Brahmin family of Varanasi (Banaras), resident of Mohalla Gauri. In 1905 it was produced before the City Magistrate by one Mangal Pandey, son of Gopi Upadhyaya's daughter. It drew attention of the scholars and it was published for the first time in the *Journal of the Asiatic Society of Bengal* in 1911. And since then it has, been often quoted by the historians. Without realizing the real importance of the farman, they accuse Aurangzeb of banning the construction of Hindu temples.

This farman was issued by Aurangzeb on 15 Jamadi, 1 1035 A. H. (10 March, 1460) to the local officer of Banaras in disposal of a complaint made by some Brahmin, who was the custodian of a temple and was being harassed by some persons. It runs as follows:

> Let Abul Hasan worthy of favour and countenance trust to our royal bounty, and let him know that since in accordance with our innate kindness of disposition and natural benevolence, the whole of our untiring energy and all our upright intentions are engaged in promoting the public welfare and bettering the conditions of all classes, high and low. In accordance with our holy law, we have decided that the ancient temples shall not be destroyed, but new ones shall not be built.
>
> In these days of our justice, information has reached our noble and most holy court that certain persons interfere and harass the Hindu residents of the town of Banaras and its neighbourhood; and the Brahmin keepers of the temples, in whose charge these ancient temples are; and that they further desire to remove these Brahmins from

> their ancient offices, and this intimidation of theirs cause distress to that community.
>
> Therefore, our royal command is that, after arrival of this lustrous order, you should direct that, in future, no person shall in unlawful way interfere or disturb the Brahmins and other Hindu residents at these places, so that they may as before remain in their occupation and continue with peace of mind to offer prayers for the continuance of our God-gifted Empire, so that it may last for ever. Treat this order as urgent.

This farman is explicitly clear on the point that Aurangzeb did not issue any new order against the building of the new temples. He only referred to the practice that was already in continuance and he simply affirms to adhere to that practice. As regards the already existing temples, he is explicitly against their destruction. The farman further shows that he was keen on his Hindu subjects being able to live in peace.

It is not the only farman of its type. Banaras has one more farman to show that Aurangzeb was really very keen that the Hindus should be able to live in peace. It runs:

> "At this auspicious time an august farman was issued whereas Maharajadhiraj Raja Ram Singh of Ramnagar (Banaras) has represented to the most holy and exalted court that a mansion was built by his father in Mohalla Madho Ram, on the bank of Ganga at Banaras for the residence of Bhagwat Gosain who is also his religious preceptor, and as certain persons harass the Gosain, therefore, our Royal Command is that, after the arrival of this lustrous order the present and future officers should direct that in future, no person shall in any way interfere or disturb the Gosain, so that he may continue with peace of mind to offer up prayers for the continuance of our God-given Empire, that is destined to last for all time.

> Consider this as an urgent matter. Dated 17th Rabi, 11, 1091 A.H.

> Some other farmans with the Mahant of the Jangambari Math, show that Aurangzeb never tolerated any encroachment on the rights of his subjects whether they were Hindus or Muslims. He dealt severely with the culprits. One of these farmans, refers to a complaint filed in the court of Aurangzeb by the Jangams (i.e., the followers of Jangam sect-a Saivite sect) against a Muslim resident of Banaras named Nazir Beg and the imperial order thereon says: "The officials of Haveli Muhammsdabad-known as Banaras Subah Allahabad, are to be informed that these days Arjunmal and Jangams, residents of Pargana Banaras, have appeared before (the Emperor) and have made complaint that Nazir Beg, a resident of Banaras, has by force taken possession of five Havelis, which they had in Gasba Banaras. It is, therefore, ordered that if their case is found true and the title of the complainants proved, Nazir Beg should not be allowed to enter the said Haveli, so that in future the Jangams may not appear as complainants before me to seek their redress.

This farman is dated 11th Sha'ban San 13 Julus (1672 A.D.)

The other farman in the possession of the same Math, dated 1 Rabi-akawwal, 1078 A.H., relates to the restoration of the possession of the land that was granted to the Jangams. It runs

> "All the present and future Jagirdars and karoris in pargana Haveli Banaras subah Allahabad are informed that according to the order of the Emperor dated 9 Amardad Illahi, 178 bighas of land has been granted to the Jangams to help them in their maintenance. The old officials have verified this fact, before this. On the present occasion also they have produced evidence bearing the seal of the Malik of the said parganas to the effect that they are, as before, in possession of the land and their title is clearly proved. Therefore, according to the order of

> Emperor, the same has been left to them as the sacrifice (Nisar) for the head of the Emperor. The said land should be returned to them from the beginning of the kharif crop of San 10 as it was before and they should not in any way be interfered with, so that these Jangams may utilize the income of every crop in their maintenance of the kingdom of the Emperor. Herein they shall fail not and act otherwise."

This farman does not only show that justice was inherent in him, but also that he made no distinction in distributing the Nisar to Hindu mendicants. The said land of 178 bighas was in all probability donated to the Jangams by Aurangzeb himself as we have another farman dated 6th Ramadan 1071 A H., which refers to this-land in following terms:

> "The present and future officials of Pargana Haveli, Banaras, subordinate to Subah Allahabad, are to be informed that under the order of the Emperor to the effect that 178 bighas of land in pargana Banaras is allotted to Jangams to help in their maintenance. The Jangams have appeared at this time also in the Darbar of the Emperor. Their rights are proved and that the same persons are alive and in possession of the land. Therefore, the said land has again been given to them as before as a sacrifice for the head of the Emperor. The said land should be treated as a mufti land as detailed below, so that they may utilise it and may pray for the continued existence of the kingdom of the Emperor."

Another land-grant to a Hindu religious preceptor in the town of Banaras was given by Aurangzeb in 1098 A.H. which is as follows:

"At this auspicious time an august farman was issued that as two plots of land measuring 58 dira'. situated on the bank of the Ganga at the Benimadho ghat, in Banaras (one plot is in front of the house of Ramjivan Gosain and .on the bank of the central mosque, and the other higher up) are lying vacant without any building and belong to Bait-ul-mal we have, therefore, granted the same to Ramjivan Gosain and his son as *inam*, so that after building dwelling houses for the pious Brahmins and holy faqirs on the above mentioned plots, he should remain engaged in the contemplation of God and continue to offer prayer for the continuance of our God-gifted Empire that is destined to last for all time. It is, therefore, incumbent on our illustrious sons, exalted ministers, noble umras, high officials, daroghas and present and future Kotwala, to exert themselves for the continual and permanent observance of this hallowed ordinance; and to permit the above mentioned plots to remain in the possession of the aforesaid person and his descendents exempt from all dues and taxes, and not to demand from him a new *sanad* every year."

Aurangzeb seems to be very careful to respect the religious sentiments of his subjects. We have a farman of the Emperor issued on 2 Safar of the ninth year of his reign, in favour of Sudaman Brahman, the Pujari of Umanand temple of Gauhati in Assam. This temple and its Pujari, were granted a piece of land and the income of some forest for the bhoga (offering to God) and the maintenance of the Pujari by the Hindu rulers of Assam. When Aurangzeb occupied the province, he immediately issued the said farman confirming the earlier Hindu grant of the land and income in favour of the said temple and its Pujari.

The text of the Gauhati Farman runs as follows

> Be it known to the present and future administrators of important affairs, Chaudharis, Qanoongos, Muqaddams and peasants of patta Bengesar in the Pargana of Pandu in the Sarkar A Dakhinkul that 21/2 Biswa of land out of village Sakara, the Jama (total revenue) of which was thirty rupees, was settled on Sudaman and his son, the Pujari of Umanand, according to the orders of the previous rulers. At this time the truth of the title (claim) out of the aforesaid maintenance rupees twenty cash out of the Mahsul (collections) of the said village and the rest of it the jungle-land exclusive of the Jama from Intakhali village being

> settled as the maintenance of the aforesaid grantee. It is incumbent upon them (officers) to leave the cash and the land in possession of the above-mentioned perpetually, permanently and for life-time after separating from both the Mahals so that they may utilise them for their maintenance and bhog and engage themselves in prayers for the continuance of the kingdom to eternity. They should not allow any let or hindrance on account of revenue taxes and other cesses or demand a fresh Sanad and if there be they should not rely upon it. Considering this as binding upon them, they should not swerve from it. Written on the 2nd of safar in the 9th year of the Accession of His Majesty."

That Aurangzeb hid the attitude of tolerance towards Hindus and their religion, is further supported by the priests of the Mahakaleshwar temple at Ujjain. This is one of the chief temples of Siva, where deep' light is burnt day and night, continuously without any break. This deep is known as Nanda deep. Four seers of ghee used for this Nanda deep, was provided by the state from the remote past. And the priests of the temple say that it continued in the Mughal period also; and even Aurangzeb honoured this ancient tradition. Unfortunately they have no royal order to support their claim. But they have a copy of an order issued by Mural Bakhsh, during .the reign of his father dated 6th Shawwal 1051. A. H. This order was issued by him on behalf of the Emperor on the petition of one Devanarain, who was the then priest of the Mahakaleshwara temple. Hakim Muhammad. Mehdi, the Waqianawis, looked into the old records and testified the claim of the petitioner. Thereupon, it was ordered that four seers (Akbari) ghee be provided by the tahsildar of Chabutrd Kotawali for the said deep of the temple.

The copy of this order was issued by Muhammad Sa'dullah in the year 1153 A,H, i.e., 93 years after the original was issued.

The present priests infer from the issue of the copy after such a long interval that the original order continued to be carried on during all this intervening period which covers the reign of Aurangzeb also. Had this order no worth at this late period, no one would have cared to obtain the copy of a dead letter. Some other royal papers deposited in the archives of the said temple were brought to my knowledge by the then Mahant Lakshmi Narain who also possessed a few papers of the time of Auranqzeb.

Generally historians talk of the demolition of the Chintaman temple constructed by the Nagarseth of Ahmedabad but they turn dumb on the fact that the same Aurangzeb gave lands for the Shatrunjaya and Abu temples to the same Nagarseth.

The sanad granting land to the Shatrunjaya temple runs: "(and) the end of which will be happy, Satidas, the jeweller has represented to that noble, most holy, exalted and elevated presence through persons who constitute the holy assembly of the court, that whereas according to a Farman of His Majesty, the exalted (and) as dignified as Solomon, the protector of the office of the successor (of Muhammad), the shadow of God, dated the nineteenth of the holy month of Ramadan, in the year, thiRyone, the district of Palitana, which is called Satranja in the jurisdiction of the Sorath Sarkar, a dependency of the Subah of Ahmedabad (and revenue of which two lacs of Dams) has been settled as a perpetual Inam on the petitioner (and) that he (the petitioner), therefore, hopes that a glorious edict may also be granted by our court. Therefore, in the same manner as before we have granted (to the petitioner) the above-mentioned district as a perpetual In'am. It is, therefore, incumbent on the present and the future managers of the Subah and the above-mentioned Sarkar, to exert themselves for the continual and permanent observance of this hallowed ordinance (and) to permit the above mentioned district to remain in possession of the above-mentioned person and of his descendants in the lineal succession from generation to generation, and to consider him exempted from all demands and taxes and all other dues and not to demand from him in respect hereof a new sanad every year, and they shall not swerve from this order. Written on the 9th of the month of Telkkand in the Hijra year 1068 (1658)."

The Nagarseth helped Aurangzeb in some war, and being pleased with his services he gave some land-gift at Girnar and Abu to the temples therein. It runs as such:

In the name of Allah, the compassionate and merciful. (Tughra) O ye Faithful, obey God and obey the Prophet and those in authority among you.

"(Seal) Abul Muzaffar Muhy-ud-Din Muhammad Aurangzeb 'Alamgir Badshah Ghazi.

"At this time, the exalted Farman is issued that since Shantidas Jawahari, son of Sahasbhai, of the Shrawak community has solicited and been hopeful of special favours, and has greatly helped the army during its march with provisions, and expects to be honoured with special rewards, therefore, the village (*deh*) of Palitana, which is under the jurisdiction of Ahmedabad, and the hill of Palitana famous as Satrunja, and the temple on it, all those we give to the said Satidas Jawahari of the Shrawak community, and the timber and fuel which is to be found on the hill of Satranja should belong to the Shrawak community, so that they may utilise these for whatever purpose they like. Whoever guards the hill of Satranja and its temple should be entitled to the income of Palitana, and they should continue in prayer for the maintenance of the eternal government. It is necessary that the administration and officers and the Jagirdars and the karoris of the present and future should absolutely not allow any deviation or alteration in this.

'Besides this there is a mountain in Junagadh famous as Gimal (Girnar), and there is another hill at Abuji under the jurisdiction of Sirohi. We give these two hills also to Satidas Jawahari of Shrawak community as a special favour, so that he may be entirely satisfied. It is necessary for the officers that they should not allow any one to interfere with these, and no one among the Rajas should obstruct him and they should always help him as such action will bring to them royal pleasure. And they should not demand a new sanad every year, and if any body makes any claim about that village and the three hills, which we have given to him, he will be liable to the censure and curses of the people as well as of God Another separate sanad has also been given to him.

"Written on the tenth of great Rajab, the Hijri year 1070 (March 12,1680)."

But there are instances which prove beyond doubt that Aurangzeb did order demolition of Vishwanath temple at Varanasi and the Jama Masjid at Golkunda, and the reasons that were given out for the demolition of the temple and the mosque may give benefit of circumstances to Aurangzeb. The story regarding demolition of Vishwanath temple is that while Aurangzeb was passing near Varanasi on his way to Bengal, the Hindu Rajas in his retinue requested that if the halt was made for a day, their Ranis may go to Varanasi, have a dip in the Ganges and pay their homage to Lord Vishwanath. Aurangzeb readily agreed. Army pickets were posted on the five mile route to Varanasi. The Ranis made a journey on the Palkis. They took their dip in the Ganges and went to the Vishwanath temple to pay their homage. After offering Puja all the Ranis returned except one, the Maharani of Kutch. A thorough search was made of the temple precincts but the Rani was to be found no where. When Aurangzeb came to know of it, he was very much enraged. He sent his senior officers to search for the Rani. Ultimately, they found that the statue of Ganesh which was fixed in the wall was a moveable one. When the statue was moved, they saw a flight of stairs that led to the basement. To their horror, they found the missing Rani dishonoured and crying deprived of all her ornaments. The basement was just beneath Lord Vishwanath's seat. The Rajas expressed their vociferous protests. As the crime was henious, the Rajas demanded exemplary action. Aurangzeb ordered that as the sacred precincts have been despoiled, Lord Vishwanath may be moved to some other place, the temple be razed to the ground and the Mahant be arrested and punished.

Dr. Pattabhi Sitaramayya, in his famous book, *The Feathers and the Stones* has narrated this fact based on documentary evidence. Dr. P. L. Gupta, former Curator of Patna Museum, has also corroborated this incident.

Now, about the demolition of Jama Masjid : The Ruler of Golkunda, the famous Tanashah, after collecting revenues of the State, did not pay his dues to Delhi. In a few years they were accumulated into crores. Tanashah buried this Khazana and erected a Jame Masjid over it. When Aurangzeb came to know of it, he ordered the demolition of the mosque. The buried khazana was seized and utilised for the benefit of the people. These two examples are sufficient to show that Aurangzeb did not make any distinction between a temple and a mosque, in the matter of judicial finding.

Unfortunately, the incidents and characters in the Medieval and Modern History of India have been distorted and falsified in such a way that distortion and falsification are being accepted as God's own truth, and an accusing finger is raised against those who try to discriminate between facts and fiction, between reality and distortions, between truth and untruth. The vested communal interests continue to distort and falsify history.

It is most unfortunate that the fundamentalists on both sides are somewhat busy distorting not only medieval Indian history but also misinterpreting vedic and Quranic tenets and injunctions. Unscrupulous politicians are sowing winds of hatred forgetting that their countrymen will have to reap the whirlwind.

I would humbly draw the attention of such misguided politicians and biased historians to the 19th century band of: reformers headed: by Rammohan Roy, Mahadev Gobind Ranade, Swami Vivekanand and Ram Krishna Paramhans on the Hindu side, who by their liberal interpretation of Hinduism showed the new generation the human values of religion, and on the other hand the Muslim band of humanist reformers led by Sir Syed

Ahmed who set the pace of Muslim renaissance. Sir Syed was a devout Muslim. But he was concerned with the religious and cultural downfall of his community. He found sanction from Islam itself for his progressive and secular approach. He was aware that in India Islam needed a Luther. His secularism and rationalism was based on a saying of the Prophet

"I am no more than a man; when I order you anything respecting religion, receive it, and when I order you anything about the affairs of the world, then I am nothing more than a man."

He concluded that Islam has nothing to do with wordily affairs. According to him it is wrong to believe that Islam is directly related to all worldly matters and that, therefore, nothing can be done without obtaining a religious sanction. The regulations and the laws of Islam should not be identified with Islam itself. They can be replaced by better laws. "It is also wrong", Sir Syed said, to hold the books of jurists incorporate infallible truth and are sufficient for the guidance of our affairs. Reason is the only weapon which can decide the value of social and moral code of Islam." He held that the principles advocated by Islam are more ethical and are common to all other religions. He vehemently criticised the Ulema, who made all the institutions established by the Prophet as a part of Islam.

Sir Syed stood for keeping the political life separate from religion. He asserted that neither the people are required to know the religion of the ruler nor the government should interfere into the religion of the people. Every good government follows this principle. Any government which refused to follow it cannot be described as civilized government. By emphasising this principle, Sir Syed clearly shows that State should not be a religious state and it should not make any distinction between the people on the basis of religion. In the context of India he believed that all the people irrespective of their faith constitute one Nation. Religious difference should not undermine the vital unity of the people. The progress of the people demanded that the leadership should be in the hands of the secular persons. This attitude was responsible for Sir Syed's opposition to the Pan-Islamic movement of Jamaluddin Afghani as well as the protagonists of Hindi-Urdu controversy, a blow to his concept of composite culture.

Sir Syed's legacy of secularism was carried forward -by Mohsin-ul-Mulk, Chiragh Alt and. S: Khuda Bakhsh. Mohsin-ul-Mulk took Sir Syed's rationalism to its logical end. This was a great encouragement to the secular thinking of a section of Muslims. These religious ideas found expression in one of his letters he wrote to Sir Syed:

"The light and glare of scientific knowledge and enquiry has driven out irrational and obsolete concepts. The modern mind is illuminated by the lustrous and bright ideas and regards such concepts as superstitious and preposterous. And now such irrational and barbarous ideas are hardly amenable to the sensible and rational mind. The only unfortunate victims of such funny superstitions are those who indulge in the luxury of childish talk and here say.

"Divinity, mercifulness and omnipresence-the qualities ascribed to Supreme Being are all a magnificent humbug. Worship and prayer springs out of fear and apprehensions on the part of the brutes and unlettered. Intuition is but a nightmare. It should better be understood, that the so-called soul or spirit is not immortal. The Day of Judgement is an absurd unreality. Hell and Heaven are concepts without any substance, reward and punishment is the work of superstition. Death is the final emancipator of every complication and agony and misery . . Such, for instance, are the reflections of those who are rational, strong of will, and swim in the ocean of sciences."

Even Ameer Ali due to the influence of Sir Syed asserted that:

"To suppose, therefore that every Islamic precept is necessarily immutable is to do injustice to history and to the development of human intellect."

He also argued that certain injunctions of the Quran are historically relevant only to the Prophet's day. It means that Islam as preached by the Prophet is not wholly applicable to all the spheres of life. According to Ameer Alt, no law is immutable. It becomes out of date after a radical change in the society. Therefore, law should be in consonance with the exigencies and the requirements of the time.

It is significant that Ameer Ali supported the abolition of polygamy. He regarded it -as much opposed to the teachings of Mohammed as it is to the general progress of civilized society and true culture. Ameer Ali held that polygamy is abhorrent to the laws of Islam. He also opposed the existing practice of divorce.

"The prophet looked upon the custom of divorce with extreme disapproval and regarded its practice as calculated to undermine the foundations of society. He repeatedly declared that nothing more displeases God than divorce," said Ameer Ali. These ideas regarding the Muslim personal law impel a change which permits polygamy as well as divorce. The change perhaps will be more in keeping with the spirit of Islam than the maintenance of the status quo.

Chiragh Ali's view of Islam was also strikingly secular and liberal. To him.

"Islam as a religion is quite apart from inculcating a social system. The Mohammedan polity and social system have nothing to do with religion. Islam is 'so sufficiently elastic that it can adopt itself the social and political revolutions going on around it. It is not a barrier to the political, social or moral innovations. Chirag Ali regarded the Prophet primarily as a reformer who supplanted ancient Arabian superstitions by monotheism, elevated the moral standard of Arabs and other people and improved the lot of women by restricting polygamy, discouraging slavery, and abolishing infanticid. To Chiragh Ali, the Mohammeden common law or Shariat is by no means unchangeable or unalterable. The Prophet did not compile any code, but permitted the Muslims to frame any code of Civil or Common law and to found systems which would harmonize with the times and suit the political and social changes going around them. The Prophet, Chiragh Ali believed, never combined the Church and the State into one. The ideas supplement Sir Syed's view on Islam.

S. Khuda Bakhsh also forcefully advocated the separation of religion from social and political life. He attempted to free Islam from the "fetters of Authority and the Dead Hand of the Past". He held that "it would be merely a front to contend that religious and social systems, bequeathed to us thirteen hundred years ago, should now be adopted in their entirety without the slightest change or alteration." He did not consider Quran as *Corpus juris civilis* to be accepted for all time. His view was that the subordination of religion to the State is a step forward in the direction of reform and progress.

S. Khuda Bakhsh was a supporter of secular politic. He did not consider the institution of Khilafat a basis of the unity of the Muslim world. On the contrary he commented that the abolition of the Khilafat ended a fiction and laid the path open for the development of Nationalism and finally removed once for all the embargo upon liberalism. What is also significant in Khuda Bakhsh was that he opposed the idea of the promotion of Muslim unity in isolation with the Indian solidarity. This makes him politically different from Ameer Ali and Mohsin-ul-Mulk. He wanted that the Muslim solidarity should be merged into a higher, nobler Indian solidarity. Badruddin Tyabji's views were similar to those of Khuda Bakhsh. He also advocated the separation of worldly and financial affairs from religion, and pleaded that in their own interest the religious leaders should keep themselves aloof from all purely financial and mundane matters.

Sulaiman Nadvi, another great scholar, admitted the separation of Church and State in Islam. It is to be noted that the liberals in the last quarter of the 19th century and in the beginning of the 20th Century were guided by scientific developments. Their effort was to decide the validity of the social laws on the basis of science. Mohsin-ul-Mulk declared that "science can submit to no confines or limitations; it is not merely speculative, it is pragmatic, demonstrable and experimental ... . It has confuted the traditional concepts of religion to such an extent that only two alternatives remain : either to allow religion to die a natural death or to interpret religion in the light of the new knowledge." Thus the scientific approach and the ineffectivity of religion in non-spiritual matters should be considered as the foundation of secularism among the Indian Muslims.

For the first time in the history of Islam in India, liberal ideas were propounded that religion should not come in the way of social progress, and that it should concern itself with spiritualism rather than with the temporal sphere of life. 'therefore, they discarded the traditional notion of Jihad, Darul, Harb and Darul Islam, and political pan-Islamism. It was the first concerted attempt towards the modernization of Islam in this country.

Political Strategy of Muslim Rulers

The Turko-Afghans who had established themselves firmly as Delhi Sultans had no firm or consistent religious policy. In the then prevailing political situation, their own position, to say the least, was precarious. On the one hand they were in a land which was not a small country but was rather of the size of a sub-continent, peopled by highly civilized, stubborn races, who practised a bewildering variety of faiths—from extreme monism to extreme paganism; on the other, they were caught in the vortex of the then Central Asian turbulence caused by Mongol depredations. Iltutmish, to secure legitimacy of his rule, did secure a robe of honour and a patent of investiture from Al Mustansir Billah, the reigning Caliph of Baghdad, but it was only his diplomacy which saved his territories being overrun by the great Chingiz Khan, the Mongol chief. The Mongols continued to inflict depredations in Central Asia and north-west India. In 1257 A.D., Halattu sacked and captured Baghdad and murdered the reigning Caliph AI-Mu'tasim and the very institution of Khilafat, the symbol of secular and religious unity of Islamic brotherhood had come under a cloud. The Muslim sultans and potentates of different lands could now, not only contend and compete for khilafat, but very many of them could now abjure allegiance to the very institution of khilafat itself with impunity.

Again, succession to the throne in a Muslim kingdom was a matter of personal fortitude and the ability to outwit other contenders, rather than a product of secular or religious authority of innate nature. This was different from the state of affairs in medieval Europe where rulers derived their legitimacy from ecclesiastical overlords or from 'emperors'. There was a close tie between the noose in the neck and the crown on the head and personal adventure and enterprise was the route to kingship. But it was clear: fortune favoured generally those who deserved it. The so-called 'slave' kings who ruled in the early part of Turko-Afghan rule were thus all deserving, having risen from slavery to kingship.

Slavery was, however, an old institution. In Athens, only one- fifth of the population were citizens, i.e. free men who could cogitate and decide over public matters; others were slaves. A redeeming feature of the institution, however, was that those slaves who showed promise were educated and trained. Thus, some of them turned out to be remarkable personalities both as savants as well as soldiers. Epictetus, the celebrated stoic philosopher was a Roman slave, and his "Dissertations", along with "Meditations" of Emperor Marcus Aurelius are the stream of thoughts which water the beliefs of the Christian Church. In Islamic brotherhood, we do come across slave savants, and also great soldiers and statesmen. India had not only the so-called slave kings, but also such outstanding slave-soldiers as Malik Kafur and Malik Ambar. It was Malik Kafur, the former slave, who penetrated into far south for Allauddin Khilji and his campaigns were always crowned with success. In fact, the ascent of former slaves to supreme political authority illustrated the democratic character of Islamic polity.

The religious policy of the Turko-Afghan rulers, therefore, depended largely on their personal predilections and the political situation then prevailing. Large-scale and forceful proselytization of the Hindu subject population was out of question. For one thing, their own position was never secure, and what they termed as conquests of the new territories were but in the nature of forays in which the local chiefs were humbled by arms and they submitted by paying tributes. The actual administration remained in the hands of local Rajahs or chiefs. Even those Muslim nobles who were appointed as governors could not administer directly, and had to depend on local chiefs. The imperial capital at Delhi, and the various provincial capitals of the new conquered territories were no better than military camps, albeit permanent, which remained in a state of permanent alert in the midst of danger, both internal and external. The nobles or Umera were always busy fostering intrigues which surfaced frequently in open rebellion. Then, it was not considered advisable to alienate the large number of Hindu chiefs by pursuing a vigorous discriminatory policy, as the rulers were wise enough to realize that such a policy would be suicidal.

The nature of Hindu polity was a factor which prevented the rise of a totalitarian theocratic state in India. For the Hindu society religion was a highly personal affair. There was no organized Church, and shades of faith within the Hindu fold were more than even the customary colours of the rainbow in the sky. Alberuni, the celebrated intellectual who flourished during the time of Sultan Mahamud Ghazni was an eminent scholar of Sanskrit, Arabic and Persian, author of Kitab-ul-Hind, a compendium of Hindu science, philosophy and religion, mentions an enigmatic aspect of Hindu religion. He wonders how the Hindus who worshipped idols of clay as God Himself for days and months together could ultimately immerse the same in water to dissolve and mix with the elements as if they were no better than lumps of clay! For the Hindus, he writes, life and death are in one continuous process, the two faces of the same truth. While living, they always remain conscious of the shadow of death and it is this quality which makes them practically indestructible, and vibrant with life. The Turko-Afghan rulers found to their chagrin that conversion of the Hindu Rajahs or the nobles to Islam could never mean automatic acceptance of the faith by their subjects or their dependants, as was generally the case in other countries. Here rulership was functional, and the ruled were under to obligation to take to the faith of the ruler. Proselytizing as a state activity was not feasible in Hindu India, and it stands to their credit that the Muslim rulers were able to grasp this essential fact of life in India.

Another great impediment was the peculiar caste system of the Hindus. We have seen that even during the Vedic age when there was no caste system, certain occupational castes were recognised. Chaturvarnaya -the four-fold varna is a broad division of humanity into functional groups according to personal inclination and occupational fitness. However, in course of time, with the growth of population and expansion of economic activities and mixture of races, distinct groups based on occupation of some common characteristics emerged, and distinct classes congealed into castes. In other countries and other civilizations, castes were not unknown. Guilds were a kind of caste, but these were in the nature of voluntary associations and one could go out of the guild by choice. There were the nobility, the freemen and the serfs in Britain, but then, though hereditary, these were more in the nature of classes than castes. However, what started as a scientific division of functions according to inclination and fitness degenerated in course of time into exclusive and hereditary continuity with fixed rules about commensality, endogamy and exogamy, marital relations, untouchability, purity, pollution etc. At what point of time these characteristic crystallized is difficult to say; but this much is clear that the feeling of exclusiveness and superiority in relation to other castes started with the Brahmins, who not only made their position, and the position of their progeny, safe by making Brahminhood dependent on birth, but also secured many privileges and perks. Their economic privileges of being provided for livelihood by gifts and settlement of rent free land in lieu of priestly functions were secure and they had not to worry for livelihood. Beside these, a Brahmin was granted certain discriminatory privileges; for example, he was exempt from military duties, had not to pay for ferry across rivers, and could not be given capital punishment. Even for tilling land, he was to give land-tax to government at a lower rate than others. Both Lord Buddha and the Jain Tirthankars, in starting their reformist movements, tried to stem caste privileges of the Brahmins but the tide proved too strong for the Buddhist and the Jain preachers.

Paradoxically enough, one of the reasons of petrifaction of caste system was the spirit of tolerance that pervaded the Hindu society. The acceptance of the inevitability of razor-sharp differences in metaphysical speculations that characterized the evolution of Hindu thought, tended to broaden the mind and to engender a universal catholicity in social relations. Foreigners like the Greeks, Bacterians, Sakas, Huns and a host of other foreign elements came to be absorbed within the Hindu fold. In India itself, there were tribes and groups in various stages of cultural development, and these were always trying to fit in with the general social order. Then again, the system of *anuloma* and *pratiloma* marriages, i.e., marriages between males from the higher casts and females of the lower caste, and marriages between males from the lower caste and females of the higher caste, respectively, were responsible for coming into existence of a number of castes and sub-castes whose position in the hierarchy of castes was determined according to the economic condition and occupational status of the members of that particular caste. So, ultimately, the varnas became the archetype, and the various castes were fitted into their cadre. There was a scramble by various emerging castes and sub-castes to be declared either of the Brahmin or at least of the Kshatriya varna. The obliging Brahmins invented ancient lores to support their claims and mythological stories were interpolated in the Puranas. The leaders of the racial groups among the foreigners were declared to be Brahmins, and some ancient rishis became the proginator of their gotra or clan. The Rajputs traced their ancestry to the lineage of ancient kings of solar and lunar dynasties and were classed as Kshatriyas. Even the Sudras who captured powers were declared Kshatriyas, albeit degenerate Kshatriyas. The Palas were Sudra in origin, but were declared to be Kayasthyas, as degenerate Kshatriyas (the Bengali Kayasthyas in spite of their high social position are still classed as Sudras in Bengal). The occupational classes, like the carpenters, blacksmiths, weavers and others, traced their ancestry to the legendary architect, Vishwakarma, and the goldsmiths and some other cultivating classes styled themselves as Kshatriyas. This state of affair led Raghunandan, the Nibandhkar of Hindu Law in 16th century to declare that no Kashatriya was left in India, a view later on endorsed by Kamlakar Bhatt in 17th century and Nagesh Bhatt in 18th century.

Caste exclusiveness was marked by a certain pride and, even when graded low, each caste and sub-caste considered itself to be superior to or at least equal to other caste and sub-caste of the same varna. These castes and sub-castes were organized on a local basis and lacked even regional or all-India character in many cases. Howsoever much insular they might have been in outlook and in other characteristics, they were by no means a welter of incoherent social groups, certainly not a flotsam or an inchoate mass of small units. They had a certain organic unity. The bonds were neither physical, nor economic or political; the bonds were made of that spiritual fibre which inspires people with a common purpose of life and makes people of different faiths hang together in mind, heart and spirit in crises of life. It was perhaps the ingrained belief in the divine law of retributive justice, karma, which made people bear with trial and tribulations of life cheerfully and in a spirit of resignation, and accept their social status, however lowly, as just and proper.

Spengler makes a distinction between Estate and Caste: Estate is the form that living must itself unfold, but caste is absolute finishedness, the phase in which development has been succeeded by immutable fixation. From this point of view, Estate is the varna of which caste is the finished product. But it has not been so simple in the case of India. Plethora of castes and sub-castes, both regional and iocal, have been traced, apart from other historical and incidental factors including the fact that they were so many social organizations based primarily on an agricultural economy, to an in-built device for dissent. Dissent, whether of form or of spirit in other societies has, however, entailed a struggle between the dominant and dissenting groups, resulting in ultimate extermination of one or the other. The whole history of the bloody and barbarous struggles between Catholics and Protestants in Europe during the last few centuries would show this. Not so in India. Here any minority, whether religious, social or economic, was free to form its own group which in course of time crystalized into a caste or sub-caste, reflecting its peculiarities and idiosyncrasies in social and group behaviour. Ultimately it was difficult to exist in India without belonging to a caste. What is skin to the body, so caste has been to the Indian society; it is caste which gave identity, and cohesion to social groups in the country. One could say that for the Indian peoples caste was a stronger bond than religion itself. The Muslim settlers in India, even if they were firm and well-knit and zealous to spread their faith in the country, came against this perplexing wall of caste system which they did not know how to penetrate.

The Turko-Afghan rulers had also no clear-cut guidance from Islamic precedence. God had bestowed on them a country to rule where they and their kinsmen were the only believers; the vast mass of the people were professing their own religion or religions with well-established philosophical systems and well-defined rules and institution of social behaviour. Being basically tribal in nature, these settlers were under the cultural influence of Persia, and had little first-hand acquaintance with Arabic or Islamic traditions of the Caliphs and the Abbasids; they had to rely on Muslim divines and ulema who, more often than not, differed among themselves. As befits a civilized and growing society, Islamic law during the course of five hundred years had become vast and complex. Besides Quranic injunctions and Sunnah or Hadith or Sayings of the Prophet, second in importance only to the Quran, there were Fatwas or previous interpretations of the Holy Law by eminent jurists, and finally the digests prepared from time to time by the learned doctors of the four schools of Islamic Law viz the Hanafi, the Malaki, the Shafi and the Hanbali. Beside these, the Urfi laws, or customary laws were also recognised in many instances. However, there was no established 'Church' in Islam with its deadening uniformity and universality, suppressing all deviations. In this respect Islam was more akin to Hinduism. The differences of interpretation of the doctrines and dogmas lead to sects and factions, but being puissant and more full-blooded, the schisms and disputes in Islamic sects and factions have often been so deep and bitter as to lead to bloodshed and war.

We have noted that Islam does not admit conversion to the faith by force, fraud or coercion. It is a religion which lays down elaborate injunctions for protection of people professing other faiths. The concept of Dhimmi, which means a non-Muslim, for the safety of whose life, property, mode of worship and customs, the Muslim ruler is responsible, is peculiar to Islam and a product of historical processes through which Islam passed and progressed. But Dhimmis in Muslim States were definitely minorities and Islamic laws provided for their protection, both as a matter of conscience as well as of policy in the interest of peace and stability of the kingdom. But the situation which the Turko-Afghan rulers and later on Mughal rulers faced in India was quite different. In the Muslim kingdoms whether at Delhi or in the south where most of the time they existed independently, the position was just the reverse: the Muslims were in a minority. They were still called upon to administer territories populated largely by peoples of different non-Islamic faiths. Thus, from the beginning of Muslim rule, it was realized that in the prevailing condition it was neither feasible nor desirable to apply strictly laws and injunctions promulgated for the Arab societies; the rulers took a pragmatic view. Iltutmish, who was the first of the Delhi Sultans to have ruled securely for a considerable period, expressed his inability to follow the advice of the Ulema in the matter of imposing Islam on the Hindus by force. This policy was largely followed by Balban, Allauddin Khilji, Mohammad Tughlak, Shershah and then the Mughal Emperors generally. Alauddin Khilji's dialogue with nazi-ul-quzzat, Moghisuddin, is an illuminating account of the Khilji ruler's straight-forward non-theocratic approach in State policy. However, some of the Sultans were carried away by religious zeal and tried to secure additions to the fold of faithful; some even tried to rule according to the injunctions of the Quran and the Hadith. Feruz Tughlaq was one such early example. Feruz devised taxation strictly according to the spirit of the Quranic Law, abolished all vexatious cesses imposed by previous regimes holding them to be un-Islamic, and allowed imposition of four kinds of taxes sanctioned by the Quran i.e., the Kharaj or one-tenth from cultivated land instead of the customary 1/3. The Zakat or alms, the Jizia or poll-tax on the non-Muslims and other heretics, and the Khums or one-fifth of the spoil and of the produce of mines. In consultation with canonists, he also levied an irrigation tax at the rate of 10 per cent of the produce of the fields. He allowed four-fifth of the spoils of war to the soldiers in accordance with the Quranic injunctions. The merchants were relieved from payment of irregular and oppressive octroi duties. The result was that both agriculture and trade flourished. It also showed that if the Quranic injunctions are followed in true spirit, the result was bound to be beneficial for the ruled. However, Firuz came down heavily on observance of non-sanctioned religious practices like congregation and Urs at the shrines of Muslim saints which had then come into vogue in the country, and many were put to death for uttering blasphemies.

However, it was Allauddin Khilji who firmly laid down the state policy in regard to religious matters. According to him, the safety of the kingdom and security of the throne mattered most, and not the personal religious inclination of the king. His simple argument was that Allah had bestowed the kingdom, and he knew no higher duty than governing this kingdom ably. This very principle was reinforced and given a dominant and more concrete shape by Akbar later on, who, tried to give equal respect to all religious denominations. Of course, even during his time Islam was the first amongst the equals. But most of the Muslim kings were devout Muslims and sometimes their religious zeal got the better of their political discretion. One of the sacred duties in Islamic scheme of things is the duty laid down on every faithful to exert himself in the path of God. Thus, it behoves every Muslim to make efforts (Jihad) to convert land of non-believers (dar-ul-barb) into holy land (dar-ul-Islam) The rider is that it should be Jihad (striving) and not Qatl (destruction). Kufr (non-belief) shall be extinguished and not Kafir (non-believers), for if Kafir was eliminated nothing would remain against which Jihad could be made. Moreover, the conversion of non-believers into believers must be by way of persuasion and not by coercion. In practice, sometimes, there is a thin demarcating line between persuasion and coercion. Thus, against Iltutmish, Balban, Shershah, Akbar, Zain-ul-Abdin of Kashmir and Hussain Shah of Bengal, who were permeated with a spirit of liberalism and tolerance and who did not allow their personal religious beliefs to intrude into matters of State, we have also Ibrahim Lodi and Aurangzeb who interpreted their 'religious' duties so narrowly as to inhibit their status as rulers over a great and diversified society, like the Indian society. Such narrowness ultimately harmed the stability of their regimes. In between them were rulers who were more or less neutral in the matter.

The city of Benaras was the seat and symbol of Hinduism. Ascetics of every order of Hinduism from all corners of the land flocked there, and no Hindu learning or philosophical theory could pass muster unless Benaras recognised it. Its importance in the Hindu world was, therefore, immense and hence it attracted the attention of both the Hindus and the non-Hindus, the former with devotion and the latter, occasionally, with hostility. It would, therefore, be interesting to note the trials and tribulations of Benaras during the period of Muslim and foreign rule in India. Being situated on the sacred Ganges, it has not only been a city of temples and monasteries, but also a great centre of trade and commerce and arts and crafts. It was here that Lord Buddha came to mount his first sermon, and it was here that Sankarcharya established the modern phase of Hinduism. Since the recognition of Lord Buddha as the ninth avatar (incarnation) of Vishnu, Vaishnavism has no doubt, imbibed many of the features of Buddhism, but so far as the personality of Lord Buddha is concerned, Lord Siva, in popular mind, replaced Lord Buddha as the ascetic, par-excellence, specially, when Buddhistic and Saivic and Tantric ceremonies intermingled and became conjointal with each other. In all the Jatak stories - birth stories of Lord Buddha, it is Benaras which is the scene and the background of Lord Buddha's previous births. Benaras thus came to be associated with salvation, both Lord Buddha and Lord Siva being firmly associated in people's mind with salvation. Thus Avimukteshwar, or Lord of Salvation came to be regarded as the presiding deity of Benaras. Built on the banks of the Ganges, the temple of Avimukteshwar was a noble building, twelve storeyed high; many of the higher storeys are said to have been constructed by the Kalchuri king, Gangeya, a great devotee of Lord Siva. During the invasions of Muhammad Ghori, Benares was under Jaichandra, the Gahadwal king. After the battle of' Chandawar leading to the defeat of Jaichandra, in 1193 A.D. Benaras came to be occupied and the city was looted and temples including that of Avimukteshwar here destroyed. In 1197 A.D. Benares was occupied finally by Qutubuddin; Malik Imamuddin became the governor of Avadh whose general, Mohammad Bakhtiar, completely destroyed even the remains of temple of Avimukteshwar, and no trace of it can be found. During the reign of Iltutmish, however, the Hindus were permitted to erect another temple. The temple of Visheshwar (universe) was now constructed and Lord Vishwanath (Lord of Universe) came to be the presiding deity of Benares, devotion to whom was said to bring salvation. Sikandar Lodi destroyed this temple, and many other temples as well; the city was destroyed and it took another hundred years for the city to recover its lost glory. His putting many holy men to death evoked protests from many Ulema and divines since such an act is considered reprehensible in Islam. Sikandar Lodi's repression of Hindus has to be regarded as un-Islamic since Benares was in his kingdom and the holymen and the common people were entitled to his protection. In 1585 A.D. however, Narayan Bhatt, one of the foremost learned men of Benares, got another temple of Vishwanath constructed with the help of Govardhan, son of Todarmal, one of the ministers of Akbar. In 1669 A.D. again, on the orders of Aurangzeb, the temple was destroyed and a mosque was constructed on the site which is still standing at Gyanvapi. The present temple of Vishwanath was constructed by Maharani Ahilyabai. It speaks of the cosmopolitan spirit and the tolerant culture which by then had emerged that Muslims contributed liberally towards additions to the building adjoining the main temple. Warren Hastings also provided funds towards construction of the Naubatkhana (Music tower) of the temple.

The so-called religious policy of the Muslim rulers was not uniform, and was mostly guided by self-interest or political interest rather than any religious suzerainty from above as in Europe. Some levied Jizia, some abolished it or lessened its rigour. Some accepted the supremacy of the khilafat, but most of them ignored it. Some were very generous with the Hindus, but then some were quite indifferent. For example, the bonhomie with the Hindus specially the Rajputs, started by Akbar, became lukewarm during the time of Jahangir (though he was born of Hindu mother) and Shahjahan, and was completely reversed by Aurangzeb, even though Aurangzeb too had a Hindu wife. It is clear, however, that Islam in course of time lost its alien character, and came to be recognised and accepted as a noble faith worth being adopted by Indians. Its democratic character, its conception of equality and brotherhood, its vigorous and manly outlook, the simplicity of its religious observances could not but make a deep impression on the Hindu mind. This impression was caused not by pressure of the rulers, but through the saintly example of Sufi preachers who, braving all odds and physical discomfort, poured into India in large numbers in the wake of Muslim conquests. It is true that many Hindus of the upper castes turned Muslims for political reasons and made history and even founded new kingdoms. Their list is impressive, but so far as progress of Islam in India is concerned, the force of authority was seldom used for the purpose.

The real impact was made by the Sufi saints who won the hearts and minds of simple folk, including a large number of literate Hindus. Islam in many ways took an Indian character so much so that Babar was struck by it and in his autobiography termed this as 'Hindusthani way', Islamic faith moulded in Hindusthani social system. It must have appeared remarkable to him that the Muslims of Indian origin not only retained many of the customs of their former faith, but even characteristics of their former social caste system, with the result that even the Muslims who came from outside the country fell under the charm of these systems and tried to form a separate class by themselves as distinguished from neo-converts, or Muslims of Indian origin. Thus, while the Muslims of foreign origin, took Indian wives, they were reluctant to marry their daughters to Muslims of Indian origin. If a Brahmin got converted into Islamic faith, he tried to pass off as a 'Saiyad', a Rajput or a member of any other martial class as "Khan", and so on. No one was satisfied with being a simple 'Shaikh'. Even those Muslim settlers who came from outside tried to distinguish themselves from other Muslims by assuming the title of 'Saiyed' , and went so far as to call themselves as 'Hashmis' or the scions of Hashamite line of Baghdad. Some assumed the title of 'Quraishi' as if they belonged to the tribe of the Holy Prophet. Qutubuddin Mubarak, son of Allauddin Khilji, who ruled for a short while, not only shook off allegiance to the khilafat and proclaimed himself the supreme head of the religion of Islam, the Khalifah, the Lord of Heaven and Earth, but also took the pontifical title of "Al-Wasiq-Billah", on the analogy of Caliph Mustasin Billah, the last Abbasid Caliph of Baghdad.

The ruling Muslim elite, whether of foreign or of Indian origin thus tried to become a distinct class by themselves in the right royal Indian tradition, the entry to the charmed circle being determined by birth and occupation. They tried to pass off as Islamic Kshatriyas, as it were. Of course, there was not so much rigidity in them as among the Hindus, but there were layers within layers in the new hierarchy of 'Khans' and 'Khan-e-Khanas' A new class of Saiyads and 'Shahs', educated in Islamic lore also emerged and these two formed the upper echelon of the Islamic society in India, like the Kshatriyas and Brahmins in the Hindu society. They generally appropriated to themselves certain social privileges not open to the common mass of Muslims. Thus, what the Sultans could ultimately achieve by way of Islamic propagation was an addition to their own rank of retainers and supporters. Mass conversion, in the prevailing condition, was beyond their competence. Aurangzeb tried to achieve this following a discriminatory State policy against the Hindus -the temptation of service and preferential treatment, in case of acceptance of Islam, being one of them. But he, also, in the end had to accept failure. In his *'Ahkam'* (precepts) collected by Hamiduddin Khan, a favoured officer well-known by his sobriquet 'dagger of Alamgir' (*Nizncha-e-Alamgiri*) the following significant lines occur:

"What have the worldly affairs to do with religion? And why should bigotry intrude into matters of religion? 'For you there is your religion, and for me mine' (*lakum dinukum wa liyadin* - Quran). If the law were followed it would have been necessary to annihilate all the Rajas and their subjects"

Another of his precepts was:

"What concern have we with the religion of anybody? Let Jesus follow his own religion, and Moses his own".

The above lines appear to symbolise the sum of state efforts for propagation of Islam during the Turko-Afghan and Moghul periods. But Islam did spread, and became part of the warp and woof of the beliefs, hopes and aspirations of the Indian people, providing sustenance and strength at a time of spiritual emasculation in northern India, verily a shaft of light in a period of darkening gloom and despair.

Overall Prosperity

The armies of the Delhi Sultanate had started with over-running the Indus-Gangetic valley, a small part of this vast sub-continent, but this still brought to the rulers a prestige disproportionate to the territories actually conquered. Sindh had been under the Muslim rule from before, but it was never considered a viable alien intrusion on the Indian political scene and existed on the sufferance of mightier Pratiharas, Baghelas, and Rastrakutas. The Delhi Sultanate, however, was a different proposition, being the successor of Indian imperialism and conqueror of Patliputra. For a thousand years, Patliputra had occupied a pre-eminent position in the Indian polity. It was from Patliputra that imperial addicts had gone out, not once but many times, to the distant corners of the country and outside. The Maurya and the Gupta rulers had been Chakravartis (king of kings) in the true sense of the word. This pre-eminence now got transferred to Delhi. However, it was Allauddin Khilji, who can be said to be the first, and perhaps, the only Muslim Chakravarti in the true sense who secured for Delhi the pre-eminent position which imperial Patliputra once occupied. He defeated one by one the disunited and warring Hindu Kingdoms of the south as well as of the west. Though the major portion of the country continued to be effectively governed by local kingdoms, some being as rich and powerful as the Vijayanagar Empire or the Bahmani kingdom in the south, in no way subordinate to the imperial Delhi for a good length of time, the fact of Delhi being the seat of imperial power came to be recognised and accepted generally. The image was maintained not withstanding the jurisdiction of Delhi Sultanate shrinking many a times to a small territory around it. Delhi became a symbol of India as an entity, and not merely a geographical expression. It did not matter who was the ruler of Delhi, whether an indigenous prince or a foreign invader, whether of a faith of the soil of India or a faith born in an alien land. In popular parlance "the Lord of Delhi was the Lord of the universe", as Jagannath Panditraj said.

In Hindu political thinking, man was not considered to be a political animal in the Aristotelian sense; in fact he was not considered an animal, whether political or otherwise. Man had no doubt animal instincts in common with higher species, but overriding them was his innate sense of discrimination, which made him a moral being able to discriminate between right and wrong. It was this rod of righteousness which could keep the fabric of life in order. All the institutions created by man for collective life, social, political, cultural or economic, functioned by this cardinal principle. This political arrangement in the Hindu view of life were purely functional. The Hindu outlook is not imbued with any sense of awe and wonder for the superiority of polity over the individual : it is eclectic and tentative, not dogmatic or assertive. It ensures respect for the individual over the herd, and is thus the inspiration behind the spirit of tolerance, considered *sine qua non* of any institutional arrangement. In the Hindu view of political economy, what is of importance is not the form of government or who forms the Govt. but the quality of the ruling elite. As 'Atharva Ved declares':

"That nation is protected whose ruler (ruling class) is enlightened and abstemious" - Atharva Veda II-15-17.

Thus not only the regime has to be enlightened, that is, based on moral and spiritual values wedded to the weal of the people, but the ruler himself must be capable of carrying out his policies of protecting the society at the cost of his personal comfort. Enlightenment and unselfishness were the hallmarks of the class, the Kshatriyas, whose main job was to protect the nation, ensure internal peace and afford freedom from external dangers. The community was expected to self-regulate its affairs according to moral precepts laid down by seers, the same precepts being capable of revision in the light of new circumstances from time to time. To punish the wicked and reward the worthy was the universal law laid down for the ruler, and it was his duty to punish a wicked even neighbouring king and save his subjects from oppression. The principle of 'Chakrauartya' was recognised in this context. The conquered kingdoms only made token submissions, and were free to govern as before, and this conception perhaps operated to ensure all-India character of the nation.

How far is all this in accord with the Islamic concept of polity? A careful analysis will show that there is no basic difference between the two. The dissimilarities are incidental to their areas and the circumstances of origin, and the emphasis put on certain aspects according to circumstances. It may be noted the conception of life in Islam is all-embracing as it seeks to lay down norms for its followers in all aspects, for individuals as well as for institutions. There is nothing like temporal and spiritual to be considered separately, temporal is spiritual and spiritual is temporal. The main point, however, is that the overriding norm according to Islam is righteousness. The teachings of the Prophet are momentous landmarks which a true believer is expected to follow in his life in all aspects, such guidance is purely ethical and humanitarian and, therefore, of universal appeal. This brings us very close to the dharma of Hindu thought. In a sense, dharma and *iman* are both rooted in the consciousness of values, rather than in any theological precept. A momin is a person of faith, not subject to any external authority except to the conscientious regulation of his conduct by the tenets of Islamic faith. The Caliph is the symbol of this regulating force, but the regulation is of Islam, and not of the Caliph personally.

It is thus that Hindu thought and Islamic tenets both reject any theory of 'divine right: It kings'. However, most western writers have sedulously projected this as the prevailing oriental concept probably in an effort to justify the peculiarly absolutist Greco-Roman conception of the state. The myth of oriental despotism, Muslim or Hindus, was promoted by the British Utilitarians of the 19th century and the historiography that arose out of this. In some ways, an image of Asian or Indian rulers as despots served the purpose of the ideologies of British imperialism, such as James Mill, by investing the British occupation of India with the aura of a liberalising force of great historical importance. "His emphasis on Oriental Despotism suited the requirements of an imperial government," says the noted historian, Romila Thaper.

There was, however, in Hindu-Islamic political thinking, the need to obey the absolutism of righteousness, the king being the chief governing functionary to uphold the primacy of 'righteousness. He was powerless to prescribe or create what 'righteousness' was this had been prescribed by the `Dharam Shastras' and the Holy Quran and the Hadith already. His power to legislate was thus circumscribed by these boundaries, and any departure was unthinkable. On the other hand, the typical western conception had invested the state with such a halo of mysterious, all-embracing power as to dwarf the individual as an insignificant entity. The state was considered as: "The immanent will and intelligence which maintains and directs an organized people, and a legal order, or a jurist entity, or self-determining authority which inheres in a group possessing stability and sovereignty. The state's organ through which it expresses its power is government." In the Platonic sense, the State is the idea, and government the concrete reality, which represents the `general will' of the community before which the individual 'will' is of no consequence. The `general will' governs the `individual will', and howsoever sweet or sour, what the `general will' determines is good for the individual will. Such a government, whatever its complexion, as an embodiment of general will, is necessarily absolutist in conception and in execution of its policies. It does not admit of any rival seat of power; hence the scramble for capturing Government by the various social, political or economic groups or associations even in a so-called democratic polity, or if they cannot capture it singly or jointly with other groups, at least they try to bring such weight as they are capable of on the group in possession of governmental power.

State-power, in western conception has, in effect, meant domination by a class, the complexion of class changing from time to time according to circumstances. Thus, when the Roman Emperors after the earlier persecution of the Christians, embraced Christianity, the Church underwent a complete metamorphosis. No longer it was a Church of the meek Christian martyrs seeking to establish the kingdom of God on earth, but a Church which had worn the purple gown of royalty; the Empire had passed imperceptibly into Papacy. The Romans had recognised only two classes: the patricians and the plebeians. However, St.Augustine divided patricians into Lords of the Church and the Lords of the King, and instead of two, three estates, the Church, the nobles, and the commoners emerged. There was actually no class distinction between the Church and the nobility; the Church was also the nobility, and more often than not, the nobility acted as the Church. As between the two, the Church held a greater eminence; the gown of the Church carried more authority than the robe of the nobility. The wealth and the range of influence of the Church had widened tremendously and by the tenth century, it owned one-third of the soil of Europe and its fiats and dogmas, definite and defined, held State and minds of the people in absolute grip. The common people remained as serfs, whether of the Lord of the Main or Lord of the Church being *ascripti glebae*, 'bound to the soil' though there was a kind of communion among them due to identity of common interest. The nexus was ultimately broken by the rise of the mercantile class. Laden with the wealth of plunder and piracy across the seven seas they laid the foundations of industrial capitalism as well as nation states and captured state power, in turn giving rise to militant labour who now seek to do the same in their own interest, since "the state is simply a political instrument, a machine maintaining the rule of one class over the other", according to Lenin. Both in theory and in practice, the rights of the individual citizens are what the State acting through the agency of the Government confers, and what is given at will and pleasure of another, can also be withdrawn at will and pleasure of the same agency. The history of the last about three hundred years of the Western world is a history of long, bitter and bloody struggle for assertion of human rights of liberty of life and living and of conscience by the common people; many heads have rolled and many a tears shed in the process. However, even these rights are not inalienable but are 'legal' rights in accordance with the Roman conception of law, to be enforced by courts on application by the citizens against the State. One may recall the famous dictum of Diecy, one of the eminent British constitutional authorities, "there is no wrong for which there is no legal remedy". The remedy for violation of rights is to be provided by the State agency itself, that is the courts of law. The concept is heavily loaded against the common man in the State as it evolved in the West.

In Islamic jurisprudence, the equality of every faithful in the brotherhood is enshrined; and for even those not of Islamic faith, the right to life, liberty and faith is ensured by casting such a duty on the Islamic authority. It is just possible that the Islamic injunctions were not always complied with, but by and large, their observance during Islamic history is well marked. The classic example is of the Jews, who, after dispersion, faced untold persecution at the hands of the Christians. Mobbed by the people and robbed by the kings, denied all civil rights in any Christian state, they found safe and honourable sanctuary at last with the Moors in Spain and Portugal in Western Europe. Once the Moors lost ground in the Iberian peninsula, they faced the very same difficulties again at the hands of their Christian tormenters. On the other hand, Islamic law and practice made it the duty of the Muslim kings to protect the "Dhimmis" i.e., non-Muslims for whose life, property, worship and customs, the Muslim ruler was responsible.

Thus, when the Muslim rulers established themselves firmly on the soil of India, they had the examples of the administrative rules of The Abbasid Khalifas of Iraq and the Fatmid Khalifas of Egypt before them. Wisely enough, however, while copying the administrative structure of the Khalifas, they made it sufficiently indigenous in the prevailing Indian conditions. They could not legislate for the Muslims as the law of Shariat was fixed and immutable, the Muslim divines could interpret. They, therefore, also refrained from legislating for the Hindus, and in matters of religion, custom and institutional framework, they left them alone. The criminal law, however applied equally to all, but though swift and severe, it was not always a continuation of the orthodox Islamic practices. For example, there was no casting of stones for adultery or no burden of proof being placed upon on the complainant in case of rape. The Muslim rulers in India realized clearly that these laws were for an Islamic society where "Nizam-e-Mustafa", or the Islamic rule of righteousness had been firmly established. By and large they prided themselves on being just, and their administration of justice was not only just but also equitable. No distinction was made between a Muslim and a non-Muslim in respect of criminal offences and the law applied equally to all. Elaborate instructions were issued from time to time to the Qazis posted in farflung corners of the empire impressing upon them the desirability of not only being just but also appearing to be just. The Emperor in Delhi reserved for himself the right of Capital Punishment: no authority could impose death penalty without the express sanction of the Emperor. There was no separate set of laws for officials; the wine law applied to both the officials and non-officials. On the other hand, the punishment in case of bribery, extortion and tyranny on the part of officials was more severe; being trampled under the feet of elephants was one of the typical punishments for them. The right of appeal lay to the Emperor, who was the last court for redress of grievances of the subjects. Every person had the inalienable right to petition the Emperor. The Jehangiri chain of Justice, by ringing of which any one at any hour could secure a personal hearing from the Emperor is well known. It may be noted that this right of direct petitioning by subjects was won in England after a hard fight through the Bill of Rights (1684). The civil rights of the Hindus were judged according to their own religious code and the custom of their caste for which assessors were appointed to assist the Qazi. Even those Hindus who embraced Islam were governed by their original canon laws and customs, if they so desired.

Thus, it was benevolent monarchy rather than a theocratic and despotic State which emerged in India during the so-called Muslim period. The will of the Emperor was law, no doubt, but this will itself was circumscribed by external and internal limitations. It had to be exercised in conformity with the general will of the people demanding protection for peaceful economic and social activities in a just and appropriate manner. Any departure from this principle, yielding to the temptations of personal predilections and weaknesses was likely to endanger both the crown and the head that wore it. Secondly, there being no recognised rule of inheritance to the throne, every ruler had to fight for its possession and retention. Challenges used to come from recalcitrant nobles and local chieftains and disloyal governors of the outlying provinces, and the personal skill, bravery and diplomacy of the ruler were always on trial. Thirdly, for the sake of expediency and in keeping with Indian traditions, the Muslim Emperors, performed two functions - Jahanbani (Protection of the realm), and Jahangiri (seizing of other realms). They had perforce to keep their swords bright and sharp and their armours shining, for the success of their regime was judged by both these standards - keeping their frontiers inviolate and extension of the same as far as possible. Hence there were frequent wars and skirmishes, but these hardly touched the lives of the people in the peculiar political and economic circumstances then prevailing.

In Europe during these periods the feudal Lords, both civil and religious owned all the lands and kept a vice-like grip over the peasantry with full rights over their life and liberties; the socio-economic power structure in Europe continued to be the same till as late as the eighteenth century. A system of this kind was unknown in India during that period. It is true that powerful people of status and wealth exercised sway over the common people, as is the case even to-day, and that, in the hierarchy of castes the so-called upper castes, the Brahmins and the Kshatriyas, or the Sayads, Sheikhs and Pathans had certain advantages over those belonging to lower order. But this was due to their superior social and economic status, for does not Bharatrihari, the great Sanskrit poet and philosopher declare? "all the qualities flow from wealth." In so far institutionalised serfdom was concerned, this was not the case in the Indian society. There was no system of being `tied to the land'. The class of `bonded labour' which we witness today is the outcome of the end of the old communal life and the rise of the subsequent farm-tenure system under the British rule giving rise to a class of parasite tenure land-holders and the consequent gradual impoverishment of the peasantry. It is true that Jagirdari system prevailed under the early Muslim rule, when nobles, in lieu of their services to the kingdom., were granted Jagirs i.e., the right of collecting rent to be appropriated in part or in full for their own use. But the rights of Jagirdari were not those of the feudal lords: the State's right to rent and a share in the produce of the land tilled was not extinguished. Moreover, due to unsettled conditions, and change of fortunes of the ruling dynasty, the Jagirdars were never firmly in the saddle of their estates. The Mughals introduced the Mansabdari system, a kind of Jagirdari but simultaneously the law of estate was in operation under which the private estates automatically accrued to the State on the death of the holder of the estate. The Muslim rulers never conceded the right of any intermediary class between the state and the tillers of soil. They understood it very well this would give rise to a class of hereditary nobility and potential rival centres of power. Second, and perhaps the more important reason was that the village comprising the Indian peasantry in the middle ages up to seventeenth century even early eighteenth century, was the "cornucopian store-house" from which the state drew its sustenance and on which it depended for its sinews of war, and its display of splendour. The village economy was self-sufficient, autarchical and affluent and was the pride and wealth of the nation.

For one thing, the country was sparsely populated. The flourishing settlements were around the main river basins -the Indus, the Ganges, the Jamuna, etc, in the north, and the Krishna, the Cauvery, the Tungbhadra, etc, in the south. All the urban settlements were on the river banks, and the first concern of people was to ensure perennial water supply by having a ring of tanks. The village settlements, both for the purpose of cultivation as well as for supply of drinking water, relied on irrigation channels, small ponds, replenished in the rainy season with water for use in lean seasons, and also on surface wells which was, however, a difficult affair where the soil was rocky or sandy. Impure water caused many diseases, and only those towns and villages which were situated on running streams could ensure a healthier life. Endogamous marriages within the same clan on account of castes and sub-castes was another reason resulting in loss of human fecundity. However, arable land was plentiful and could always be added to by reclamation of jungle with which the whole country was studded. Thus, Mathura was surrounded by the sacred forest of Barsana, where Akbar used to hunt tiger, according to contemporary accounts. Oudh's inhabited territory was girdled with forest belts, as was the case with most of the human settlements. The north-east Oudh was a huge tract of forests where wild beasts roamed and its marshes bred malaria. Fourth-fifth of Bihar was in the state of nature as naming of the regions as Aranya (forest), Purnaranya (Purnea), Champaranaya, (Champaran) Saranya (Saran) or simply Arnya (Arrah) indicates. Except for Mithila, the whole tract of north Bihar was a huge forest. East Bengal was a huge territory of swamps and wilderness, although West Bengal was well populated. South of the Vindhyas the country was even less populated and the peculiar terrain of the territory was studded with a chain of forts both for defence and for habitation. It is difficult to guess the population of the country in fifteenth to seventeenth centuries, but certainly it was never more than one fourth of the population at the time of independence of the country from British yoke.

Social harmony between the two main religious groups - Hindus and Muslims, and various caste groups among both the Hindus and the Muslims is known to have existed in all the economic activities of cultivation, craft and trade. The economic life of the community was centred round the village which was an economic unit, organized for production and distribution, and not for war as was the case with villages in Europe which were units of war as well as of production. The Indian village was a viable unit, which took upon itself the function of apportioning work and rewards of the various segments of society, enforcing discipline by sheer weight of custom and public opinion, promoting a *esprit de corps* by appealing to the sense of pride in the village, and presenting a joint front against external dangers. It was a world within this mundane world, a specimen of peaceful communal life. When the British came to India to see this, they were struck with wonder, for it nullified all their assumptions, and in course of time they did their best to dismantle these institutions.

What had contributed to this kind of social set up? The foremost was a spirit of tolerance which accepted dissent and division. It was recognised that biologically everybody was not fitted for the same task equally, hence division into castes according to economic activities was a necessary arrangement. But, then, everybody was entitled to a share in the common pool. Surplus, if any, was God's gift, and had to be shared with others. Both property and talents were in the nature of sacred trusts which had to be utilized for the good of others. This was the philosophy of life which animated both the Hindus and the Muslims. Indeed in this sense Islam was no longer alien in India. The Muslims, though professing a different faith, were as much a part of the community as others. On their part, the Muslims even after embracing Islam had not forsaken the mores of their forefathers. Even those Muslims who came from outside and became a part of the rural scene, though in positions of authority had become integrated and attuned to the peculiar caste system. If a Hindu did not partake of food touched by them, they did not take offence, as they knew that this was done not to offend them, but was their way of life. Rites and rituals were different, but the way of life was one.

The tiller of the soil was the linchpin of the rural economy. It was he who by his labour extracted the bounty of mother earth, and it was he on whom the community depended for its victuals. Land was plentiful, soil fertile, manure abundant, and water plentiful. The forests were there on which one could draw for lands to reclaim for tillage, and these also provided fodder for the domestic animals. They also gave sanctuary in time of need and distress. But while there was no scarcity of land there was scarcity of labour, and hence the labourers commanded not only fair wages as a part of the produce, but also care and respect from the cultivator. His condition was not only stable but also secure : the cultivator could not simply afford to alienate him. There was little difference between the cultivator and his farm hands, for a farm hand could always become a cultivator if he could muster necessary organizational skill. Thus, there was no roof for serfdom, and the condition of rural peasantry and rural labour, when compared to the medieval European society as also the present-day rural India, was one of freedom from want.

For one thing, the Indian mind did not acknowledge any proprietary rights in land. Land was for use and possession and not for exploitation of others. Mere title to land for any one, whether acquired by force or by legal rights, was useless unless one could derive profit from it. Hence those nobles who got grant of lands in lieu of services rendered to the state, in effect received the right to appropriate for personal use a part of the share of the state in the produce of the land. They could not sell off their grant of land, as there was virtually no market for land, and mortgage, sale and alienation of land were rare phenomena. If the occupier desired to part with land, he had to beg of a person to buy it, there being no legal conception of absolute and exclusive possession in land. In fact, instant occupation and use were the only attributes of property with which man was concerned. What however, mattered was the immutable right of tillage of the cultivator which was inheritable by his legal successor, and the state had the traditional right of a share in the produce of land, and the landlord, if any, of his commission for collecting this share. The Indian rural communities, not burdened with the regressive phenomenon of land-ownership, were thus well poised for a social mode of production in modern times, but before this was possible, the picture was completely changed by the agrarian policies pursued by the British administration.

In this state of affairs, it is no wonder that from the Emperor down to local chieftain, everyone had taken upon himself the task of ministering to the welfare of the peasantry, for that was the goose that laid golden eggs. Not that there were no petty tyrannies and injustices on the part of local minions of state, and also of lanky governors and nobles out to fatten themselves in the shortest possible time; but whenever these instances came to the notice of the Emperor or high state officials, the redress was instant. For, if oppressed and suppressed beyond endurance, the village community or even individual villagers had the option to abandon the arable land, seek refuge in the forest and begin life anew in a new settlement putting the state and its minions to loss of their shares in the produce. Hence even if there was a war on, both sides left the cultivators alone, and in case of change of regime or authority due to war and similar other causes, it was the minions who changed sides or were written off; the cultivator gave the share of the state to whomsoever was in authority and the spinal chord of agrarian economy remained unbroken.

The village community ran its own internal affairs in respect of maintaining peace in the community, settling personal and proprietary rights, and managing the common rights and liabilities. Only in respect of serious crimes, like robbery, murder or riot, the state would intervene. The state also reserved to itself the right of intervention, if a complaint was laid before it or before its officers, and of the right of adjudication calling upon the parties to compliance to its direction, defiance being visited upon with dire consequences. Thus the prerogative of the state, unlike Europe where it was absolute and unlimited, was defined and definitive. It was the village community that abjured its rights in favour of the state for protection from external aggression and internal disorder, and conceded a part of the fruits of its labour in favour of the state. This was the customary way of life in India, and the Muslim rulers, after settling down, entered into the spirit of this political-economic arrangement and strengthened it further.

The village affairs were managed by a committee of elders called village panchayat. Not that it was a regular body; it came in existence only when some doubts or disputes had to be resolved, because everything was regulated by long usage and custom and only a departure from the same had to be resolved one way or the other. The decisions had to be collective and by consensus. However, instances have also come to notice when the affairs of the village community were managed by a permanent body of elected members. It was the case specially in the south, where the village panchayat was an elective institutional. Dr Radha Kumud Mookerji, in his book *Local Government in Ancient India* (pp.171-72), gives an interesting account of the method of elections in the panchayats on the basis of two famous inscriptions at Uttarmalur. In an open general assembly of the village, in which all adults participated, there was secret casting of votes, the choice of candidates limited to those who fulfilled the qualifications, the ultimate result being announced by drawing of lots from amongst the choice of electors. This sensible method avoided any partisan politics in the village. However, during the period which we are discussing, this wholesome method had fallen in disuse, and the village elders by choice fulfilled the task of village 'panch'. As against this general village council charged with administration and justice in the village, there were caste panchayats of particular castes, specially of the lower order, which decided matters of purely caste interests. The village councils too decided even matters of caste interests of a particular caste; the jurisdiction of the village councils and caste panchayats touched upon each other and were not exclusive.

Thus the majority of the people came to be governed largely by themselves, unaffected by any theory or practice of prerogative of the state. It was sheer weight of adverse public opinion which deterred wrong-doers from wrong doing. However, there was enough resilience in the system. In matters of faith or conduct which went against the prevailing mood, if one was bold enough, or if one could gather around sufficient number of like-minded people, one could form one's own community. Thus dissent of conscience was not visited upon with dire consequences as in Europe. No body in India was burnt on the stakes or thrown in dungeons for dissent against the established order, either for religious or for political views. Nor did petty crimes or aberrations attract dire and cruel punishments as happened in Europe. Generally, fines were imposed and the wrong-doer given an opportunity of retributing the wrong himself. Life was held sacred, unlike Europe where people were incessantly tortured and killed throughout the medieval ages and even later. For example, during the time of impending invasion of Spanish Armada in the Elizabethan period of English History, the Jesuits flitted about in disguise, hiding in 'priest hole' in the thickness of man or house walls, pursued by Justices of the peace, occasionally caught and executed. G.M. Trevelyan in *English Social History* (p.348) notes:

"Throughout the century (18th century) Parliament went on adding statute upon statute to the 'bloody code' of English law, enlarging perpetually the long list of offences punishable by death; finally they numbered two hundred. Not only were horse and sheep stealing and committing capital crimes, but stealing in a shop to the value of five shillings, and stealing anything privately from the person, were it's only a handkerchief."

In "Joseph Andrews" of Fielding we read how when Joseph lay naked on the roadside, all the members of a passing coach, neglected him either due to prudence or modesty, all except a coach boy, afterwards decorated for robbing a hen-roost, who threw on him his coat, with an oath. In France, before Code de Napolean, there was no defined law of crime and punishment, and anybody could be arrested, confined indefinitely, and even beheaded, at the sweet will of authorities. Crime and punishment system in Muslim India appears to be far more humane than in the Western world during the same periods.

The political arrangement in the rural India was self-regulating and adequate, whether the country was at peace or not; war did little to influence the tempo of life in the village. However, the cities whether administrative headquarters, or important for purposes of trade and commerce, had a sophisticated and elaborate administrative machinery, wholly bureaucratic charged with maintaining peace and order in the regime and keeping the channels of commerce open. The Emperor was the head of bureaucracy at the capital, and so were the provincial governors in the provinces and both were expected to look into the details of the administration personally. The officers held both civil and military ranks and headed subordinate civil offices and military departments. All the paraphernalia of a modern bureaucratic machinery; like the departments of exchequer, revenue, mint, intelligence or communication, etc, were in existence. Likewise, military establishment was divided into infantry, artillery, pay, admiralty, etc. The "sadr-ul-sadr", an officer for religious affairs who acted as the spokesmen of the ulema, as in any other Islamic state was an important official but his chief task was to arrange state charities and to act as Emperor's almoner. The "Muhatasibs", were censors of public morals; their task was to see that people lived a life of rectitude, and in case of Muslims, life according to Sharia. The Kotwal was not only responsible for peace in his jurisdiction but had to keep himself in touch with state of affairs in the surrounding regions specially on highways. He had an adequate force of policemen and spies to enable him to discharge his duties efficiently. The department of Justice had three important functionaries; the Mufti expounded the law, a job something like a modern lawyer's, the Qazi made investigations into and tried cases and the Adit drew up and pronounced the judgment. These posts were prestigious, and care was taken to fill them up with men of probity, though in practice some of them were not above temptation. Generally, such posts were frequently held by men of reputed piety.

The provinces had a replica of all these offices. In important sub-divisional headquarters of the provinces. Fauzdars along with Kotwals were held responsible for keeping the highways free from robbery and looked generally after peace in the countryside. Besides, there was the system of Thanedari, according to which it was the duty of the thanedar in lieu of rent free jagirs, to keep sufficient force to police the high ways under his jurisdiction, specially where the terrain was difficult. He had also to keep boats ready at ferries for passengers and for the army, when needed.

India, during the period from the fifteenth to seventeenth centuries, appears to be a country with a cohesive social order, despite the sway of two different religions, one of them being alien but in authority, and the other the cherished faith of a vast majority. This surely reflects the humanising and non-sectarian spirit of Islam. It has become easy now, for fundamentalists of both religions, to either deny or ignore these facts of history, since the institutional character of the Indian society had been altered beyond recognition by the imperialist rule of the British in the succeeding two centuries.

Agriculture requires the aid of artisans. We have seen that even during the time of the Rig Veda certain occupational groups such as carpenters, ironsmiths and potters were recognised as distinct groups which was apparently due to their specific utility in cultivation and pastoral activities which were the chief occupations of the Vish, i.e., the people at large. The artisans were, therefore, a necessary appendage to the village economy subsisting on farming and animal husbandry, not only to fulfil the requirements of productive activities, but also to meet the daily requirements of clothing and shelter. India is considered to be first among civilized countries to have invented the spinning of cotton into clothes, also of silken fibres, though China is said to have discovered the utility of silk as wearing apparel. But in so far as finished product of cotton and silk is concerned, there was none to beat the Indian artisans in quality, smoothness, lightness and texture of the cotton and silk piece-goods they manufactured, and they justly commanded fabulous prices in all advanced countries. Dresses made of Indian cotton and silk fabrics were marks of aristocratic distinction, and till the middle of nineteenth century and before the advent of modern manufacturing processes, they commanded a high price in the world market. Indian cotton and silk, ranked as luxury goods, became common and plentiful in Europe, specially in England in the eighteenth century, England having become enormously rich on account of her overseas colonies and overseas trade. A pamphlet published in 1782, said, "As for the ladies, they wear scarcely anything now but cotton, calicoes, muslin or silks, and think no more of woolen stuffs than we think of an old almanac." Calicoes are so called because such cotton pieces were first imported from Calicut in India. Muslin was "an Indian textile, woven plain without looping of the warp threads on the weft", the like of which could be produced only by Indian artisans. India, in the plains, did not produce high-grade wool, but it was still superior to English wool, though England prided itself as the clothier of Europe, and wool trade was the chief mainstay of English commerce. However, in the highlands, specially in Kashmir, *merino* wool of very high quality comparable to the best *merino* wool of Spain, was produced and woollen garments made of goat hair reared in Kashmir were of exceedingly fine quality; no regalia was complete, either in East or in West, unless the sovereign wrapped himself in a 'Cushmera', so called because it was manufactured in Kashmir with goat's hair.

India had a vast store of minerals, gems and precious stones and the skill of her workmen in turning these into useful articles of use or of pieces of art, was legendary and excited the wonder of foreigners. Indian swords and weapons were also prized. Indians cooked and partook of their meals either in vessels and plates of silver, copper and brass, or in earthenware or on plain plantain leaves, according to their status or occasion. Thus, though pottery was advanced, it was not of that high quality as in China which justly prided itself on its porcelain wares. Copper and brass vessels from India were in great demand in Middle Eastern countries and in other areas under Persian and Turkish Empires where they were used for cooking delicacies of meat and rice. Indian filigree workmanship on gold and silver ornaments was considered unique, and such ornaments adorned the figures of royal and rich ladies all the world over. India had ivory too which few countries in the world had during those times, and its possession was highly prized. As late as the seventeenth century, Pyrard of Level, a French traveller who travelled in the East, observed, "I could never make an end of telling such a variety of manufacture as well in gold, silver, iron, steel, copper and other metal's, as in precious stones, choice woods, and other valued and rare materials ..... And what is to be observed of their manufacture is this, that they are both of good workmanship, and cheap."

Certain agricultural products like spices were regarded as exotic items badly needed in many countries, specially the cold countries of Europe, plagued by long, barren and dark winters. In England and other cold countries, come winter and all the stock of animals except those in breed had to be slaughtered and salted, for two very good reasons; firstly, there was nothing to feed them upon during the long winter months, and secondly, to have frozen meat as the principal item of food, there being nothing else to eat. Fresh meat during winter months was a luxury even for royal kitchen. For preserving and seasoning of meat, spices, specially pepper, was essential. It was, therefore, a most valued commodity in Europe from earliest times. Since Europe in those days had nothing worthwhile to sell to India, it had to pay for spices in hard currency - that is, silver and gold. Thus, the outburst of Pliny against India for "robbing" Rome of her treasure of silver annually. Spices were also grown in Far East, but India was the main supplier. These products were carried overland on camels' back across Arab and Middle East by Arab merchants up Levant, off Mediterranean coast east to Italy. Venice was then the centrepoint of trade and commerce between East and West. After the establishment of the Turkish Empire, the Turks (Arabia had come under their possession) held the monopoly of spice trade in the West. It was to free the European market from Turkish monopoly that Columbus had been financed to find out a sea-route to India, the exotic land, where `spices grew, the land being paved with silver and gold.' When Shakespeare in Macbeth: (V) (1) (53) says: "all the perfumes of Arabia will not sweeten this little land", he is speaking not of any manufactured lavender of Arabia but of Indian spices like musk, camphor, etc, carried by the Arabs, because these were the only perfumes the Elizabethan knew of. Just as Indian numerals are known as Arabic numerals, the Indian perfumes (of spices) were known as Arabian perfumes (of spices), since both came to Europe through the agency of Arabia. Indian spices were also essential ingredients for flavouring such delicacies, such as meat and *pilao* dishes and were valued highly in Middle East. Turkish Empire, and the Mediterranean lands. The price they commanded was fabulous according to the then prevailing standards. Sugar, indigo, saltpetre, and opium were other items in which India commanded an enviable position.

India appears then to have been fairly- advanced in ship-building in comparison with European countries including England. India was endowed with extensive timber, of very enduring quality wood, sturdy and water-resistant. Fahien, the Chinese traveller on his return journey to China sailed from Ceylon in an ocean going ship built in India, which was carrying two hundred passengers across the turbulent Chinese Sea. Indians had colonized the East Indies-Malaysia, and Indonesia for fifteen hundred years. The Cholas were a great maritime power carrying on war against Shailendras of Java for about a hundred years. This pre-supposes a well developed ship-building industry and an efficient navy. The maritime regions of the country like Bengal, Orissa, Andhra, Malabar, Konkan, Cambay and Gujarat, had seafaring populations. Moreover, the main arteries of communication and commerce were the perennial rivers of India, the Ganges, the Indus, the Jamuna, the Sarju, the Gandak, the

Narmada, the Krishna, the Cauvery and many others, which criss-crossed the country and sustained heavy traffic by boats. It was normal to have boats of a cargo of one thousand tons and boats of tonnage of 1500 even were not unknown. Besides satisfying indigenous needs, India supplied sturdy ships to Arab sailors; it was in Indian ships that the Arabs had carried the flag of Islam to Malaysia and Indonesia in the fifteenth-sixteenth centuries. England, which became an advanced maritime power in sixteenth and seventeenth centuries with an enviable merchant navy - her life-line extended to the Atlantic Ocean in the West and the China Sea and the Pacific in East - was not able to build ships capable of carrying more than hundred passengers and cargo, as against India which during the fifth century could boast of building passenger ships capable of carrying even two hundred passengers Godfrey Davies in his *Early Stuart* (p. 337) notes: "Between 1630 and 1643, 200,000 sterlings was spent in conveying 20,000 men, women and children to New England in 200 ships. This gives one hundred persons in one ship on an average. According to Parkinson, "In ship building, they (Indians) probably taught the English far more than they learnt from them". Even an imperialist historian like Moreland, referring to Medieval India says "it is still to my mind indisputable that in the matter of industry India was more advanced relatively to Western Europe than she is today".

Obviously, the industrial activity embracing over this vast country was organized on a two-tier basis, rural and urban. The village remained the basic unit, and the village artisans supplied the necessary manufactured goods to the community in exchange for grains and other items of necessity. Cash nexus was almost nil, thus guarding all concerned against wide price fluctuations. In times of famine and distress, the artisans took their wares to such parts as were relatively affluent, and were able to purchase or exchange the manufactured items. The artisans, both Hindus and Muslims, were organised as occupational castes. However, cloth manufacturing artisans were mostly Muslims. For historical reasons which we have already discussed, these occupational castes of Bengal and Northern India had accepted Islam, and were scattered now all over the country either in the countryside or in urban manufacturing centres. Then again, carders, spinners, dyers, etc, comprised distinct sub-castes. Similarly, metal workers were mostly Muslims, and their rank was swelled by artisans from Persia and from the Turkish Empire, who came to India attracted by the high reputation of Indian craftsmanship. In course of time, they were absorbed in the Indian milieu; but, sometimes, they still comprised distinct sub-castes of their own. Ironsmiths were mostly Hindus and so were goldsmiths. Those village artisans who could excel in their calling and whose wares achieved distinction so as to command better price generally migrated to urban manufacturing centres. These were generally the capitals of provincial governors and local chieftains, places of pilgrimage where people congregated in large numbers periodically, and were commercial centres. There was free movement of artisans from one part of the country to another and it was very seldom that any restriction was put by any local ruler and chieftains on emigration of the artisans from their territory on any ground, religious or otherwise. It appears such restrictions were the common practice in medieval Europe where guilds of artisans had to function under control and restriction of the local nobility either temporal or ecclesiastical.

India, thus was a bee-hive of industrial activities the different regions specialising in different products, depending on the availability of raw materials but more so on availability of expertise of artisans. The artisan's skill was the mainstay of the country's industrial wealth. Textile was the most important industry -almost every village producing its own clothing needs. Important urban textile manufacturing centres were Dacca, Murshidabad, Patna, Banaras, Agra, Jaipur, Multan, Burhanpur, Lahore, Ahmadabad, Baroda, Broach, Surat, Coimbatore, Kanchi and Madurai. Fine Muslin was the speciality of Dacca; silk and brocade of unrivalled quality were the speciality of Benares and Madurai; Lahore, Multan, and Agra were famous for fine metal works armory and precious jewellery; while Cuttak and Jaipur, specialized in filigree and gold and silver ornaments. India could develop such expertise in manufactured goods because the producers were all hereditary skilled workers, engaged for several generations in the same traditional skills. Under such conditions work was not an imposition but a source of satisfaction, , the products partaking something of a work of art. Compared to the guild system of Europe and England, there was no practice of apprenticeship, and journeymanship; the calling was inherited, the artisans being a member of a particular occupational caste. Those who did not want to stick to the calling of the caste had always the alternative of taking to cultivation, and thus the industry had never - an unwilling worker or a worker at variance with his own calling as was often the case in the European guild system.

This industrial complex seems to be organized on a somewhat modern system of financing and marketing. Merchants had their agents in almost all important manufacturing centres; in the village the local grain merchant who dealt in village commodities was generally the agent of some prosperous merchant also. The artisans generally borrowed raw materials against sale of their products at a price mutually agreed upon but there was nothing to deter the artisan selling his surplus in the ready market at the going price, if it was more handsome. Certain castes like Banjaras, Sahus, etc, specialised in transportation of goods from one corner of the country to another. Then there were Bhats and Kroris, so named because they were so honest that goods and bullion of the value of crores of rupees could be entrusted to them safely for transportation (originally, 'Krori' was the name given to officers appointed to collect revenue of one crore *dams*). The usual transportation was river navigation. It was estimated that in Bengal alone there were 40 to 50 thousand boats in the sixteenth century carrying both passengers and goods. There were flourishing entrepots all along the river coast. Administration took special care to police river navigation, and river piracy, though not unknown, was not widespread until we come to the 18th century when the writ of central authority ceased to be strong. The Mughal rulers had a department of Admiralty which looked mainly after internal navigation. Similarly, the authorities on the Coromandal and Malabar coasts had their system of policing internal navigation. However, in Gujarat, on account of its extensive trade with Arabian coasts, the authorities also maintained navy. On the roads, horses and palanquins carried passengers but goods were carried on pack animals. A special breed of bullocks, called Nagori Bullocks, were bred for speed and load and were employed for carrying cartloads of goods swiftly; many of them out-raced even horses. Thus, the country was a big industrial and commercial unit. The whole country from Orissa to East Bengal was one huge cotton factory, all villages and towns being concerned in the production of cotton, yarns, and finishing of the goods and making them ready for home and foreign markets." The volume of production and trade was massive. As Tavernier observed, the total output of silk in Bengal in the middle of the 17th century "was about 2.5 million pounds out of which one million pounds were worked up locally, 3/4 million were exported raw by the Dutch, and 3/4 million distributed over India, most of it going to Gujarat, but some being taken by merchants from Central Asia."

In the seventeenth century, India could perhaps be rated as the largest producer of industrial goods in the world. Neither China, nor the Turkish Empire nor Europe would compete with her in the variety, excellence or volume of her products. She had the largest working force in the world, with a family pride in the excellence of their products. Such an institutional framework ensured that there was no unemployment or lay off. The occupation of the industrial worker was hereditary and a joint family affair, and so was the case with the merchants who financed and marketed their products, both being tied down with each other in a long, enduring relationship. The city merchant was a familiar figure in India from times immemorial, and occupied a position of trust and responsibility in the economic and social hierarchy. The city-merchant called Nagar Seth (Chattiyar in the south) used to be on the advisory council of the Hindu kings, guiding and advising them on economic policies. In both Buddhistic and Jain literature they have been pictured as vastly enterprising, adventurous, and enormously rich, parsimonious and self-denying in their personal habits but generous and self-sacrificing for common cause. As a matter of fact, according to Buddhistic traditions, the princes of Benaras were among the first ones to succumb to the charms of Lord Buddha's personality, renouncing their all to take refuge in Dharm Sangha. The Muslim elite were generally not interested in trade and industry being by inclination and occupation, soldiers and administrators. They did not want to embroil themselves in the intricacies of finance and commerce. Merchant-princes of Central Asia and Persia were interested more in trading in merchandise than in production of goods. Of course, during the beginning of the Muslim rule, trade and commerce had suffered enormously due to unsettled conditions in the country as also due to the encrustations of the marauding Central Asian herds who were pouring into the country, compelled out of their own home and hearth by the stronger herds of Mongols and other Homeric tribes. By fifteenth-sixteenth centuries, however, conditions had settled down in the country and the lines of communication had become stable and safe.

The city merchant, either singly or organized into a co-operative unit or a part of joint-family unit, was the financier, supplier of raw materials and purchaser of finished products of the artisans, all rolled into one. Thus, generally, the artisan did not have to worry about supply of raw materials and the marketing of his goods. In times of distress, it was in the interest of the merchants themselves not to allow the artisans to suffer in any way. This was better than the guild system of Europe which was not in the word of C.R. Fay "favourable to capital accumulation", so vital for the rise of capitalism and Industrial Revolution. It is noteworthy that from seventeenth century onwards, England freed itself from the European style guild system and adopted a similarly personalised system of finance and production until the Industrial Revolution gave rise to the Joint-Stock Company system as agency of capitalist and financing of production and trade.

The city merchants, just like the merchant capitalists of latter day England on their part, had links with marketing outlets, both internal and external. At the apex were the hyperbolic Jagat Seths or "world-merchants" in the various centres such as Bengal, Benares, Multan, Gujarat and Maduri. The Houses of Jagat Seths of Bengal, Nathji of Gujarat and Chettiers of South were widely known. The Jagat Seths of Bengal, however, hailed from Marwar, and Nathji of Gujarat from Benaras. These merchants performed all the functions of a modern bank-receiving deposits, giving loans and issuing hundis (bills of exchange)—much before a Rothschild or a Russel. They had acquired a world-wide reputation of probity and stability in the financial world and commanded great confidence and credit. Of them Nathu Kothari Chetty of South carried on business in Burma, Ceylon, Malaya and the Eastern Islands and Nathji of Gujarat had trading links with Arabia, Egypt, Damascus and Istanbul. From Multan and Kabul caravans went to China and Central Asia; Khotan was an important clearing centre where caravans from India, China and Central Asia assembled and exchanged goods. Muslim merchants also had a fair share in the trade particularly in Lahore, Multan and Kabul. Khwaja Wajid and Istamuddin of Bengal were noted Muslim businessmen of the times.

Manufacture of fire arms and field artillery was, however, a state enterprise, if not a state monopoly. The Muslim rulers before the Mughals depended largely upon fire arms and artillery of Central Asian make. The Chinese had been pioneers both in the manufacture of rustless steel and gun powder. However, Indian artisans later on improved upon the Chinese technology of making steel, and India came to be justly reputed as the manufacturer of finest rustless steel (Qutub Minar is an example). However, Indian rulers, both native and foreign, failed to appreciate adequately its military significance, and did not give attention to have effective projectiles made of steel, even though there was adequate supply of saltpetre, an essential ingredient of gun powder. Akbar was conscious of this deficiency and he set up state manufacturing units for armoury. But the effort was half-hearted; the Mughals continued to depend for their guns and field artillery on Turkish and Central Asian 'suppliers. It was ironical, however, that these guns and artillery pieces were made of steel imported from India. The artisans of Damascus had discovered an alloy which when mixed with steel made it fire resistant. Barrels made of such steel could fire continuously for hours together without the barrel being heated. The Damascus barrels made history and artillery using such barrels won for the Turks not only the Byzantine Empire, but enabled Sulaiman, the Magnificent, to subjugate Eastern Europe and knock at the doors of Vienna. The Indian army depended on such Turkish artillery. The artillery-men were also drawn mainly from that region; Rumi or Turkish. The Europeans had, however, countered the Turks by their growing sea power, and the Spaniards fought the Turks the great sea-battle at Lepanto in 1571 A.D. which, however, did nothing to diminish the land power of the Turkish, as their artillery continued to be superior. Later, the Europeans also were employing the same tactics and importing Damascus-barrelled guns for their army. That the Turkish artillery and artillery men were superior to those of Indian or European origin as late as eighteenth century was proved at the third battle of Panipat. Ibrahim Khan Gardi, a clever artillery man who had been trained in European methods of fighting under Bussy in the Nizam's army, was the head of artillery of the Maratha army, but he cut a sorry figure before the more potent and efficient Turkish artillery and artillery men heading Abdali's Afghan army. The Indians paid a heavy price for this technological deficiency in spite of their much vaunted rustless steel.

While the world needed India's spices, cotton and silk piece goods, saltpetre, indigo, boats, fine rice, steel, steel weaponry -all items of necessities beside items of luxuries for kings and nobles, India imported a limited quantity of rugs from Persia and Turkey, steeds from Arabia, pieces of artillery from central Asia and Turkey, and raw silk and porcelain from China. With unhindered and free flow of goods from one part of the country to another, and a single point taxation levied by the authorities on sale and purchase of goods-duties only on the frontiers and place of sale within the kingdom -introduced by Shershah, and continued by the Mughal rulers, India was one single big mart for trade and commerce. Export of bullion - silver and gold - was strictly prohibited but India having a favourable balance of trade, the foreigners had to pay in bullion, mostly silver when they had no worthwhile goods to give in exchange. Opening of sea-route to India round the Cape of Good Hope had brought European traders to India in search of

Indian goods directly, at the source instead of through circuitous routes of Arabia, Turkish Empire and Levant. However, Europe then did not have much worthwhile goods to give in exports and had, therefore, to pay in cash in shape of silver. It has been estimated that by 1621 A.D., England had exported 1,00,000 sterling in bullion to India, brought back wares worth five times in terms of English and European level of prices, and consuming one fifth at home, sold the rest abroad and received a profit of 400%.

The wealth of India understandably excited the envy and greed of the enterprising nations of the world. The drain of precious metals into India in exchange for her goods, reached a peak in the seventeenth century with the direct participation of Europeans in Indian trade and commerce. In the picturesque words of Terry, "many silver streams run thither (India) as all rivers to the sea, and there stay". Bernier ruefully complains, "silver after circulating in every other quarter of the globe, comes at length to be swallowed up, lost in some measure, in Hindusthan."

It appears India emerged as the foremost industrial nation of the world during the fifteenth to seventeenth centuries, a position subsequently occupied by Britain and by USA. There is suspicion that England adopted Indian organisational systems, discarded the guide system and allowed the Statute of Artificers enacted in 1563 A.D. to fall in disuse gradually, and encouraged cottage production units to grow. This enabled England to be nearly a hundred years ahead of Europe in achieving an industrial revolution. Colonial historians like Smith, Moreland, Elliot and Erskine, have done their best to paint a somewhat gloomy picture of Indian economy and Indian commerce during this period.

That the wealth of India and Indians was legendary is borne out of constant reference to it by some of the great English poets. Thus, Christopher Morlowe would have nothing less than Indian gold:

"I'll have them fly to India for gold,
Ransack the ocean for orient-pearl"
(Dr.Faustus 110)

Shakespeare would find no better compliment to praise Rosalind than to say.

"From the east to western India
No Jewel is like Rosalind."

Finally, Milton, the true Christian of firm faith, has heard of the celestial city in the Revelation of St. John "The street of the city was pure gold", (21 : 21). Milton refers specifically to India:

"... the wealth of Ormus and of Ind,
Or where the gorgeous East with richest hand
Showers on her Kings barbaric pearl and gold."

How this picture of economic prosperity got transformed and the wealth planted elsewhere is another story to be discussed in the following pages.

Fall of Muslim Authority

As the seventeenth century passed into the eighteenth the web of affluence which India had been able to spin of and build up into an edifice of peace, power and prosperity had begun to crumble, due to both external and internal forces.

We shall take up the external forces first, because these were the product of certain historical processes, over which perhaps, human agency has no control, and which remain mysterious and elusive of any definite assignment. Gibbon laments the fall of the Roman Empire, but, then, Rome Empire, or at least its ghost or ghost of its idea, is still alive and kicking and keeping its hold entrenched over human mind. The Roman Empire, instead of finally dying, had passed into Papacy, and as Hobbes said "the Papacy is not other than the ghost of deceased Roman Empire, sitting crowned upon the grave thereof." When Papacy declined in power and glory, it gave rise to numerous nation states in the West who hold aloft now the banner of the West and the Empire. In fact it is the decline of the East that one has to mourn - and human misery and political emasculation which has gripped China, India, Arabia, Iran, and the Middle East, once acclaimed as the seed-houses of ideas and movements and pioneers in science and technology. They now lie humbled, living off the crumbs and left overs of the West; the result has been that the East is becoming puny and irrelevant - a deadening sorrow its destiny:

> "To sorrow I bade good morrow,
> And thought to leave her far away behind
> But cheerly, cheerly, she loves me dearly,
> She is so constant to me, so kind."

In India, at least, sorrow has been our constant and kind companion for the last three hundred years since the country was taken over by traders, merchants mercenaries and other adventurers from a foreign country. Aristotle held merchants and financiers unfit to be "citizens", much less able to govern but it became India's destiny to be governed by foreign capitalists and they still influence its ways of living and thinking. The question is: how this misfortune came about? For the foreign merchants did not come with an expeditionary force. They came as welcome merchants to the vast mart of India to carry her finished goods, and bounties, with which nature had generously endowed her, to the four corners of the world, but ultimately they stayed back as masters and arbiters of her fate. These merchants were from a tiny country who took about a year to sail from their country to reach India and who till the fifteenth century were quiet insignificant in the comity of even European nations, with no national cohesion or purpose. An inexplicable historical spectacle indeed!

Of all the important European countries, England had certain advantages due to circumstances, as well as due to the character of her people. A nation originating in Roman bandits, Viking pirates, Norman conquerors, Saxon Freemen and Bondsmen, the English people, bold, enterprising and adventurous, emerged by the fifteenth century as an aristocratic commonalty with national pride in their king and country. The fine balance between aristocratic pride of the elite and the craving for democratic rights of the common people has since informed all their institutions and made them win the race of power, leaving their other European competitors behind, who unfortunately for themselves realised the need for balance in their political, social, and economic arrangements very late, or at least later than the English. It is not for nothing that makes Macaulay recall with pride "thus our democracy was, from an early period, the most aristocratic, and our aristocracy the most democratic in the world." In common with other Teutonic countries of the continent, England did shake off Papal supremacy and scholastic crust of mind, not in the way of Luther or Calvin, but what her own Wycliffe preached and what Erasmus (1524-83) laid down i.e., the Church must be controlled by the State and be made an arm of it. England, in her own peculiar genius, founded a national church of her own without much tear or travail, ensuring a large uniformity in religious teachings and practices. Of course, as in other Christian countries, there were persecution and religious conflicts, even regicide, in course of a power struggle for religious ends but not on the scale and to the extent as on the continent. England, generally, steered clear of extremes, allowing dissent, and eventually tolerating sects which were Christian but no part of the establishment of the state Church. The national Church, however, maintained a hierarchy of churchmen in offices under the state. The Bible and the Book of Common Prayer were source of ultimate spiritual solace, and it was proclaimed that "the Bishop of Rome hath no Jurisdiction in this Realm of England. Proud of their national heritage, swearing loyalty to their king and their country, whom, however, they sought to control and govern, liberated from the yoke of Popish mental serfdom, the Englishmen harked at the callings of their ancestors - Viking sea-pirates and Norman and Anglo-Saxon adventurers.

The lure of the riches of India had taken Columbus to America, and Vasco de Gama had ultimately discovered India by sea. England was ready to take full advantage of new vistas of trade with distant and unknown lands. England has ever been a sea faring nation: mainly a pastoral wool-raising country, a spinner of yarns, clothier of the continent, an island trader, and sailing for trade in her own ships. By the sixteenth century, England was as great a maritime nation on the European continent as the Dutch or the Spaniards or the Venetians. The sea had been with her and remained with her. As T.S. Eliot puts it, "the river is within us, the sea is all about us." Sporting on the wide bosom of the seven seas, the English sailors along with the Spanish and other continental seamen pirates were on prowl, looting, pillaging, and raising the flags of their country on virgin lands or founding settlements and colonies for their country men on distant lands. Their greed and lust were insatiable and freed from bounds of inhibition of any kind, they indulged in unspeakable treachery, trickery and brutality against unprepared, unfortunate inhabitants of the new found world. "Plus Ultra", "more beyond" was their motto. Kant, the great German philosopher, gives a graphic description of the situation. He says:

"If we compare the barbarian instances of inhospitality ... with the inhuman behaviour of the civilised, and especially the commercial States of our continent, the injustice practised by them when in their first contact with foreign lands and peoples fills us with horror; the visiting of such peoples being regarded by them as equivalent to a conquest. America, the Negro lands, the Spice Islands, the Cape of Good hope, etc., on being discovered, were treated as countries that belonged to nobody, for the aboriginal inhabitants were reckoned as nothing .... And all this has been done by nations who make a great ado about their piety, and who, while drinking up iniquity like water, would have themselves regarded as the very elect of the orthodox faith. "

Verily, history was being repeated. For a thousand years back, Central Asian barbarians riding their stallions and armed to the teeth, had been embarking on forays of plunder, loot and settlement in other more prosperous and civilized lands, and had ultimately exhausted themselves by destroying the Byzantine Empire and founding the Turkish Empire, bringing under their sway the holy lands of Arabia, Syria and Palestine. Now the neo-barbarians or "northern barbarians", as George Santayana calls them, had started on a spree of feeding themselves on destruction and desolation of less fortunate lands and peoples, the echoes of which have still not died down. It is thus that a philosopher like Schopenhauer finds the motto of history running as: "*Hadem Sed Aliter*", "the same thing, true in different ways". So, the ships were now the stallions of the European marauders, and, happily for them, the ships had not only more effective teeth to fight against others, but the very mode of naval warfare had changed for the better. Until the sixteenth century, ships had been used for transportation of soldiers, and generally the fight had taken place deck to deck, hand to hand, rank to rank, and formation to formation as if they were on land. It is thus that the Greeks and the Persians had fought the naval battle at Sa1G.nis, the Cholas of India against the Shailendras of Jave on the breast of the Indian Ocean, the Spaniards, in keeping with Mediterranean traditions concerned with soared galley and the grappling of the ship, against the Turks at Lepanto in 1571; and Phillip of Spain out to conquer England in the English Channel. The English had, however, learnt to have broadside on their ships, rows of cannons protruding between the timbers, and thus naval warfare from a game of soldiers became, instead, a game of sailors, manoeuvring their ships so as to fire their cannons with utmost effect: the ship ceased to be a platform for a storming party and became a moving battery of guns. The role of the ship was changed from one of a transport vessel to an engine of war; the credit for this transformation goes largely to England. It is, thus, that in the race of founding new colonies and carrying on world-wide trade, the English finally could establish their supremacy over the Spaniards, their chief opponent in the Atlantic, and against the Portuguese, their chief opponent in the East.

On discovery of new lands and new routes, the Pope at Rome had drawn a line on the globe across the continent of Europe from North to South, and generously assigned the East to the Portuguese, and the West to Spain, "to conquer and spread the gospel of the Lord among the heathens!" Armed with this Papal Bull of 1493 A.D., the Portuguese had come to India and East Indies in the East, but found the going too tough as there were well-established empires and kingdoms before whom they could do nothing more than carry on trade, found a few settlements, and make conversions wherever they could. The Spaniards were, however, more fortunate in the west as under Pizarro and other conquistadors, they conquered and ransacked Mexico and Peru, "where streets were paved with gold." The great Maya and Aztec civilisations, in a state of very high degree of development - at least superior to the Hispanic one itself -were completely devastated, and Incas the Peat Princes, physically eliminated by trick and treachery by the invaders. It is in this context, perhaps, that Becon relates : "Solon said well to Croesus (when in ostentation Croesus showed him gold), Sir, if any other come that hath better iron than you, he will be master of all this gold" - All the gold of Peru could not hold against the Spaniards who had better iron.

English freebooters, like Hawkins, Drake, Frobisher and Raleigh, were out on the seas, for booty and trade. They fought for freedom to sail the seas, which was sought to be denied to them by the Spaniards, and freedom to worship God in their own way which was not liked, again, by the Spaniards, and to colonize empty lands where the Red Indians-as they termed all such natives - would be the only persons aggrieved. They did not want any of the Spanish lands on the new continent: they were content to loot, harass, and destroy the Spaniards on the high seas, and thus despoil the despoilers. Later on, they discovered a more profitable source of trade - the negro slaves caught and tricked and sold into slavery from the coasts of Africa, being carried on by ships into the new settlements, and colonies, and even into Spanish America. Their ships were lighter, capable of better manoeuvring, and the discipline on their ships was better than on the continental ships with their penchant for democratic behaviour, they required even the gentlemen volunteer sailors to haul at the ropes along with the regular mariners, and all were treated alike. "There was no gentleman among seamen, and no seaman among gentlemen." On the other hand, the Spaniards should not lay aside their military and aristocratic pride even to save the ship. The Broadsides, the lighter ships, and better discipline and operational efficiency of the English seamen made them successful against the Spaniards in the struggle to found colonies in the new lands, and empire in the old world.

Meanwhile, the booty of plunder and the plums of piracy as well as the profit from extensive trade and commerce continued to enrich the English society over a period of time. There was a spirit of romance, adventure of the unknown and an air of expectancy for the whole nation. The hazards were many but the prize was also great. England had no standing army, but a 'royal' navy and a growing and strong merchant marine. The British aristocracy and the British monarch himself, or herself, had a direct interest in the maritime activities combining trade with piracy. The various Navigation Acts were making it compulsory for British merchants to trade in English ships. Wealth was thus pouring in, and there was a scramble for a share by all and sundry.

Though a 'nation of shopkeepers', the English were no mean fighters, and had a reputation on the continent with 'bow and arrow'. The sturdy rustic from the English countryside, who joined on voyages abroad, had his own pride, but was amenable to discipline and team work and had 'respect for the superiors'. The English sailors and soldiers were no doubt 'the scum of the earth', as Lord Wellington, the victor of Waterloo, once said, adding "it is really wonderful we should have made them the fine followers they are". Their naval military commanders would transform them into efficient and enterprising band, who could achieve given tasks.

The Englishmen established trading posts on the Indian coast along with other Europeans such as the French, Portuguese, Dutch, Danes, etc. In about one hundred years, they consolidated their position in such a way that they began to be considered a power to be reckoned with, ultimately emerging as the paramount power on the sub-continent of India, administering directly a very large part of the country and exercising effective control over the rest through native princes. In the above paragraphs we have referred to some of the factors which made them successful. These traits were such as to make them superior to other continental nationalities in the race for power, but in so far as India was concerned, it is doubtful how far these contributed to their success in this country. For example, the founding of a national Church and tolerance of dissent might look progressive in the context of the Jesuit-Calvinist bitter feuds raging on the continent of Europe till the end of eighteenth century, and with the burning of dissenters at stakes on mere suspicion of supposed heresy, but this quality leaves us cold as there was far greater amity and tolerance of each other amongst the Hindus and Muslims in spite of five hundred years of Muslim rule in the better part of the country, and in spite of constant wars that were waged for territorial aggrandizement and supremacy amongst different powers, both Hindu and Muslim. These wars were never religious wars, and though there might be religious persecutions even, here and there, there never was any organized and collective persecution of opposite faiths as was the case say in France even up to the latter part of the eighteenth century. To give an example:

"In the city of Toulouse, the seventh city of France, the Catholic clergy enjoyed absolute sovereignty there; the city commemorated with frescoes the Revocation of the Edict of Nantes (an edict which had given freedom of worship to Protestants), and celebrated as a great feast the day of the Massacre of St.Bartholomew. No Protestant in Toulouse could be a lawyer, or a physician, or an apothecary, or a grocer, or a book-seller, or a printer; nor could a Catholic keep a Protestant servant or clerk in 1748 a woman had been fined 3000 Francs for using a Protestant midwife."

No Huguenot (Protestants of France and the low countries) could settle in France or Canada. Social and political ostracization on such scale, deliberate and discriminatory, was never practised in India. In England itself, most of the civil wars were religious and denominational in nature, and though dissenters were tolerated, there was a limit to toleration, and persecution for holding different opinions was not unknown. Nobody could enter into the portals, of the establishment without conforming to its tenets. England could by no means be said to be a country of greater mutual tolerance than India. The Muslims had been ruling over an appreciable part of the country, but the proportion of the Muslim population never went beyond 12 to 13 per cent. Even in urban centres where the Muslim presence was most marked, such as Murshidabad, Patna, Lucknow, Agra, Delhi, Lahore, Bijapur, Multan or Burahanpur, the majority of the population still was Hindu, which shows there could be no social or political ostracization, or discrimination against them. The English therefore, could not have reaped any political benefit in India on account of the fact that they were a tolerant race. In fact they were not tolerant enough according to Indian standards.

The naval superiority of the English was not of much relevance in a predominantly land mass like India. The English ships with their broadsides and easy manoeuvrability might have been like so many floating fortresses on the coastline of the country, but generally ineffective in land battles. The English were certainly not better fighters than the Indians; man to man this was proved so many times during the wars the English waged in India. However, they were certainly better organized and amenable to perfect discipline. The criminality prone sturdy rustic from England, out on a fortune-hunting expedition in a distant foreign land like India, was a model of tact and discipline, very much conscious of his own honour and the honour of his country; while the Indian soldiers were generally an ill-disciplined mass, inclined to take soldiering easy. This made all the difference, and we find again and again the Indian soldiers being humbled by better formations during the English-Indian wars. A stronger factor, however, was the failure of Indian leadership to understand the political and economic forces that were operating around the world at that time. Just like a cub grown into a wolf, the Europeans were sniffing and prowling all over the world. The English had entered Persia as commercial traders through the river system of Russia, thus defying the difficulties of old routes. The Portuguese had taken over Ormuz,.a port in Persian Gulf well-known to the Indians. Tales of Negroes being whisked away from the coast of Africa must have reached India, and it is impossible to believe that conquistador's savagery and butchery in the New World had not reached India and its rulers. Still the Indian leadership could not discern any danger from these foreign traders who were swarming over the country and fighting among themselves to secure better privileges and trading rights from the native princes and potentates.

These traders had nothing worthwhile to offer in exchange for the Indian goods; they, rather, offered to act as carriers of Indian goods into foreign lands to earn ready bullion, for which they sought concessions in custom duties. The Indian authorities out of misplaced generosity as also instant greed easily granted such concessions as also permission to build port facilities of their own on the Indian coast-line. The trading stations on the coast-line were soon converted into forts to be put to military use. The Indians should have treated the offers from these traders as if they were in the nature of Greek gifts, made out of treacherous motives, as Virgil says:

"I fear the Greeks, even though they offer gifts."

The foreigners began to show their teeth early. The Portuguese defeated a combined Egyptian-Indian fleet at Diu, in 1509, and forced Mahmud Begarhe of Gujarat to permit them the site for a factory at Diu. The rivalry among the various European nations seeking commerce in India took the form of open war on Indian soil without caring for the territorial sovereignty of the Empire of the Indian rulers. During the times of Shah Jahan and Aurangzeb, punitive action had to be taken against such defiance. In fact, the very wording of the charters granted to the foreign companies by their home governments, showed that these were sought to be State within State, empowered "to make war, conclude treaties, acquire territories, and build fortresses, Dutch, French, and English - from the very beginning had not only commercial interests in view, but also territorial ambitions in India, and were ever on look out for opportunities. Let us consider the advice of Sir Thomas Roe, James, It's Ambassador and East India Company's Agent at the court of the Moghal Emperor:

"A war and traffic are incompatible. Let this be received as a rule that if you will profit, seek it at sea, and in quiet trade; for without controversy it is an error to affect garrisons and land wars in India."

Implicit in the advice is the ambition of territorial aggrandisement, though Roe advises against this for the sake of earning profit. Indians certainly failed to see the evil face of Europeans in the garb of traders. It was the elite the political leadership that failed completely in India in the eighteenth century. The eminent historian, J.N.Sarkar, thus laments, "Nothing is more striking than the decline of the peerage. The heroes adorn the stage for one generation only and leave no worthy heirs sprung from their loins. Abdur Rahim and Mahabat, Sa'ddullah and Mir jumla, Ibrahim and Islam Khan Rumi who had made history of India in the seventeenth century were succeeded by no son, certainly by no grandson, even half as capable as themselves." The reason was not far to seek: Indian nobility both Hindus and Muslim had become too soft due to the "haram culture". A life of ease and indolence, of easy virtue and instant riches, had deprived them of cultivating the manly qualities of vigour, vision, and the ability to foresee and meet vicissitudes. Francisco Pelsaert, the chief of the Dutch factory at Agra in the time of Jahangir, certainly not suffering from any anti-Indian bias, observed "the mahals of the rich were adorned internally with lascivious sensuality, wanton and reckless festivity, superfluous pomp, inflated pride, and ornamental daintiness", and this was not the atmosphere in which `bravery abides, vision resides, and success is crowned'. The Mughal, Afghan, and Rajput princes had lost much of their old shine, involved in petty intrigues, mutual rivalries and jealousies, taking the imperatives of peace and war just in their stride. Expediency became the rule of life, loyalty was at a discount, and self came before everything.

It is true in a federal polity like India, balance has to be maintained between local autonomous entities, and central authority. The moment both or any of them become unbalanced disaster is bound to overtake the whole fabric. It was true then, as it is true now; any other arrangement, political, social or economic, is simply not possible. Whenever the central authority has become overbearing or weak, the local autonomous entities comprising of local conjoint authorities, as well as the articulate masses have withdrawn their allegiance to the central authority. No central authority in India has been able to impose its will for long on the country or a major part of it, unless it was able to maintain this tenuous bålance - be they the Magadhans, Mauryans, Guptas, Imperial Pratiharas, Chalukyas, Cholas, Cheras, Pathans, Afghans or the Mughals. In the Indian psyche, which includes both Hindus and Muslims, no feeling of sacredness is attached to the imperial authority: it is simply an arrangement to govern effectively but justly. No divinity was attached to the person to foster this myth. As long back as the times of Harshavardhan, Bana, the writer of *Harshacharit*, pricks the bubble of the divine right of kings in these words:

"Though subject to mortal conditions, kings look on themselves as having alighted on earth as divine beings with a superhuman destiny; they employ a pomp in their undertakings only fit for gods and win the contempt of all mankind. They welcome this deception of themselves by their followers from the delusion of their own divinity established in their minds, they are overthrown by false ideas."

In India the idea has persisted that the kings existed not for their own good, but for the good of the polity. The Islamic idea equally went against glorification of the royal personage. In the Indo-Islamic ethos, the king was but a *mustafi*, upholder of righteousness. There were causes higher than the State as represented by royal rulers for which one could sacrifice and lay down ,life; but to die for the king as a personification of the country was not built-up in the character of the Indians. In England, on the other hand, was the primitive idea of feudalistic allegiance to the Lord of the Manor that had grown into the modernistic idea of allegiance to the king. An Indian would die for his king only for a cause and at a price; though he would gladly die for his religion, his clan or for his honour. If the king failed in his kingly duties and in the duty of protecting the realm and upholding the scales of justice and traditions, there were others eager to fill up the vacuum, and he who succeeded in filling up the vacuum automatically secured the allegiance of the people. It is this that happened in the eighteenth century in India. The extravagance of Shah Jahan and Aurangzeb, the former in glorification of himself by erecting memorable monuments, and the latter in costly wars and exhausting campaigns had weakened the central authority. The symptoms of the gradual collapse of Indian federal strength were many; the neglect of the administrative apparatus, the unnecessary needling of an important segment, the Hindus, by overzealous practices of some fanatical rulers, the failure of the imperial forces to suppress local risings, the loss of Kandhar to the Safvi rulers of Persia exemplifying weakness of the kingdom, the loss of confidence amongst the trading community after the sack of Surat by Marathas, two times, the fleecing of the peasantry through unbearable burden of additional taxes and, finally the sheer incompetence of later Mughal kings in retrieving the situation in any way. All these had alienated the classes and masses from the imperial authority. The Golkunda and Bijapur kingdoms would have been a rallying point, but they had been extinguished. Powerful local forces tried to fill in the vacuum, and the English, after having worsted their European competitors entered the scene for supremacy, and fate willed them to succeed. For one thing, the eighteenth century was a dark period in Indian history in as much as in no field of life, either politics, or religion, or morals, or social organization, India had any notable personality who could give guidance to the nation. For it is only great men who can act as pilots to steer clear the fortunes of a nation through troubled times. The Marathas, who had emerged as the strongest contenders to fill in the vacuum, very soon earned odium from the Hindus and the Muslims for their depredations, and exactions in the shape of Chauth, and Sardesmukhi, which they levied to protect local authorities from their own raids in future. In the long run, the common people suffered: agricultural operations were halted, industries were ruined, communications were disrupted and a feeling of insecurity pervaded all around, the golden boughs of prosperity nurtured in sixteenth centuries got withered and shrunken. The Marathas failed to build any goodwill for themselves even among the Hindus, though they had tried to whip up religious feelings which, however, fell flat as there was no communal feeling per se in the country. For the folly of not opposing effectively foreign invaders like Nadir Shah, and Ahmad Shah Abdali and allowing the Mughal Emperor to be humbled, even though accepting his nominal suzerainty and being duty bound to protect him, the Marathas had to pay dearly. In turn worsted by Abdali, they have ultimately to concede prime place to the Britishers who had in the meantime become strong both economically and militarily.

Wealth in England was pouring in from the four corners of the globe. The English were carrying the commerce of the world, or at least a major portion of it, in their ships. In 1622 A.D., they had captured Ormuz from the Portuguese, and though ousted from the Spice islands by the Dutch, were casting their covetous eyes on the Chinese coast and on trade in Chinese silk, tea, and porcelain. They were carrying merchandise to and from Russia, Persia, and the Turkish Empire, and reaping profits from the 'oriental splendours of the wondrous East.' The naval superiority of the Europeans had checked the expansion of the Turkish Empire further into the West. It was the Atlantic trade, however, which enriched or finished Africa; these ships were the 'slavers' as they exchanged cotton goods for captured Negroes, took the slaves across the Atlantic and returned with cargoes of raw cotton, besides tobacco and sugar. The planters of the West Indian Islands and the American mainland bought Lancashire cotton goods to clothe their slaves, and the supply of Negro slave labour from Africa enabled them to provide the raw material of the great Lancashire industry. In 1771 A.D. as many as fifty eight "slavers sailed from London, twenty three from Bristol and one hundred and seven from Liverpool. They transported 50,000 slaves that year". The heavy coarse cotton goods of England could not at that time be sold into India as they were no match to the finely woven Indian fabrics. Hence efforts were made by English merchants to purchase Indian goods as cheaply as possible and to sell in the world market, and in this the political subjugation of the country was greatly helpful.

The English were gaining valuable expérience in the art and science of warfare and in military tactics on the continent of Europe where they were engaged in fighting of and on with European powers, mostly in pursuance of trade rivalry. Though England had had no regular standing army, their expeditionary forces were better motivated and disciplined than those of other European powers. Besides, after the union of the crowns of England and Scotland and the admittance of the Scots into the English prosperity of trade and commerce, the Scotish Highlanders, proud and haughty and used to enduring rigours of life, had become a valuable addition to the English army; they were a match to the toughest Indian soldiery, and played no mean part in upholding the superiority of English army on battlefields. However, the England enormously prepared Ships with cargoes Lancashire cotton goods went from Liverpool to English had superior arms and had access to the best arsenals in the world. An analysis of English campaigns against the native powers of India during the period shows that the English had better arms, better discipline, high morale, and the will to succeed, which above all is the *sine quanon* for success in wars. The Indians, on the other hand, were disunited among themselves; the generals, prey to petty ambitions and intrigues with the least compunction in betraying their principals at crucial moments; the army personnel were loyal only to their local commanders rather than to any unified command with whose fate they never linked their own. In many cases, the native armies did not command even the sympathy of the local population on account of their predatory habits. Thus, though the English were fighting on foreign grounds, they were not adversely placed.

The Sepoy Mutiny or the first war of independence in India, was the last occasion when any semblance of a united military stand against the English was put up by Indians. Very late in the day the Indians awoke to the fact that the English had been fighting against them with the soldiery of the native land itself. The disaffection of the Indian Sepoys was thus channelled into a mutiny. The adroitness with which it was done evokes some admiration. But except for northern and central India where the leadership fell into the hands of defeated and displaced Maratha chiefs, it did not evoke much response in the Punjab, Bengal, or in the south. This would not have mattered much, had there been some kind of unified command and some sort of discipline among the soldiery. For, success begets success, and had the rebellion succeeded, others sitting on the fence would have surely joined later on, and the English would have been certainly driven to the seas from where they had come originally. But this was not to be. The same weaknesses which the Indians had shown so long in lighting the English surfaced again. The rebellion was crushed, and the inevitability of English rule over India and the invincibility of the English arms were accepted as facts of life; India became a dependency of the British crown.

Four

Impact of Islam

Islam inevitably recalls the memories of Arabia — The Arabs like to call this desolate country as the Island of the Arabians. No country could be imagined geographically, economically and culturally less suited than Arabia for the leading role on the stage of history. A country about four times the size of Germany. It was but a population of seven millions-less than that of greater London chiefly on the fringes of the southern and western coast on which people could subsist. The principal industry of the kingdom that now acknowledges the away of Iban Saud is undoubtedly the dispensation of religious merit to the many thousands of pilgrims who annually foregather in the sacred places, to feel, even if it be for a few fleeting moments, the spark of inspiration which fired the ancient world in the first half of the seventh century. Arabia is undoubtedly an interesting country for a brief pleasure trip, just to realise the step-motherly treatment which nature can vouchsafe to some parts of the world.

Life is hard and by no means a joke; and the Arab is nothing if not serious and what is more, practical, for the limitless horizon of barren sands act as a constant reminder to the realities of the surrounding world and leaves but little time for day-dreams about the nature of the world and the ultimate end of existence. Arabia is geographically but an extension of the Sahara desert, and when you have seen what the modern settlement of Aden with its elaborate water supply and salt-work arranged by the organising genius of the British people is like, you feel that the 'Island' of

Arabians is better as a place of pilgrimage than as a land for a life of ease or a place for earning one's livelihood.

The Backdrop

All this presents a complete contrast to our own Hindustan. If one is to believe history and the records left by the Chinese travellers, life here must have been at the end of the 7th century by no means difficult. When Harshvardhana of Kanauj, or rather Thaneshwar (the latter is now one of the most desolating wildernesses in the neighbouring district of Karnal, quite close to the sacred but singularly depressing battle-fields of Kurukshetra) died in 647 A.D., Buddhism had already spent its force. The ascetic creed of the Buddha-the Enlightened one had been transformed by the interpretative genius of the Indians into vast organization of jolly monks and nuns, who despite their yellow robes, did not look askance at the pleasures of the world. Monastic life was gay. It offered the best of both worlds. External piety coupled with a sufficient stock of high sounding platitudes and precepts for popular consumption is an excellent preparation for a successful life, especially in a country where religion is one of the major and all comprehensive vocation and absorption of the multitude. Princes found ample leisure for Shastric disputations, enlivening their spare hours occasionally by composing verses of an erotic nature and a few centuries later having them even translated into the sensuous language of the plastic art. All this was undoubtedly fascinating and even to this day the sumptuous, if rather salacious decorations of the temple-walls at Bhuvaneshvara and Khajuraho leave us spell-bound with the versatility of this medieval civilisation, and incidentally furnish one of the explanations of the astoundingly easy progress of the Islamic incursions. Islam knocked at the gates of Hindustan early in the eighth century and within two centuries had practically the entire country at its feet. Small wonder that the highly cultured princes who had found literary and artistic activities more interesting than the dry routine of administration, quickly made up their minds that the dark age of Kali Yuga had set in with the advent of these 'Mlechchhas' from across the borders. The quality of these early raiders was unmistakeable and the pattern for all times was furnished by Omar the second Caliph. The Prophet had died in 632 A.D., and the great Abu Bakr two years later. But those were the days of mighty achievements. Persia had already been overwhelmed. Egypt had changed its allegiance and Jerusalem surrendered in 638 A.D.

Caliph's Idealism

But the condition of its surrender was that the Caliph must himself receive the homage of this cradle of Christianity. Omar did the journey of 600 miles with a solitary attendant mounted on an Arabian camel with a bag of barley and dates and a wooden plattar and a water-skin. When he reached the eternal city by swift marches, he met his splendidly appareled officers mounted on gaily caparisoned chargers. The Caliph was overcome with rage at this transformation of this simple soldiery and did not ride round the city with the Christian patriarch before he had told these gentlemen what he thought of them and pelted them with the stones that he could pick up on the spot. This was a characteristic incident in the early history of Islam.

Spread of Islamic Culture

At the beginning of the seventh century, the 'Island' of the Arabians showed no signs whatever of its emergence from its desolate obscurity. Mecca, a town of about 20,000 souls, was even then a place of pilgrimage on account of the famous shrine of Kaba which was in charge of the Bedouin tribes who found the piety of the pilgrims a profitable source of income. Medina, the home of the Prophet, was a pleasanter place situated round an oasis and boasting of about 15,000 inhabitants. It was here that the founder of Islam spent most of his time till he was 51. It was difficult to imagine then that the petty bickerings that were going on between Mecca and Medina were but a portent of a world revolution in a few years' time. The flight of the prophet in 622 A.D. marked the beginning of an epoch in the history of making. What appeared as arid theological disputes in an unimportant and rather backward community composed chiefly of Christians,

Jews and Mazdeans was but the release of a new and elemental force in the history in the world. Within 25 years of the prophet's death Islam had already overwhelmed the adjoining kingdoms of Persia, Armenia, Syria and Egypt. By the middle of the eighth century, it had spread from the Indus to the Atlantic in Spain and from Kashgar on the borders of China to upper Egypt. "It prevailed because everywhere it found politically apathetic peoples robbed, oppressed, bullied, uneducated, and un-organised and it found selfish and unsound governments out of touch with any people at all. It was the broadest freshest, and cleanest political idea, that had yet come into actual activity in the world, and it offered better terms than any other to the mass of mankind. The capitalistic and slave-holding system of the Roman Empire and the literature and culture and social tradition of Europe had altogether decayed and broken down before Islam arose; it was only when mankind lost faith in the sincerity of its representatives that Islam too began to decay". (Page 320-30 'H.G. Wells' *The Outline of History*.)

A pious Muslim from my audience, who suggested at the end of my discourse that I should now embrace the Islamic faith! My Muslim friends have been most generous in their appreciation of my attempt to summarise some of the results of the impact of Islam on India of today. I quote a few excerpts from some of the letters that I received:-

Khan Bather Hafiz Hidayat Hussain. C.I.E., M.L.C., Cawnpore wrote to me as follows:

> "I have been asked by several members of my community to congratulate you most warmly on your brilliant paper read (I spoke extempore) at Muzaffarnagar and now published in the *'Leader'*. You expected to get this issued in a book form: What is your idea now? If you do not intend to do so authorize me to do so. I want to broadcast it. I also ask for your permission to translate it into Urdu and Hindi for the benefit of both Urdu and Hindi knowing people".

I quote a further letter from an unknown friend. Mr. Abul Rahman Adhana of Gorakhpore:

"Allow me to thank you most heartily as an humble Muslim for your contribution of Islam to Indian culture published in the *'Leader'* of Allahabad of the 12th, 14th and 16th instant. Let me also congratulate you for your vivid and frank description of the activities and contribution of Islam on the culture of other countries and specially of India."

"Your appreciation of Islamic teaching has given great delight to the Muslim hearts and from the core of which they pray the Almighty to shower His blessing on you. It was really unexpected and extraordinary in these days of communal animosities and it was heartening to find a Hindu scholar eulogizing the tenets of Islam and speaking well of the great prophet of the Arabian deserts and of Umar the great "Caliph of Muslims".

I have refrained from further quotations from these as well as from other letters as I feel that my Muslim men have been overgenerous in their estimate of an humble attempt at the hands of a non-Muslim in appraising the contribution of Islam to our common culture.

My Muslim friends are therefore really responsible for this reprint of articles which were originally published in the *Leader*. I have touched a few of the paragraphs here and there and I hope that the reprint will be found useful to some of my younger friends in this country, who will have to try and understand the component elements of the great Indian culture, as it is today and as it will be tomorrow. If text books of Indian History are a dull and tedious record of never ending feuds and fights, bloody battles and massacres, anarchy and incomprehensible follies; it is because the learned have gone astray and fastened their attention, not on what is of a permanent, spiritual or cultural nature that matter most to the life of the people, but on the transitory, the conventional and often insipid and uninspiring accounts of individual lives or of dynastic happenings. The History of India-a-vast and ancient continent-is certainly not the record of individual princes or imperial "houses", but of its various peoples with their unique traditions and cultures. I sometimes feel that the old-fashioned Puranic chronicler had a juster perspective as to the places of kings and royal "houses" in the historical scheme of India than the assiduous and scientific historian of the present day, who laboriously attempts to piece together the broken fragments of the lives of kings and their courtiers and proceeds to base on them the life story of a great country. The puranic chronic on the other hand was more concerned with the life of the people as he found it and was content merely to give chronological tables of ruling families.

The life-history of a great and ancient land such as ours is primarily a chronicle of thought-movement and a few outstanding and epoch-making personalities. It becomes meaningless and dreary only if it is allowed to degenerate into a bleak record of ruling individuals or families. If Indian history is dull, it is because no scholar has yet essayed the task of surveying in a broad and majestic sweep the periods of out mighty achievements and inevitably also of relative quiescence over a period of the last five thousand years.

This is not a question of mere academic knowledge. It goes to the root of some of our most knotty problems of the present day, which would be very much nearer their solution if only there had been a little more understanding and mutual insight as regards our historical past. My present attempt is to lay before the readers especially those of my countrymen who have not yet taken to wearing communal glasses, in bare out-line, the momentous reactions of a Revelation in desert of Arabia thirteen centuries ago on the life-history of Hindustan. My purpose has been neither to preach nor to justify, it is only to understand and to appreciate, if possible.

I am grateful to the editor of the *Leader* of Allahabad for permission to reprint the articles which originally appeared in its issues.

The genesis of the present pamphlet may perhaps be of interest to some of my readers. I had agreed somewhat reluctantly and with diffidence at the instance of my friend. Nawabzada Muhammad Liaquat Ali Khan, Deputy president of the U.P. Legislative Council, to speak at the Provincial Muslim Educational Conference held in November last in Muzaffarnagar on the subject of "Contribution of Islam to Indian Culture". It was, however, just as well that I made the attempt, for when the time came to collect my thoughts on the subject, I was more and more excited as I began to ponder over the cultural achievements of Islam, and spent some sleepless nights in puzzling out some of the conundrums of Indian History. In other words, the preparation of my lecture at the Muslim Educational Conference helped to clarify my own ideas on the subject of Indian culture which is necessarily a synthesis of many a diverse element - indigenous as well as alien. As I went on working on the subject, the history of Islam in India appeared to me in totally different light. I was impelled, as a matter of necessity, to look for the real impulse for the achievements of Islam in India in the early history of Islam and above all in the life of Muhammad Rasulallah - the prophet of God. The result has been so far as I am personally concerned, an almost new and more vivid understanding of the Islam then I had ever thought it possible.

The attitude of Islam is in some ways so novel, so rational and in some ways so modern, particularly in contrast to the Hindu attitude in matters secular as well as religious, that an analytical and elaborate study of its influence in the world of today would be worth attempting, if only to gauge the possibility of future progress among a substantial section of the modern world professing the Islamic faith. It is true that the days of orthodox and rigid creeds are gone; but there is and will always be room for impassioned Faith especially when it is translated into action and enlisted for the good of the common humanity. The prophet of the desert was a unique personality. His was a chequered life of repeated hardships and occasional triumphs. A carpet-merchant, a faithful travelling agent of the Khadija the widow, a devoted lover, a visionary, a merciful ruler and considerate master, a generous but sometimes an implacable foe. A practical and uncompromising legislator-Muhammad to give his full name, Abul Qasim Muhammad-bin-Abdullah-bin-Abdulmottalib-el Hashimi) was altogether a singularly colourful personality. Muhammad was a posthumous child whose principal patrimony was his mother Amina who passed away when he was six leaving five camels, some sheep, and an old Negress. "Ignorant of all things save absolute truths, not so much illiterate as pure natural and supernatural, freed from all prejudices, inspired either by the intelligence or the heart, a perfect prophet and simple soul stepped forth to explain to the learned what they had been discussing, to straighten out the tortuous roads in which the so-called wise men had lost their way. In listening to this Prophet's inspired discourse and his parables suited to the period, men again felt themselves before God and learned how to arrange their fleeting lives so as to either satisfy or disobey Him, therein finding a living rule such as neither the advice of philosophers nor heads of state could give. Mahomet appeared on the scene at one of the darkest periods in all history when all the civilizations, from Merovingian Gual to India, were falling to ruin or were in a state of troubled gestation." (From the life of Mahomet by Emile Dermenghem (1930) pages (147-48).

The life of Rasul Allah - the Prophet of God is indeed a fascinating one which inspired a story in the history of mankind. Mohammad was no ascetic and no philosopher. He was a practical idealist, fully conversant with the intricacies of life and the conflicting motives that dominate it. His attitude towards Life was therefore eminently rational and modern. He had no faith in mortification of the flesh nor did he view in the highway to a life of eternal bliss hereafter. It is noteworthy that Muhammad alone among the religious prophets of the world, did not consider sexual abstinence as a virtue in itself and looked upon celibacy as something holy and indispensable for the attainment of a 'higher' and more 'spiritual' life. The Prophet himself had known the intimacy of a remarkable woman-Khadija, his first wife and his senior by fifteen years in age (she married him when she was forty) who had been a singularly devoted wife, lover and mother fused in a single personality - during the many vicissitudes of his career. He had became Muhammad Rasul Allah the exalted Prophet of God with the fullest and most affectionate collaboration of Khadija. He never had any occasion therefore to prove his exceptional strength of mind by remaining steadfastly insensible to the feminine charms. Women to him were neither vile nor the root-cause of the fall of the innocent Man. His whole attitude consequently, towards women tinged with an unusual sympathy and practical common sense for the like of which one may search in vain in the annals of the ancient world. He never lost sight of the practical problems of life, specially in so far as they related to women of his times. At a time when unrestricted polygamy and promiscuous relations between the sexes, on the one hand and exaltation of celibacy on sexual abstinence as such were the fashion of the day, this shrewd man of the world preached for sanity in matters sexual and recognised the rights of women to inheritance. It was a revolution of the first magnitude in the history of women's right. At a time when status and birth were matters of supreme importance, Muhammad arranged for the marriage of his erstwhile slave Zaid Ibn-Harith to Zainab—a lady of the Qureish aristocracy — his third cousin and later his own wife. Zaid was later appointed, much to the chagrin of the aristocratic scions and friends of the Prophets, to lead the armies of the Faithful against Basra.

Bilal, a negro slave, "long, thin, bent with the face of a crew under the head of thick grey hair, his lance in hand," used to walk in front of his master on the day of Id. It was Bilal who became "the first official muezzin of the Prophet, first muezzin and the patron of all the muezzins who for 13 centuries have called forth five times a day from all the minarets that Allah is the greatest". It was truly an amazing personality that of the prophet, Muhammad Rasul Allah who changed the face of the world by his uncompromising insistence on action as contrasted to the mere letter of the Law. He undoubtedly made the ordinary man to rise above the cramping superstition, the irrational fears and the unaccountable taboos which surrounded him at every step. It was as if a new and powerful spark of energy summoning man to reassert his manhood had suddenly gone forth thirteen centuries ago from the desert of Arabia, and the world was never the same thereafter.

That my attempt to estimate the contribution of Islam to Indian culture was not altogether in vain, was proved by unique compliment that was paid to me.

Practical Religion

It is sometimes forgotten that the value of ideas is chiefly important to the extent to which they are translated in practice. It is undoubtedly correct that the older civilisations of India and Persia, of Greece and Rome had known the ideas to which Islam gave prominence in the middle of the seventh century. The contribution of Islam therefore was not so much in the originality of the ideas as in making them impulses of farreaching revolution in the minds of men. Doctrine of monotheism was not new, especially in Hindustan, but it has not prevented the growth of idolatry in its extremist form. The change of emphasis was a matter, therefore, of the utmost importance.

The strength of Islam lay in its kindliness, simplicity and above all, its call to action and uncompromising insistance on the harmony between practice and precepts. Its toleration had certain limits. While the great brotherhood of Islam recognised and what is more, tolerated no distinctions—social or racial, it refused to compromise with idolatry, superstition or barbarity masquerading in the name of religion. All newcomers to the Islamic fold were offered absolute and practical equality of worship and social status. Anybody who believed in the oneness of God and Muhammad as the Prophet was qualified to join this great fraternity which transcended racial and geographical frontiers and yet existed as a real unity, for the Prophet had exhorted. "Know that every Muslim is the brother of every other Muslim. All of you are on the same equality."

It is not easy to visualise the shock which must have been caused to the ancient civilisations of Byzantium, Iran, India and China by the simple teachings of the Prophet, who unlike the learned philosophers of the age was tremendously serious and called upon the faithful to translate his teachings into action.

Equal Rights for Women

He was undoubtedly a revolutionary, for did he not say that women were to have the rights of inheritance, if only to the extent of half of what the man would get; that even slaves were to be fed and clothed with the stuff that their masters used and that knowledge was to be sought even in China?

I am sure that the adventurers from beyond the borders professing this new faith would have been welcomed in India if they had contented themselves with the spoils of the country without trying to introduce in the Empire their ethics of action which though simple challenged the fabric of Hinduism at every point. Let me just glance at some of the important points on which the cultured Hindu of a thousand years ago must have felt the intolerable interference and also folly of these outlandish people. Woman is Shakti-the power. Gods have their abode where woman is honoured. But why should this store house, if not incarnation of Divinity be recognised as a civil entity especially if she happens to be a wife, a widow or a daughter? Is it not pulling down the Divinity off here pedestal by conferring on her independent rights of inheritance instead of keeping her under the loving tutelage of her masculine devotee? Immolation on the funeral pyre of a husband was the crown of a woman's life, it was the apotheosis of conjugal love and established beyond doubt the superiority of the Hindu wife in the cause of disinterested sacrifice and devotion to Shastric injunctions. But here too, the Hindu must have felt, the vision of the Musalman to be narrow and materialistic. The Muslims did not care for these fiery-ordeals as the test of feminine virtue. Islam is in this as in many other things more practical and rooted to the earth than the older creeds of Hinduism and Christianity. Islam has been in India for over a thousand years and though there is and can be no disputes about the theoretical admissibility of the claim of women to succession and inheritance along with men, the question has not yet reached the stage of urgency or of practical politics so far as the Hindu Society is concerned. The Hindu mind is supple it will concede or score a point to its logical limits, so long as it is not called upon to harmonise theory and practice.

No Right by Birth

Every imaginable latitude in the matter of worship or doctrine is permissible to a Hindu but for the uncompromising insistence of Islam on correct practice, Hinduism would have absorbed the new faith from Arabia. There was nothing in Islamic doctrine which could be repugnant to a catholic citizen of Hindustan of a thousand years ago. But the Muslim made himself obnoxious like the present day communist by harping on the necessity of weaving the simple but unambiguous injunctions of the Prophet into work a day fabric of life. His philosophic interest were limited, he was far too engrossed in matters mundane to interest himself in the philosophical inquiry as to the ultimate reality of the phenomenal world which had engaged the attention of the Hindu saints and seers for so many centuries past. Islamic monotheism was but a simple affirmation of faith in the oneness of God as compared to the subtlety of Sankar's Vedantic monism or its own later Sufistic embroideries which found such a congenial field in Iran and India. The Prophet was a man of the people, an extraordinarily gifted psychologist, for he knew that mankind is moved by a few elemental urges and can only be uplifted by right action. Though Islam is free from an anointed priesthood, it did not long escape the influence of the times and the curious desire of the common human beings who apparently want a special class of spiritual guides to settle doubts and give correct interpretation of the sacred text. Pursuit of theology undoubtedly offers an easy career and though its usefulness may be disputed, it must not doubtless be taken too seriously as regards its ultimate influence or power over the minds of men. The Ulemas - learned theologians of Islam did sometimes wield and do so even now considerable influence over the people and in the Councils of State, but they never attained the inviolable sanctity of the Brahmin priest or the ubiquitousness of the Christian clergy, for they never constituted a separate privileged class.

To revert for a moment to the monotheism of Islam, the early Muslims were after all the Christian Jewish or Mazdean converts of Arabia.

Rise of the Downtrodden

They were not even all Arabs. Negroes and Abyssinian slaves were also incorporated and admitted as full members of this revolutionary fraternity. The name of Ballal, the slave, is well-known as one of the early followers of the Prophet and apostle of Islam. Such was however the magic of the new message of the Arabian Prophet that even slaves - whose very existence was assumed as a mere instrument of service, found themselves roused to a new consciousness of their lives which swept at least some of them to the highest peaks of wordly achievement. Not a few of the enterprising slaves humbled the pride of many a monarch of ancient lineage, and founded their own "houses" of rulers in India, Iran, Egypt, and elsewhere. The slave dynasties of India in particular have left imperishable monuments of their rule. Qutub Minar - is a memorial of one of these slave-rulers of great valour and undoubted taste. If Muhammad Ghazni - the fierce iconoclast and the parsimonious patron of Firdausi Al Beruni was a slave, so was Ahamad Shah Abdali who vanquished the vast Maratha army of the Peshwas at Panipat. The achievements of these slaves of Islam are indeed unique in the annals of the world. They had the fire of a new revelation and a vivid experience of the popular handicaps of idolatry, superstition and myths. The latest symbolism of all these could not always escape at least the more gifted of them but they knew that the popular mind is generally incapable of looking below the surface. The result was inevitable. The Indian Muslims looked upon the numerous and sometimes enormously wealthy shrines of the Hindus as abodes of darkness and did not have any scruples in filling them and utilising in the earlier centuries of its history, the building material of the demolished shrines-the richly carved columns and ornamental slabs for the construction of mosques. What was desecration in the eyes of orthodox was according to the Muslims, merely a more useful and enlightened conversion, The iconoclastic zeal of the Musalman was from his standpoint merely a meritorious attempt at cleaning the Augean stables. People were then enormously interested in religion, for it impinged on life in numberless ways.

Respect for Hindu Culture

While the Muslim rulers of India have been known as idol-breakers, it is perhaps not known so widely that it was a pious Muslim sovereign -Firoz Tughlak who with infinite care and piety removed the edict-pillar of Ashoka from Meerut to Delhi. He was perhaps the first prince to be interested in Indian archaeology. I was agreeably surprised to see the marvellous temples of the Mysore State untouched by iconoclastic hands, contrary to the impression made on me in my school days regarding the character of Tipu Sultan. Coming to modern India who does not know the noble work of conservation done by H.E.H. The Nizam of Hyderabad for the Buddhist and Brahmanic monuments of Ajanta and Ellora. Muslim piety is seen here in its noble aspect, for nowhere in India are the memorials of the past looked after with so much care and affection as by Nizam Government under the guidance of Sir Akbar Hyderi and supervision of Mr. Yazdani the Director of Archaeology and gifted artist Syed Ahmad, the curator at Ajanta. This should however occasion no surprise; for Islam in India did not bring or settle new race of inhabitants, but merely brought a torch of dazzling light with which to illumine and banish the dark shadows that had gathered round the life of the ancient world, where old civilisation was decaying and noble ideals had come to be a matter of mere doctrine or of meaningless polemics. Islam's greatest conquests in India as elsewhere were therefore not so much in the sphere of worldly power as in the realm of mind and the mighty empire of Islam today is purely a spiritual community knit by ties of faith the common acknowledgement of the oneness of God and the equality of all believers.

Political Influence

It was perhaps unfortunate that the history of Islam in this country is identified for centuries with the possession of supreme political power, for the latter has tended to obscure its real nature and its achievements - actual as well as potential. It was not an accident that Islam within three or four centuries had spread to the major portion of Asia including Java, Sumatra and the far off China on the east to Spain and the gates of Hungary in the West.

The ancient cultures of Egypt; Asia minor and Persia had surrendered early, for the life sap of the ancient traditions had dried up and the sheer virility of the new faith had swept the people off their feet.

It is perhaps futile to conjecture the probable evolution of Islam in India, had it come in the guise of a new revelation unaccompanied by the flaming sword and the indubitable valour of its adherents. It is possible that the new dispensation would have either swept the whole country within its fold or lost its identity in the thick jungle of Indian faith. It is likely, however, that apart from the total number of its adherents it might have solved the problem of the untouchables, destroyed the 'don't touchism' which Swami Vivekananda described as the most characteristic feature of the present-day Hinduism, and raised the Indian woman to a new level of economic independence and dignity.

It would probably have prevented the bringing of religion into the market place and kept the animals including the cow in their proper sphere, for it is well known that while the Egyptians thought of ascending the Heaven on the horns of a cow, the Hindus till about the eighth century did not look askance at beef as an item of their dietary. Cow worship is in fact one of the later and amazing developments of medieval India. It is possible that

Muslim India while professing its own distinctive creed might have retained its loyalty to Indian culture to a greater extent than is the case at present, for Islam as such acknowledges no fatherland and knows no limiting or exclusive frontiers. In other words, Islam might have been merely an accession to the Indian culture, as happens in the East Indies - especially in Java.

It is of course untrue that Islam brought the pardah system into this country. Seclusion of women can be traced in all ancient communities, and it was particularly right among the aristocracy during the palmy days of the Hindu civilization. It is perhaps truer to say that Indian Muslims followed the custom of the country and adopted the prevailing hall-mark of gentility. The question of inter-marriage may be touched in this connection. Royal intermarriages between Hindus and Muslims did not work for unity, for the common ground between a free Islam contemptuous of and indifferent to the meaningless restrictions as to food, drink and worship. It could not meet on level ground with a society which was vitally interested in matters of ceremonial purity. Intermarriages were therefore from the Hindu point of view not a gesture of friendship. They were merely a measure of their degradation and incapacity to keep their own people within the ambit of their social gradations. Royal descendants therefore of mixed marriages were, if anything at all, even more intolerant of the idolatrous Hindu than the full-blooded Musalman. I need only mention the names of Feroze Tughlak and Shahjahan.

No Hereditary Rights

The essence of Hinduism lay in its social gradation established on the basis of birth. Hinduism could not in practice conceive the equality of a Prince and a peasant. The Brahmin and the Shudra stood at two opposite and unalterable poles of social gradation. It is true that the voice of poets, saints and reformers was occasionally heard in favour of the outcast; but the stigma of birth was one that could not be washed away in the present life at all. The whole conception of Hindu society was and is foreign to the fundamental tenets of Islam, which not only proclaims but uncompromisingly insists on the absolute equality of all Muslims irrespective of their birth, status or race, in matters social and religious.

There can be no doubt therefore that the conquests of Islam in the religious sphere, were won primarily by voluntary allegiance, especially of the poor classes, who naturally saw a new future spreading out before them as members of a virile community, which judged men on merits and ignored accidents of birth or race. The power of the sword and the allurements of social and preferment as well as the exclusive snobbery of the high-caste Hindus did also contribute to some extent in swelling the ranks of the Musalmans. It is however probable that, but for these adventitious aids the progress of Islam would have been even more rapid than it was. Hindu society maintains such an immense reservoir of the socially depressed classes with no apparent future within the Hindu fold that any creed which offers them a hope of human equality and some social rise is bound to mark a powerful appeal to them. It is from these classes that all the new creeds. such as Islam, Sikhism and Christianity have drawn their greatest support.

Al Beruni had noticed the exclusiveness and the arrogance of the Hindu Civilisation. He had also commented on the impossibility of fusion, so long as the Hindus insisted on the imaginary purity of food and drink and refused to meet the alien on terms of social equality. The old causes even after well-nigh a thousand years, still persist and are largely responsible for the division between the two great communities. The medieval Musalman was something like the westernised Indian vis-a-vis the common folk. He did not believe in the world old superstitions and had no patience with them; being in a position of power he was able to influence the people partly by example and partly by compulsion. But sword is no substitute for conviction. I have sometimes felt that the usefulness of Islam was greatly circumscribed by its early and prolonged association with political supremacy.

Sphere of Religion

The uninterrupted success of Islamic arms produced a widespread searching of the heart. Polytheism which had to meet the higher needs of the people and had been found to be particularly profitable as a profession by the priestly class, received its greatest challenge. Religious movements of one kind or the other were one of the most outstanding features after the advent of the Arabs in the eighth century and before the appearance of the Moghuls in the sixteenth. The trend of all these movements was more or less democratic. Less emphasis was laid on mere learning as such. Love and devotion to the deity were the principal passport to a spiritual life, the avenues of which had hitherto been closed to the people or were only accessible through the agency of a special priesthood. The common man found himself suddenly raised to the level of the highest, so long as he had the proper spirit. The cult of Bhakti-devotion undoubtedly received its vogue as the result of Islam, Bhakti made light of all ritual and intimate acquaintance with the Sastras. It did not even need images or magnificent temples; simple devotion was all that mattered, and incidentally Bhakti presupposed the existence of a loving entity. Here also the influence of Islam is to be traced. Kabir, Ramanand, Dau Dayal, Malukdas, Namdev and countless others sprung from the ranks, spread the gospel of the oneness of God and the equality of all his devotees.

The proselytisation to Islam on an extensive scale gave an impetus to the Hindu Society to bring out all its defences. Its genius for pliability was tested to the utmost. It was easy to incorporate the Islamic monotheism. So a conservative community as the Jains also recast their doctrine and towards the end of the 17th century one Lonka Shah founded a sect called the Sthanakvasis which dispensed with temples and image worship altogether. This Puritan sect survives to this day. The movements however that were even more important were the offshoots of the peripatetic singers and saints such as Ramananda, Kabir, Nanak and others. The lower strata of the Hindu Society were galvanized into life by a new spiritual message, which, while conserving their ancient traditions, gave them back their manhood. The great Khalsa of the Sikhs was the most remarkable of these popular achievements.

Persecution in the name of religion brought forth unexpected developments and a Catholic and Unitarian movement while it accepted some of the fundamental tenets of the Islamic faith, it refused to embrace Islam formally. All the imperial might of the later Moghuls broke in vain against the spiritual forces that had been released among the masses. A new community with all the simplicity and vigour of the earlier Muslims themselves was brought into being out of the poor, the lowly and the dispirited. This was one of the unintended though major achievements of Islam in this country. Popular Vaishnavism which had been heralded by Chaitanya in Bengal and Vallabhacharya in Muttra undoubtedly did something for the poor people, but Vaishnavism lacked the fire and the fibre of Islam or Sikhism. The common man has but little scope for emotional luxuries or sentimental flabbiness. The cult of Rama that was preached by the great Tulsidas was unfortunately too puritanical and idealistic in nature to find widespread acceptance among the people. Krishna-worship was undoubtedly more popular and more in consonance with leisurely nature of the people. In brief, the very existence of the Hindu Society and its time - honoured organization was challenged by Islam. With its genius for compromise and religious experiments the fury of the storm was for a time averted, but not without having to effect changes of a radical nature within the social body.

In this connection mention must also be made of the Arya Samaj which was also a movement though late in time inspired by the decadent condition of the Hindu society and the intrinsic strength of the Islam.

An Organised Way of Life

Apart from the simplicity of the Islamic teachings the one quality which struck and strikes every non-Muslim to this day is the development of an overwhelming sense of discipline among the adherents of the Islamic faith. And this discipline is noticeable whether at prayer or on the occasion of communal festivities. The congregational worship is of course impossible without a certain modicum of discipline and organization. What is more, congregational prayer meant a veritable revolution in mental posture, for at prayer the equality of all Musalmans was not merely a scriptural commandment. Like most things in Islam, it was a precept of practice and has been the conspicuous as well as the unalterable feature of the Islamic world. The prophet had rightly said that the whole of this earth is a mosque. The portals were open to all who·chose to come in and within these precincts no distinctions of any kind were tantamount to the enlargement of the individual ego into a higher social and spiritual entity.

It was on the strength of this innate discipline that small armies of 3000 to 4000 people emerging from the deserts of Arabia had literally smashed through the powerful battlements of older and more prosperous but effective civilizations. Communities under the sway of Islam were not slow in realizing the secret of latters's strength, and in some cases the lesson was learnt with conspicuous success as by the Sikhs and to a smaller extent by the Arya Samaj. It is an extraordinary peculiarity of the Islamic faith, perhaps not noticed by the Musalmans themselves on account of its extreme familiarity that even their few festivals and the sacred month of Ramazan are like congregational prayers, so distributed and designed as to knit the entire social fabric more strongly than ever. Fasts and festivities are like the prayers of the Id-uz-Zuha, an integral part of the social organisation. There is a heightening of the social sense which renders the compliance with the injunctions of the Prophet to treat all Muslims as brothers easier and practical on account of the identity in ritual.

What Islam achieved in the seventh century by uniting in worship has not been achieved by the Hindus to this day with the result that the most actively pious section of the professing Hindus is rigidly excluded from the places of worship. The democratic surge in the religious sphere had important repercussions in other fields. Sanskritic culture had hitherto held undisputed supremacy and by its very nature was the monopoly of a small class-principally of Brahmins.

Five

Islam's Influence

Late Dr. Shafa'at Ahmed Khan, a well-known scholar of modern Indian history, rightly said that, "for the scientific student of history India is a fallow field beneath which lay buried a civilization and a culture which were to become objectives alike of admiration and respect. Indian historian must consequently, reach forth across the gulf of ages, and base his work on the severe framework of abstract truth."

History demands a clear vision of the world in which we live. History is capable of changing our vision of the contemporary world. History requires imagination, yet it is not a mere romance. History demands philosophical background, yet it cannot be achieved by philosophic speculation. History rests on the belief that we are the products of our past and that it is desirable and necessary that we should know how we have come to be, what we are. But we have to acknowledge the fact that each veneration creates its own past. Under the stress of nationalism and national aspirations of India the past is being re-examined and reinterpreted in accordance with new interests.

When the followers of Islam came to India they must have seen that the entire country lived upto high tenets in regard to religious tolerance, perhaps the highest for the age in which they were living. They must have wondered all the more that the people, who were so tolerant to outsiders and so free from all racial and political bias were the most conservative in the world and rigidly exclusive in their social habits and customs. The mosaic of their caste system with its political replica of independent and conflicting units had to be built up anew into harmonious structure. The people had to be welded into common brotherhood and corresponding political unity had to be evolved to serve their common needs and save them from unending conflicts. The need of the hour was religious tolerance, social and cultural synthesis, political integration and a secular outlook. Destiny had ordained the Mughals to play this unifying role, and in spite of disruption which followed at the end of Aurangzeb's rule, the convulsion of policies could not overwhelm the synthesis of social life, and Hindu-Muslim relations continued the same upto 1857.

The Universal surge of loyalty and devotion towards Bahadur Shah, the symbol of political revolution conclusively showed, for the first time in history, that India had become politically self-conscious and that the foundations of Indian nationalism had been truly and deeply laid.

Throughout the medieval ages the Muslims took enormous pains to acquaint themselves with the religious literature of the Hindus. They translated books of important texts into Persian, the Vedas, the Upanishads, the Mahabharata, the Ramayana, the Dharma Shastra, the Purana, the Yoga Vashistha, the Yoga Shastra and the Vedanta Shastra.

Among the later writers may be mentioned the name of Mirza Mazhar Jan Janan (1699-1781 A.D.). Mazhar said about the Hindu worship of idols:

"In idol worship the process is similar to the Dhikr, contemplative ritual, which is prescribed by the Muslim Sufis."

Mahmood Shabistri (A.D. 1317), the well-known writer of *Gulshan-e-Raz*, writing on the theme of the idol worship, explains the difference and similarity between it and Islam:

"The idol is the expression of love and unity in this world, and to wear the sacred thread is to take the resolve of service. As both faith and unfaith are founded in existence, unity of God is the essence of idol worship. As things are the expression of existence, one out of them must at least be the idol. If the Muslim knew what the idol is then he would understand that religion consists in idolatry and if the idol worshipper understood the idol, he would not go astray in his faith".

Sir W.W. Hunter in his book, *The Indian Musalmans* quoted fatwa of the Gazi of Jaunpore in which he declares that Muslims should regard regions under the Maratha rule as Dar-ul-Islam, on the ground that the Rulers permit the Muhammedens to say their Friday and Id Festival prayers and maintain the laws of Islam although the Musalmans have to ask them to appoint their qazis and governors.

In spite of the existence of two religions, there were net any deep cultural differences between them. They took pleasure in the study of each other's religion, philosophy and science. Their arts were common. They had no prejudices in regard to participation in the fairs and festivals of each other. They spoke the same language, wore similar clothes, furnished their houses in the same style, had similar outlook upon the life of this world, if not also the next. Their industry and commerce, urban and rural occupations were parts of one economic system.

While in the middle ages, under Muslim rule, Hindu and Muslim reformers had led movements of religious and moral purification concerned with both communities, the reformers of the 19th century were exclusive; for example, compare Kabir, Nanak, Chaitanya, Dadu, Tukaram, Basveshwar, Pran Nath and others with Sir Saiyed and Swami Dayanand. The medieval religious leaders cared essentially for the substance and reality of religion and deprecated emphasis upon external acts, doctrines and dogmas; on the other hand, the modern reformers have been concerned chiefly with the philosophy and tenets of religion rather than its inner emotional and spiritual content.

No account of cultural synthesis is complete without a discussion of religion. Of the Muslims attitude towards religion other than their own, a great deal of misunderstanding prevails on account of the false propaganda spread by their enemies, especially European writers belonging to Church; and the result has been that the non-Muslim world has almost come to believe that Islam has been a religion of violence, of force, of uncompromising rigidity and bigotry. But the facts are, however, quite contrary to the popular belief. Long before Europe had learnt to enquire about religion under scientific and detached spirit, many Muslim learned men had compiled books on comparative religion in which they displayed an amazingly true and rationalistic attitude of mind. Among them was the most eminent scholar, Abu Raihan al-Beruni.

The underlying forces for this strong social synthesis were the great precepts of religion that acted as powerful brakes. The Quran teaches tolerance. "Let there be no compulsion in religion" is its eternal commandment. And beautifully has the reason for this commandment been given: "But if my Lord had pleased verily all who are in the world would have believed together wilt thou then compel men to become believers?"

The Bible teaches tolerance and forgiveness in these noble words : "Whoever smite thee on thy right cheek turn to him the other also," The commandant in the Quran "Recompense evil with that which is better" is almost a paraphrase of the Christian commandment. The same idea is expressed with greater fullness of imagery in the following words of the Quran "and a paradise; vast as the heavens and the earth, was prepared for those who mastered their anger and forgave others".

The *Bhagwad Gita* says: "However men approach Me, even so do I welcome them, for the path men take from every side is Mine, O Partha." And again, "O Son of Kunti, even the devotees of other deities who worship full of faith, they also worship Me, though not according to the established custom.

In Akbar's time a unity was reached in the national consciousness which extended from the cottage to the throne. Akbar's efforts to give it the form of a new religion were bound to fail because religions could not be created through politics; and, also because a movement whose essence consisted in transcending all religious formalism could not be imprisoned in new bonds though cast in gold and set with diamonds. But, after this, politics could not be an obstacle in its path; and we find that throughout the Mughal period, though thwarted for a while to some extent, the movement continued to widen and deepen in its course.

It will be conceded by everybody that, so far as race is concerned, the Muslims of India, with the exception perhaps of a very microscopic minority, are wholly indistinguishable from the Hindus. There is scarcely any trace of the old Arabs, Turks and Persians left. It is impossible in the population of Sind to distinguish the vestiges of the Arab soldiers who invaded it under Muhammad Bin Qasim or of the Arab families which ruled over the valley for hundreds of years. The Central Asian clans which entered India in the wake of the Ghaznavides, Ghoris, Mughals, Turks and Afghans and whose descendant continued to exercise authority and dominion for five hundred years and more, have similarly disappeared almost completely. The Muslim conquerors have not maintained their racial identity or clan organization and have merged themselves into the general mass of the Indian people. Tribes, clans and families whose names make such a noise in the annals of the Muslim rule are today barely known and are all but forgotten. The process of assimilation has been continuous throughout the centuries. Conversion, marriage and settlement in India without any desire to return to or have relation with the peoples of the homelands have removed their differences and brought about racial homogeneity.

Socially the Musalmans of India developed an organization similar to that of the Hindus. Muslim societies in India, unlike Muslim societies in other countries, became divided into castes comparable with the Hindu caste system. Sayyids correspond with Brahmins, Mughal and Pathans with Kshatriyas, Shaikh with

Vaisyas and the group of artisans craftsmen and labourer with Shudras. The distinctions between the four divisions were based not merely on economic and vocational considerations, but also on heredity which was recognized throughout the middle ages as a factor of supreme importance among both the Musalmans and Hindus.

In every social system woman holds a characteristic position. Arab and Turkish societies differ considerably from Hindu society in this matter. Yet in India the Muslims followed not the customs of Arabia and Turkistan but those of India, In toilet, dress, ornaments, ways of social intercourse, daily routine of life, they adopted Indian ways and manners. The Muslim marriage ceremonies were adopted from Hinduism Nisbat, (Haldi, Mehndi, Tel, Mandwa. Barat, Jalwa, Kangan, etc. were Muslim adaptations of Hindu ceremonies). The only difference that remained was, that in the Hindu marriage bride and bridegroom went round the fire to the chanting of Vedic Mantras while in the Muslim marriage they were joined together in bonds of matrimony by the Qazi who read appropriate verses from the Quran. Early marriage of girls, prohibition of widow marriage, dependence and subordination of woman and the use of the veil were common to Hindus and Muslims.

It is true that the religious fasts and festivals of the two communities were different but the manner of observing them was more or less similar. Muharram celebrations were assimilated to Dussehra, Shab Barat to Shivaratri, Ramzan and Id to Navartara, etc. Besides there were many fairs and festive occasions which were common; and even so far as the peculiar communal festivals were concerned, the Hindus and the Muslims participated in both, e.g. Holi and Muharram.

The Muslims adopted many Hindu funeral ceremonies, for example, the Tija, the Daswan, etc. Then ceremonies concerning pregnancy and childbirth like the seventh month, sixth day of child birth, the shaving of the child's head (Mundan=Aqiqa), licking of Khir, boring of ears, birthday, anniversary, etc., were common to both. Even such purely Hindu practices as the immolation of the widow on the death of her husband and Jauhar were occasionally resorted to by the Muslims. Ibn Batuta relates the story of the defeat of Ainul Mulk by Muhammad Bin Tughlaq and tells how his wife plunged into death after her husband. Again the *Zafar Namah* describes the Jauhar committed by wife of Kamaluddin, governor of Bhatnair, when he proceeded to fight against Timur. Amir Khusru's admiration is evident from his famous lines:

chun Zan-a hindi kase dar Ashiqi dlwana nest
sokhtan bar sham'-a shauhar kar-a parwana nest;

Dress is the most outstanding expression of the inner character of a society-of its grades and classes, of its psychological values, tabus and reticence. From this point of view it is important to notice how Muslims in India largely discarded the garments worn in Arabia, Iran and Central Asia and mainly adopted Indian costumes and clothes. The use of Arab *amamah, juhba, ridah, tahmad* and *tasma* and of Central Asian *kulah, nima, moza,* etc., .disappeared, giving place to Hindu *pagri* and *chira, kurta* and *angarkha, patka* and *dopatta pajama* and *juta*.

If we turn from such externals to the cultural aspects of life, we find the same kind of fusion there. Let us consider the sacrifices the Musalmans have made for the evolution of a common culture in India. Take the question of language which is of fundamental importance, the chief medium of expression of the intellect and of the spirit. Arabic is the sacred language of Islam. It was also the mother tongue of those early invaders who came to Sind. It is not now the language of any group of Musalmans in India although it is studied by the learned for obvious reasons. Turkish was the spoken language of the Muslim conquerors from Central Asia; Persian was the language of the court from the beginning of Muslim rule till its final overthrow. Neither of these languages is today spoken by the Indian Muslims, nor has the conqueror imposed them on the conquered.

On the contrary, the Muslims adopted the Indian languages and enriched them with words drawn from their languages. The Muslims of Punjab speak Punjabi, of Bengal Bengali, of Gujarat Gujarati; in other words, they speak the dialect of the region where they reside, and there is no difference between them and the Hindus in their forms of speech. There remains one language regarding which much controversy rages today, namely, Urdu. Now Urdu is not a Muslim language, it is not spoken in any of countries where Islam is or has been the religion of the majority of the people, the homelands of the conquerors of India. Urdu belongs to Aryan branch of languages, its basic structure, grammar and the greater part of its vocabulary are Indian. In fact, the origin of Urdu is the dialect which is spoken round about Delhi and which is known to linguists by the name of Khari Boli. It became the spoken dialect of the Musalmans also when they settled in and about Delhi. The spoken dialect evolved into a literary language and both Hindus and Musalmans have made it as such throughout the centuries. In fact, it may be truthfully said that, before the use of English among the Indian educated classes, Urdu occupied the position of the lingua indica of India.

According to Havell, a great admirer of Hinduism, Islam influenced the Hindu social life in two ways. There was a rise of rigidities in the Hindu society: Islam also gave the depressed and downtrodden masses the prospect of improving their social status and economic lot. Havell says that the Muslim success in India cannot be explained away by external factors alone. It became possible owing to the political disintegration and moral degeneration of India since the death of Harsha. Havell has emphatically observed that it was not the philosophy of Islam but the democratic nature of the Islamic society that attracted the attention of the Indian people.

The Arabs were the first among the Muslims to come to India, and they had settled down firmly in South India by the end of the tenth century. Henceforth Muslim influence began to grow rapidly. They were heartily welcomed as traders and were allowed by the local princes of Malabar to acquire lands and to practise their religion freely. Islam is essentially a missionary religion and the Arabs experienced no difficulty in preaching their gospel and winning converts from the local people. They created a great stir among the Hindu populace as much by their peculiar beliefs and worship as by the zeal with which they professed and advocated them.

Islam found a congenial atmosphere in South India. Religious conflicts had been going on in South India as Neo Hinduism had been struggling with Buddhism and Jainism for ascendancy. The religious atmosphere bewildered the common people; and it was at such a juncture that Islam appeared on the scene with a simple formula of faith, well-defined dogmas and rites. The result was a large number of voluntary conversions of unsophisticated people to Islam followed by the conversion of the last of the Cheraman Perumal Kings of Malabar to the new religion in the first quarter of the ninth century. According to some, it was with a view to propitiating the Arab traders so that they might enrich the Kingdom of Malabar by their prosperous trade and commerce that the Perumal King embraced Islam. Whatever might have been the motive of the Malabar King, it cannot be gainsaid that the Muslims came to acquire great influence and importance in Malabar region under the patronage of the local princes. The number of Muslim settlers in the dominion of the Zamorin of Calicut continued to increase by leaps and bounds, and in his eagerness to train his men as expert mariners and sailors, the Zamorin "gave orders that in every family of fishermen in his dominion one or more of the male members should be brought up as Muhammadans."

Marco Polo, Ibn Batuta and Abdur Razzak noticed a large number of Muslim settlers along the Western coast with their mosques and flourishing centres of trade. Each settlement of the Muslims in the Eastern and Western coasts grew into a centre of religious propaganda. It is really surprising that within the course of a few centuries, before the advent of the Turks, large areas in the Eastern and Western regions turned into centres of Islamic civilisation and culture without the least resistance from the sons of the soil. The rise of the Bahmani Kingdom in the South offers a glaring instance of the impact of Islam in South Indian politics and culture. This impact is much more glaring when we take into account the rise of Bijapur and Golkonda as two other great Muslim kingdoms in the later days.

Northern India came into direct contact with Islam from the time of Muhammad bin Ghori. From the thirteenth century onwards Hindu imperialism, based on loose confederation of autonomous principalities gradually gave way to Turkish suzerainty and paramountcy. Hinduism came face to face with a dynamic religion which threw a challenge to the philosophic basis of Hinduism, attacked its social structure and denied its pantheistic doctrines.

Speaking of the moral effect of Muslim conquest, Cunningham writes:

"The influence of a new people who equalled or surpassed Kshatriyas in valour, who despised the sanctity of Brahmins, and who authoritatively proclaimed the unity of God and His abhorrence of images, began gradually to operate on the minds of the multitudes of India . . . New superstition emulated old credulity. Pirs and Shahids, saints and martyrs, equalled Krishna and Bhairav in the number of their miracles, and the Muhammadans almost forgot the unity of God in the multitude of intercessors whose aid they implored".

In the words of Cunningham again:

"The first result of the conflict (between Hinduism and Islam) was the institution about the end of the fourteenth century of a comprehensive sect by Ramananda of Banaras. He seized upon the idea of man's equality before God, and admitted all classes of people as his disciples".

Islam entered Kashmir in the fourteenth century A.D. The people welcomed its exponent, the great Shah Hamadan, with open arms, and the synthesis of Hindu and Islamic religious thought found its greatest exponents in Lalleshwari and Sheikh Nurud-Din, who continue to be held in great esteem by both Hindus and Muslims. Kashmir has witnessed dark periods of religious persecution but the people, true to their tradition have lived like brothers, giving solace and shelter to their brothers in distress.

Two names that come very easily to an average Kashmiri's lips are Lalitaditya (724-760 A.D. and Zain-ul-Abedin (1422-1474 A.D. Lalitaditya ushered in an era of national glory, prosperity and peace. He was tolerant towards all schools of religious thought. Buddhism and Hinduism, the two prominent creeds of the time, received patronage at his hands- a Hindu ruler, who constructed temples for the Buddha as well as for Shiva, Vishnu and other gods. The king offered liberal patronage to men of letters. Learning flourished, and Kashmir became the "cynosure of foreign scholars, and many cultural missions set out from the country." His faults, as recorded by Kalhana, notwithstanding, he was above religious bigotry. His commander-in-chief was a Buddhist and so were many of his high officials. To talented men of all nationalities he showed great respect and regard. He brought from Kanauj the two famous poets Bhavabhuti and Vakpatiraja and installed them in his capital in Kashmir. Zain-ul. Abedin popularly known as Bud Shah (the great king) was not a conqueror but remains a beacon light for the people of Kashmir for their cherished principles of tolerance and fraternal living. 'Possessed of a broad and tolerant outlook", says Pandit Anand Koul, "and dominated with a desire to benefit mankind, he rule(with such equity and justice and did so much to improve the material prosperity of the people that one cannot fail to admire him...Zain-ul-Abedin was deservedly surnamed 'Bud Shah' or great king. In spite of six centuries having rolled by since he lived, his name is still remembered with genuine reverence and gratitude. Take the name of Bud Shah before a Kashmiri and at once he will, with a happy countenance, rhyme with 'Padshah'.

During the reign of Sikandar Zain-ul-Abedin's father, the Hindus suffered enormously through the persecution of his minister Siya Butt, a new convert to the Muslim faith. It is said that the Hindus fled away and only eleven families remained in Kashmir. With Zain-ul-Abedin's ascending the throne, confidence returned to them. He sent messengers to them inviting them to return to their homeland. They responded with pleasure. He gave the pride of place in his court to Shri Butt, a great physician, and Jonaraj, a great historian who updated the chronology *Rajatarangini*. Himself a scholar of Persian and Sanskrit, he encouraged the translation of a major portion of the Upanishads from Sanskrit into Persian. The *Katha-Sarit-Sagar* was also translated into Persian during his reign. A general toleration of all faiths was proclaimed and practised. The king built temples and penalized the killing of cows and himself abstained from meat eating during the holy festivals of the Hindus. The *Rajatarangini* gives a detailed account of how the king took part in the annual Nag-yatra festival when he would don the robes of a Hindu mendicant and perform the journey in the company of other pilgrims.

Two other names that come easily to the lips of a Kashmiri are of Lalleshwari, more popularly known by the homely name of dal Ded (Mother Lal), and Sheikh Nur-ud-Din, better known as Nund-Rishi. They are believed to have been contemporaries. Both of them as mystics saints and poets, continue to have an equal claim on the affection of both Hindus and Muslims. In fact, both communities hold forth divergent views as to which community they originally belonged.

Lalleshwari was a follower of Shaivism. Born towards the middle of the fourteenth century A.D., she preached the message of truth and peace in the language of the people. Her poetry known as Yakyas, is committed to memory by thousands regardless of their religious faith. Her verses are quoted even in daily conversation, and their wide use has given a healthy direction to individual and community ideals.

In one of her sayings, she exhorted people not to differentiate between a Muslim and Hindu. "They are not different", she said, 'Know thyself, of thou art sans", she advised. In a verse she castigated the fanatical followers of so-called 'religion" and said:

> O Mind hast thou become intoxicated at another's expense?
> Why hast thou mistaken truth for untruth
> The little understanding hath made thee attached to others' religion,
> Subdued to coming and going, to birth and death

Lal Ded criticized the cold and meaningless way in which religious rituals were performed. She said that God did not want meditations and austerities. The abode of bliss could be reached only through love.

Nund Rishi, born in 1377 A.D., was a pious Man. His fame as a saint and the glory of his spiritual attainments travelled far and wide attracting to him a great number of followers. His verses have become stamped in people's memory. He preached against the snares of false preachers.

> I saw a priest blowing out fire (and)
> Beating a drum to others,
> The priests have nice big turbans on their heads,
> They walk about daintily dressed,
> Dressed in priestly robes they indulge in mutton,
> They run away with cooking posts under their arms.

The Rishi exhorted his followers to perform good actions. He wanted people to lead disciplined lives in which they cared about others. In one of his sayings, he asks:

> Thou hast eaten six platefuls, one like another,
> If thou art a priest, then who are robbers ?

No wonder, King Zain-ul-Abedin was the chief mourner at Nund Rishi's funeral. During his lifetime, he founded an order of Rishis which exercised tremendous influence on Hindus too. The last of the great Hindu mystic poets, Parmanand, who died towards the end of the last century, contributed a great deal towards uplifting people morally and spiritually.

This rich tradition in history and literature has had its impact on the life of the people of Kashmir. The family of a Hindu emissary who was deputed to negotiate with Ranjit Singh to rescue the people of Kashmir from the tyranny of Pathan rule, was given protection by a Muslim shawl-merchant who preferred death to the betrayal of trust. The holy cave of Amarnath, which was declared "lost" during Pathan rule, was rediscovered by one Malik of a village in the vicinity of Pahalgam. To this day, the Muslim Malik family receives a share from the offerings made by the thousands of Hindus who visit the holy cave annually. The shrine of Shah-e-Hamadan and the temple of Mahakali exist together at Khanqah Mohalla in Srinagar city. The shrine of Makhdom Saheb and the temple of goddess Sharika at Hari Parbat are, also similarly situated. Be it Id or Shivaratri, the, participation is not only of one or the other community but of the people of Kashmir as a whole. One may even say that the spectacle is unique to Kashmir.

Faith in the unity of God was not to them an intellectual proposition alone. It was infused with universal love. Love alone could lead to the realisation of oneness. Nizamuddin Aulia is quoted as saying:

"The main purpose and objective of man's creation is the love of the Supreme Being."

Along with the love of God goes the love for His entire creation. Nizamuddin Aulia explained it thus:

"Oh Muslim! I swear by God that He holds dear those who love Him for the sake of human beings, and also those who love human beings for the sake of God."

Their love had no boundaries. It was limitless. It took every one under its magnificent umbrella.

The universality of love of that age is well expressed in the inscription Abul Fazal inscribed in a temple in Kashmir. It runs thus:

> O God, in every temple I see people that seek Thee,
> And in every language I hear spoken people praise Thee.
> Polytheism and Islam flee after Thee.
> Each religion says, Thou art one without equal . . .
> He who from insincere motive destroys this temple,
> should first destroy his own place of worship.

Thus we find that on both the intellectual and the emotional levels, the saints' outlook extended like an ocean.

One of the distinguishing characteristics of the saints was that they were not passive seekers of truth. They actively sought to purge the community of all evils out of the fathomless love that surged in their hearts. Renunciation of the world has never been an ideal of these saints. They remained in touch with life, kindled in it a new zest and contributed to the socio-cultural and moral development of the community.

It is true that quite a number of them renounced the world and annihilated their selves (Fana fi-Allah). "Sheikh Sharafuddin Yahya Maned kept standing in the jungle for years. Sheikh Ahmed Khattu fasted for forty days continuously, each fast broken by one date. Sheikh Mohammad Ghous Gwalior spent twelve years in meditation on the mountains of Chinar." But renunciation was not the general tendency of these saints.

Sheikh Nizamuddin Aulia explains it thus:

Renunciation does not imply giving up garments or food. Renunciation requires both. One should take food and wear a dress. However, it is but essential that one should spend whatever one earns. One should not keep his heart in worldly things and should remain detached throughout.

Hazrat Khwaja Gesu Daraz in the Deccan insisted upon his disciples that they remain in service : "If noble souls gave up their missions, undesirable people would slip in, to the grief of common people. The greatest worship is to do justice with everyone and never be tempted by wealth."

"It is incumbent on everyone," says Sheikh Sharafuddin, "to serve the needy by the pen, tongue, wealth and positron. Prayers, fasting and voluntary worship are good as far as they go, but they are not as useful as making others happy."

In the same manner the values of honest labour were praised. Shah Latif of Sind proclaimed thus:

> Not sloth but honest and persistent labour
> Will win the coveted prize.
> The mountains yield no diamonds to lovers of lassitude.
> Neither the stars know any rest nor rivers any tranquillity.

How will you amass spiritual wealth if you sleep all night? Out of the eight principles that Sheikh Shaftabuddin Suhrawardi laid down with Quranic sanction for functioning of Khanqah, two were that the people of Khanqah should learn to value time and completely shake off indolence and lethargy. The whole life and energy should be submitted to do good to others.

Khwaja Gesu Daraz (of the Deccan) used to advise:

Look, the tree stands erect in the scorching heat but it provides shade to others. Wood burns itself to provide comfort to others. It is thus natural that a man should undertake pain in order to provide pleasure to others.

The outlook of the Muslim saints as well as of the Bhakti saints aimed at purifying the soul. It ridiculed formal worship. It raised the banner of intrinsic equality between man and man. It set high moral standards for society. Bodily pleasures were deprecated and the joys of the soul, truth, justice, self-sacrifice, and submission to the will of God were extolled.

It was during this period that modern regional languages developed. Love and devotion expressed themselves in poetry and music. They were instruments in bringing about union with God.

The common people flocked around the saints. The aggrieved sought solace, the guilty admitted guilt, the bereaved found peace and the frustrated a ray of hope.

The saints in turn identified themselves with the people. They picked up the folk language of the area, and used it as an instrument for preaching faith and love of God and high moral ideals. A large number of saints were poets of a high order, who turned each of the folk languages into an independent standard language with its own treasure of literature. By blending words of different stocks, expressions of different cultures, and by mixing poetic styles of Persian and Apabhramsha Prakrit, they created fine poetry.

Shah Latif Bhitai (A.D. 1690) was a Sufi poet of Sind. He is ranked by authorities of that language as one of the greatest poets of the world. His *Risalo* is a sacred work and a unique treasure in Sindhi language.

He was an ardent devotee of Sufi philosophy. He explains it thus citing Rumi:

> The whole diversity is His seeker and He
> The fountain source of Beauty-thus says
> Rumi.

In his love of God he would make no difference between man and man:

When truth is one, and the Beloved (God)
the same, why should man fight over the
means?

He expressed this theme of devotion and love in a multitude of colours and variegated musical tunes.

Shah sings of his eternal love in Sur Yaman Kalyan, in Sur Soraih, in Sur Asa, in Sur *Maazuri,* in *Sur Sarang*, in *Sur Kapairi*, in *Sur Rag*, in *Sur Doha* and many others.

He loved the beauty of Sind, its fields and dales, its mountains and rivers. His *Risalo* contains references to Lokhpat, Girnar, Jaisalmer, Thar, Ganjar, Hano, etc. He visited almost all important places in Sind and every time he had a new spiritual experience. About Ganja Hills he says:

Those who get acquainted with Ganja Hills
Become saints, forsaking all books and
scriptures.

He was a true lover of nature. The sight of the Hill and the Kinjhir Lake on the way inspired him to sing:

The water runs below, the blossoms above,
and lovely forests stand on the sides
The fragrance of Tamachi saturates the air;
With the blowing of the north breeze,
the Kinjhir becomes a cradle.

Many other saints translated Persian and other classical stories into Sindhi. *Hatim Tayee*, *Laila Majnu* and *Gul-i-Bakauli* have added to its literary stock.

Sheikh Fariduddin Shakarganj, popularly known as Baba Farid, is regarded as the first poet of Punjabi language. There were other Sufi poets before him — Masood Sa'd Salman was one of them. His name has been mentioned by Amir Khusru, and others as the first poet of Punjab. But his Divan is not available today. But with Baba Farid a new star shown on the horizon of Punjab. He granted an independent status to Punjabi, by his dohas. These dohas are highly revered and are preserved in Granth Saheb. They portray ecstatic love for God. He implores people not to be contented with outer appearances but to see within:

> If anybody hits you, do not repay him back in the same coin,
> Since you are to go to Heaven, better touch his feet (Doha 7).
> Oh, Farida, why do you wander in-the-thick of the jungle
> You are searching for Him outside yourself,
> While He is hidden within you. (Doha 18).
> How is it possible to sow kikar
> but start expecting a crop of kishmish ?
> Weave wool but aspire for silken cloth 7 (Doha 23).

There is a long array of poets who have greatly contributed to building up Punjabi language like Syed Shah Waris (A.D. 1375-1395), Qutban A.D. 1503), Sultan Baba (A.D. 1631-1691), Ali Hyder (A.D. 1690-1785), Bulley Shah (A.D. 1680-1752), Shah Sharif (A.D. 1724), and many others.

All these saints were highly catholic in their attitude. They had intense yearnings for God. In the words of Sultan Baba:

> I am not a Hindu, nor a Muslim,
> I am not a mulla nor a kazi.
> My heart does not fear death,
> Nor does it long for paradise.
> Oh God, give me Your vision,
> Everything else is false.

Hindi and Urdu, both the languages, developed out of Khari Boli. Amir *Khusrua* (A.D. 1255-1325), a disciple of Nizamuddin Aulia, is regarded as the first poet of Khari Boli. Prior to him whatever works survive they are in *Arsha Apabhramsha Prakrit* or *Saurseni Apabhramsha*.

In Khari Boli, it is said, Amir Khusru has written one lakh stanzas consisting of pahelis (riddles), do sukhna, kah-mukarnis, savnias, etc. They were so simple and flawless that they soon entered the everyday language of the people Hindi and Urdu developed in the direction that he indicated. He had an intense feeling of love for everything that was Indian. His Hindi is very congenial to Indian life. People still sit together in the village meeting place and test each other's wit through Khusru's riddles. His songs on the rainy season are still sung by young girls while swinging in the rainy season. His dholak songs are still heard on festive occasions like marriages.

Amir Khusru was deeply devoted to Nizamuddin Aulia, who was his spiritual master. When he passed away, Khusru is reported to have recited the verse:

gori sowey sej par mukh par dare kes
Chal khusru ghar Apne sanjh hui chal des

(The beloved lies on the coach
with her black tresses scattered over face.
Oh, Khusru, return to your home,
Night has fallen over the whole country.)

It is said that Khusru combined in his personality the variegated colours of Indian culture. He was poet, mystic, artist, humorist, musician, soldier, historian naturalist, linguist and above all a humanist.

In that age, Amir Khusru painted Hindi literature with many hues. In his period principles of literature were not well defined.

Poetry was harnessed for religion and politics. It was not an ordinary thing to create a literature for popular recreation.

From the thirteenth century onward, not only Khusru but a large number of Sufi saints contributed to the development of Hindi language.

Mulla Dawood (A.D. 1295) produced *Prem Katha Chandayan*. Qutban in 1501 produced *Mirgavati*. Malik Manjhan brought out *Madhu Malti* in 1345. Malik Mohammad Jaisi wrote *Padmavati*. Sheikh Rahim was known for his *Prem Ras*. Many other works of Noor Mohammed, Qasim Shah, Usman and Jan are also noteworthy. A new climate developed wherein devotional songs were sung. Nirgun Bhakti and Sagun Bhakti dominated the religious thinking of the day. Thus Hindi got a start and it flourished at the hands of these Sufis and saints.

Urdu has never been a court language. It was regarded as a language of the bazar and the lashkar. Urdu and Hindi both developed out of the interaction between the indigenous tongues and Persian, Turkish and Arabic words.

In the Deccan, Khwaja Gesu Daraz' *Mi'raj-ul-Ashiqeen* (A.D. 1422) is supposed to be the first work of Urdu. It is a philosophic treatise. *Mi'raj-ul-Ashiqeen* has a surprisingly smooth flow and it determined the future development of Urdu and Hindi both in the South and in the North.

Besides Khwaja Gesu Daraz, a very prominent writer of this common language was Shah Miranji (1496). He wrote both poetry and prose. Wajhi's *Sab Ras* is well known. Shah Burhanuddin Janam and Shah Aminul A'la were others who developed this language in the South.

Growing out of the Magadhi Apabhramsha, modern Bengali assumed the status of a standard language in the fourteenth century. During this period the entire country was waking to new religious heights. The keynote of this movement was the apprehension of the unity of God and the belief that He can be achieved through intense love. God views everyone equally, whether he is Brahmin or Chandal. Shri Chaitanya initiated the Krishna Bhakti movement. The Sufi movement in Bengal flourished through Jalaluddin Tabrezi. Shri Chaitanya had many Muslim followers who were Vaishnoi and had abundant poetic work to their credit. The close interaction of Sufism and Chaitanyaism gave rise to Baul songs (A.D. 1625-1675). They were a creation of Hindu-Muslim unity. This was a movement against all externalism whether of Hindus or of Muslims. It aimed to break all external restraints:

> You wander aimlessly:
> Mandir, Mandir, Masjid, Masjid;
> Oh, my teacher.
> What a headache it is
> The foolish, while weeping, look at me.

Among the Muslim saints whose contribution to the development of modern Bengali is recognized without question is Daulat Kazi. According to Shanti Ranjan Bhattacharya, he was the author who introduced novel-writing in Bengali. His book *Sati Meenavati* had a historic significance. Then there was Ala~ul, creator of a large number of Vaishanavite songs. His *Padmavati* is well reputed. Besides, he translated a large number of Persian books into Bengali, like Nizami's *Haft Paikar*, or *Sikandarnama*, etc. His *Vaishnava Padawalis* are very popular in Bengal. Another was Syed Sultan. Besides Vaishnavite songs, he has written books on Islamic religion like *Gyan Pradeep*, *Hazrat Mohammed Chant*, and *Nabi Bangash*. In *Nabi Bangash* he counted all Brahma, Vishnu, Shiva, Shri Krishna as Nabis, and showed great respect towards them. Mohammed Khan wrote *Maut-ul-Husain* (1645) and Hayat Mahmood wrote *Ambia Bani*. Syed Murtaza was poet of the first rank in Vaishnavite songs. His *Pad Kalpararu* is well known. Sabit Khan wrote *Vidya Sunday*. Ali Raja is known for his books *Gyan Sager*, *Saraj Koloop*, *Dhyan Mala*. He has depicted the love of Radha and Krishna, Ravan and Mandodari, and Yusuf and Zulekha. His conclusion is that one rises from the love for a person to love for the entire creation and the Creator. A volume of Akbar Shah has been discovered. It is in praise of Lord Krishna. Inayatullah translated *Chahar Darwesh*.

A reference to the Pathan rulers of Bengal like Sultan Nasir Shah (A.D. 1282-1325) and Sultan Husain Shah, and their religious tolerance, is necessary. They declared Bengali to be the official language of the regime. They got the *Mahabharata* and *Bhagavat Purana* translated into Bengali. This is regarded as the first translation during these early days. The great poet Vidyapati had dedicated his poems to Sultan Nasiruddin. The Sultans were patrons of the Bengali language and tried to enrich it in many ways. According to S.R. Bhattacharya, Shah Husain patronized *Tarja Geet*. It is supposed to be the earliest form of the Bengali poetry. (Nazr-e-Zakir)

Upto the fourteenth century, Gujarat Apabhramsha was spoken in Gujarat. Since Gujarat is situated on the western border of India, there was a direct interaction with people of Arabia and Persia. Many Gujarati Saints and Sufis became famous. Among them names of Sheikh Ganjul lim (1381), Syed Burhanuddin (1411) and Sheikj Wajihuddin Gujarati are well known. One can see in Gujarati works like *Ramal Chand* and *Kath-Da-Prabandh* the absorption of Persian, Arabic and Turkish words.

Kashmir and Persia had a long history of contacts even before Kashmir's political amalgamation in the Delhi Sultanate. The impact of Persia was direct. The Sufis loved the Kashmiri language and filled it with the romantic Sufi philosophy. Mahmood Ghani, Khwaja Habibullah Nowshaharwi and Nooruddin were the reputed Sufis of their times. In a Kasmiri Rubali Sheikh Nooruddin says:

> Don't yield before His bows,
> Don't turn your head if you are injured
> by the thrust of His sword.
> Accept willingly all the calamities that He has sent to you,

Only then would you be honoured in this world and after.

Mahmood Ghani translated many classic Persian works like *Yusuf Zulekha, Laila Majnoon, Sheereen Farhad*. Saifuddin translated *Gulshan-a Raz*.

Music has been another field to which the saints contributed generously. They came to realize that, like poetry, music also elevates emotion to the ecstatic state necessary for union with God.

Both the Chishtiya and the Qadria fraternities sanctioned Sama', musical rhythms, that enhanced the effect of poetry. They enabled the devotee to be plunged in a state of trance called Haal. The effectiveness of Sama' can be gauged by the fact that many a Sufi embraced death while listening to certain poetic lines which intensely affected their hearts. It is said that Khwaja Bakhtiyar Kaki surrendered his life while hearing the following poetic line:

kushtagan-a Khanjar-a taslim ra
har zaman az ghaib jan-a digarast.

(To those who have been killed by the dagger of submission, there comes new life every moment from the unseen world)

Akhbar-ul-Akhyar, an authoritative work of Sheikh Abdul Haq Mohaddis, shows the keen interest of the saints in same, music as a path to the spiritual realms. One of the many incidents that *Akhbar-ul-Akhyar* quotes is that of a young man who was attending an audition at the house of a Sufi, and heard the words

jan be-deh, jan be-deh, jan be-deh.
fa'ida-a guftan-a bisyar chlst.

(Surrender life, surrender life, surrender life;
It is of no avail to talk and talk.)

All of a sudden the young man burst out crying "Surrendered, surrendered, surrendered", and his life ended.

Such incidents were not few. Sometimes in order to maintain the emotional pitch, a single poetic verse had to be repeated for hours together.

In the beginning, Persian poetry was resorted to for such gatherings. Persian had been a highly developed language with the treasure of scores of Sufi poets like Attar, Rumi, Jami, Sa'di, etc.

Amir Khusru, in his devotion to his preceptor, wrote four volumes of Persian poetry. Each word of his poetry is permeated with divine ecstasy. To match it with appropriate music, he needed to be an expert musician, which he was, being well versed in both Persian and Indian music.

Hakim Mohammad lkram Imam Khan, a reputed musician of Oudh, in his book *Ma'din-ul-Musiqae* writes:

> Amir Khusru had such a mastery of Persian music and the ragas of Hindi that he was supposed to be a naik of that age. In place of the Pakhawaj he invented the Dholak, and in place of the Beena he invented Sitar. He used to teach music to boys endowed with good voice. Ohuroo, Rahwa, Matha, Chind, Persand, Dhrupad were commonly used. He introduced six new modes: Qaul, Qalbana, Naqsh, Gul, Tarana and Khiyal.

He was a master in the Persian musical system called Naqsh. Persian poetry was sung to twelve tunes. Each had two shades, resulting in twenty four ragas. Each raga was to be sung at a particular hour of the twenty-four hours of night and day. It goes to the credit of Amir Khusru that he invented novel ragas by combining Persian music with the Indian. Many of these ragas have gone out of use, but still many are a delight to musicians like

Yeman, Zulf, Sarparda and Gazgiri, etc. He also invented many musical forms like Sawani, Farodast Pashto, Qawaali etc.

After the thirteenth century, music was accepted by these saints as a sacred treasure. It was developed by reputed and dedicated musicians.

In this climate it was easy for kings and nobles to patronize music and enrich it with new forms and a new content. The name of Sultan Husain Sharqui, a ruler of Jaunpur, was second only to Amir Khusru's in this field. It became a fashion among the nobility and kings to equip their sons with instruction in music as a necessary part of education. There were Sufis and saints everywhere who were expert in music and worked for its advancement, like Sheikh Malli Khan Gujarati, Sheikh Alauddin and Sheikh Jamal Sahib. Sheikh Nizamuddin Aulia was himself a great critic of music.

Syed Nizamuddin Madhunaik was a scholar of persian and Sanskrit. He wrote two books on music expert in Arabic, Persian *Nad Chandrika* and *Madh naik Singhan.* Makldoom Bahauddin Bunnais was another Sufi who devoted his life to get an access to the Divine through music. He invented two musical instruments : Saz Khiyal and Khat Ras. He wrote a number of Zikria in praise of God which were sung in those days in the Lalit, Bilawal, Todi and Kalyani ragas.

An overwhelming number of musical gharanas (schools) of repute owe their allegiance to the early saints. These schools might have been fostered by rulers of States. Yet they drew their inspiration from saints, particularly of the Chistiya order, like Tamras Khan's Gharana of Delhi, Ustad Faiyaz Khan's Gharana of Agra, Huddu Husain Khan's Gharana of Gwalior, the Fatah Ali and Ali Bakhsh Gharana of Patiala, Aia Diya's Gharana in Kolhapur, the Mushtaq Husain and Ishitiyaq Husain Gharana of Rampur. In earlier times it was ecstatic and religious devotion to music that institutionalized a particular form of music and rendered it into a school which attracted both Hindu and Muslim disciples.

The Legacy of Hinduism

One has to take note of the fact that more than five centuries had already elapsed since the advent of Islam when by 1206 A.D. the Sultanate in Delhi got established. It was indeed not an "Islamic" army that the Turko Afghans headed, but purely an expeditionary force bent upon conquering new lands to be added to the meagre pastures in their homeland. The Islamic faith had never had a brush, not to speak of a skirmish, with Hindu faith as such. In Sindh, it was a punitive expedition that was sent by the Caliph in 711 A.D. under Mohammad Bin Qasim after the ships meant for the Caliph had been looted. More significant than the success of the Arab invasion was the fact that Dahir was defeated mainly because the Buddhists of his realm had risen against him and helped the invaders. The Muslim administration set up in Sindh was an island in a sea of many Hindu states; it was allowed by the powerful Hindu kingdoms of the Pratiharas and the Baghelas to continue to exist and was finally extinguished by the Delhi Sultanate. It would thus be a historical distortion to show that the conquest of Sindh was in any way a triumph of the Muslims over Hindus, as some western scholars have tried to do.

Other Religions

It would be pertinent to recall the state of India at the time Muslim armies embarked on a spree of victories in the Middle East, Iran, Egypt and further West in Africa and the Mediterranean. India was a large country, a sub-continent according to modern calculations, peopled by several races, chiefly the Caucasoid (Dravidians) and Nordic (Aryan), according to modern classification, all in varying stages and degrees of civilization and culture, the predominant race being the so called Aryans. However, Hindu India did not recognise such calculations and classifications. As the Vishnu Puran and Kularnaua Tantra say: In the word 'Hindu', Hi stands for the Himalayas, and Indu means the Ocean. Thus, Hindu scriptures recognised all the people living from the Himalayas in the north to the Ocean in the south as Hindus. In the east, where the Himalayas ended, and in the west, likewise, all the lands that griddled the Himalayas up to Khotan were included in Hindu India. The Hindus were proud of the land they lived in and called it 'Aryavarta', a land peopled by virtuous people. The word "Arya" stood for excellence; for people who were the stately, the noble, and the virtuous. It never denoted any race, or any distinct class of people, far less a religion, as some of the Western scholars would like us to believe. Had it been so, Lord Buddha would not have called his teachings as `Arya Satya' (eternal truths) and would not have been referred to as 'Arya Putra' which, in fact, meant `Your Excellency'. As for the view that the Aryans were those who came from outside India, the whole edifice of the myth collapses, if the correct meaning of the word `Arya' is taken into account. Western scholars have been anxious to show that the Teutonic peoples belonged to the Aryan family of races and that Indo-Europeans and the Aryans had a common ancestry; just as the Teutonic races invaded and conquered Europe, so also the Aryans invaded and conquered India. The fact remains, however, that the Aryans were a cultural group of people marked by a certain way of and outlook on life. The Vedas are a collection of their lore and wisdom, which spread in course of time among the peoples of India, Central Asia and even beyond. If there was any Aryan conquest, it was a conquest of a superior and a more civilized way of life being accepted willingly by different cultural and social groups by sheer force of its excellence.

The only group of people outside the territory of the Aryavarta who can be said to be of the Aryan cultural stock are the Iranians. There are striking similarities in the religious outlook and social organization of the Iranians and other Aryan peoples. Among the ancient peoples, it is perhaps the Aryans alone who built the norms of their social life and institutions around cultivation and tilling of land. What sustains the bounties of mother earth, sun, rain, wind and other elements of nature, also sustained them, their myths and their beliefs. 'The same divine power, a motion and a spirit, which impels all thinking things, all objects of all thoughts' is also one 'whose dwelling is the light of the setting sun, and the round ocean, and the living air, and the blue sky', as Wordsworth chose to express it in poetry. The Aryans saw one divine power in sentient and non-sentient beings manifesting itself through the elements of nature. As the Rigveda (I.CXIV.46) says "To what is one, the wise give many names, Indra, Varun..." Hence, it is not nature that they worship in order to invoke its blessings; it is verily the Divine Power itself in its various moods and manifestations that is the object of their worship.

The ancient religion of Iran, Zoroastrianism as set out in its holy book Zend Avasta, appears to be rooted in a cultivating civilization. Its invocations to sun and fire have striking similarities with many of such invocations in the Rig Veda. Contrast this with what the Old Testament has to say:

"And God blessed them (man and woman) and God said unto them: Be fruitful and multiply, and replenish the earth, and subdue it: and have dominion over the fish of the sea, and over the fowl of the air, and every living thing that moveth upon the earth."

This is evidently the blessing given to people who were still in a mainly pastoral society. Again, the story of Abel and Cain in the Old Testament indicates the same cultural stage. While Abel was a keeper of the sheep, Cain was tiller of the ground. It is significant that the Lord accepted the offering of Abel in the shape of 'firstling of his flock and of the fat thereof, but unto Cain and to his offering he had not respect.'

Aryans of the Vedic Age

The Aryans of the Vedic age were thus at a stage of cultural development which had moved ahead of a purely pastoral civilization; their social organization was, therefore, complex and variegated, representing a more 'modern' society. The peculiar characteristics of social organisation of the Aryans lay in its four-fold division, called Varna. Now Varna literally means `colour', but by Varna, they did not mean colour of the skin, but the quality of the group which a particular man may belong to. The four-fold division in India, Brahmin, Kshatriya, Vaisya and Shudra had their Iranian counterparts, in Attarvana, Rathaestra, Fshuyant and

Huite, respectively. Kalhan in *Rajatarangini* has designated Iran or Arian as Aryanaka, the country of the Aryans.

The Vish or Vaishyas were the people, the tiller of soil, and keeper of flock of animals who fulfilled the wants of the community. All the three Varnas could justify their existence only to the extent they ministered to the welfare of the Vish; the Brahmin by invoking rain-god and performing Yagna was to ensure timely rain for the crops, the Kshatriya was the protective arm of the community, and the Shudra was to provide physical help and assistance. The Aryan Brahmin should be understood to be very different from the priestly class in ancient Egypt. While the priests of Egypt enjoyed tremendous wealth and power, the Aryan Brahmins had to undergo a most rigorous discipline and had to eschew the temptations of the senses. Severe austerity was their mode of life. The respect they commanded was in proportion to their spiritual attainments and to the extent of their self-denial and simplicity of life. For example, a Brahmin to be truly called a Brahmin was prohibited, according to Apadstumb Sutra, from storing provisions for himself and his family for more than a day, or a month and at best a year, on pain of loss of his Brahminhood. The Kshatriya was more fortunate in respect of earthly enjoyments in view of the hazards of his occupation of soldiering but any excess on his part was frowned upon. The Vaisyas and the Shudras, after meeting the levies and social obligations, were free to enjoy the fruits of their labour. The rod that kept the four Varnas in position was Dharma as defined and explained in Grihsutras. Dharma was a set of duties, a code of conduct native to the genius of the Varna one belonged to. There can be no exact English equivalent of word Dharma, but, perhaps, the Greek word "entelecheia" i.e., having (echo) its purpose (telos) within (entos) would come closest. The word was used by Aristotle to explain that everything is guided in a certain direction from within by its nature. Thus, according to the rules of Dharma, a Brahmin would willingly vow a life of penury and destitution to pursue spiritual and intellectual ends, a Kshatriya would unhesitatingly sacrifice his life, ease and comfort in protecting and fighting for the country and the community, and a Vaisya will give up his all for the common good. Thus though the duties enjoined differed from Varna to Varna, there was nothing like a double ethical standard, a Herren-Moral for the Brahmin and the Kshatriyas and a Herden-Moral for the Vaisya and Shudra as in Teutonic races. Except for the esteem and honour of their callings and the veneration and respect, their personal qualities commanded, the material perks and pre-requisites of a Brahmin were meagre indeed. Dharma was a derivative of Sanskrit root dhri meaning 'holding together' and as Satpath Brahman says, the Strotriya and Rajanya (the Brahmins and Kshatriyas) were the upholders of dharma which held society together.

As economic activities multiplied, so did occupational groups of the community. The Vedas themselves mention many occupational groups. Thus we have barber (Vepta), chariot-maker (tasta), carpenter (tvasta), physician (bhisk), iron-smith (katmasa), tanner (carmanna), artisan (karmara), potter (kulala), fowler (punjista), fisherman (nishad), amongst others. By the very nature of their occupations and utility to the community, these occupational groups comprised the Vaisya Varna. It appears certain that in course of time occupational groups based on birth embodying the principle of kinship emerged as castes, differentiated and distinct, exclusive in character, from other occupational groups and castes and such caste system became the hall-mark of the Aryan society in India. For the occupation of Brahmins and of Kshatriyas also, division did not exist on the basis of birth, but by inclination, and even the two duties could be enjoined together in one man. For example, a nobleman or even a king could officiate as priest, and a priest could become a commander of forces or even a king. The ancient traditions are full of such examples. Since Brahminhood was a difficult affair, depending upon personal attainments of a high order, even those born of Brahmin parents had to take recourse to other occupations, if they did not feel up to rigours of discipline and intellectual life. Atri, the famous law-giver, smritikar, mentions ten kinds of Brahmins: these include people who performed spiritual functions, those who worked as Kshatriyas, Vaisyas, and even those who degenerated to earning their living as Malechha and Chandalas, lowest of the lowly. The rank of Kshatriyas swelled or depleted according to demands of time. For performing kingly functions, there appeared to be an intense rivalry indeed between the Brahmins and the Kshatriyas as a class. According to the Mahabharat, Parsuram had destroyed the Kshatriyas and the Vishnu Puran gives a graphic account how Mahapadma Nanda sought to destroy the Kshatriyas. Other Puranas support the story. Again, it was not unusual for war-like tribes to emerge as rulers of vast tract of land and assume a Kshatriya lineage. The Smritis mention Audhras, Abhirs, Odras, Pahalvas and Pulinds as some of these tribes. The many tribals across the Hindukush, like the Greeks, Bactrians, Sakas and Huns, who foraged in this country from time to time, got absorbed in the mainstream and added to the caste texture in their own way.

However, Rikhavadeo, the Adinath, first Tirthankar of the Jains, appears to have seriously challenged this system of social division. According to him people were either asidharma, men of sword, or masidharma, men of pen. Among the men of sword were the ruling classes, king's soldiers, magistrates and all those whose duty would be to keep peace and order for the proper functioning of society. Among the men of pen were people who enriched social life with their labour and skill, such as cultivators, artisans and traders. It is significant that he ignores the Brahmins completely, and instead advocates a class of recluse, ascetic holy men without any family attachments, devoted to pursuits of knowledge and paths of rectitude, their bare earthly requirements being met by alms. Such ideals, feeble in the beginning, took a mightily shape later on. This was the famous shraman dharma preached by Lord Mahavir and Lord Buddha, who laid the foundations of a Sangh of Bhikshus. While the code of conduct laid down by Buddhism for the laity was Vinay, it was dharma for the Bhikshus.

Doctrines of Jainism

The doctrines of Jainism, as preached by Lord Mahavir, due to their extremism, both in conception and practical application, were too exacting. The extreme asceticism and almost masochistic rigours of discipline of life as laid dawn in Jainism were for truly brave souls and hence did not attract many adherents beyond the shores of India or even within the country. Buddhism, on the other hand, had the Delphic oracle meden again, "nothing in excess", as its basic principle. The Buddhistic doctrine of balance has been compared to the Aristotelian path of the golden mean, but this was nothing but practical application of the Hindu philosophical idea of equilibrium and harmony. Lord Buddha did attack the prevailing ideas and social system, but not too violently, taking care to chalk out a path steering clear of extremes. It was this which won him adherents, both kings and commoners, the learned as well as the unlettered, the laity and the ascetics. It spread into far and distant lands, to the wilds of Central Asia and Tibet, to civilized and highly sophisticated China, and through China to far eastern Japan and Korea, and as modern researches have shown, even to the Pacific shores of North and South America. The Indians colonized and founded kingdoms in Siam, Cambodia, Java, Sumatra and Bali. The old Brahminical order had not remained idle. It mended its fences and thus grew Saivism and Vaishnavism. By the sixth century of the Christian era, there were four main religious orders in India: Saivism, Vaishnavism, Buddhism and Jainism, and emphasis was more on personal aspect of divinity. Instead of the impersonal, intangible Brahama, whom one can feel in heart and mind, but whom one cannot give a concrete shape, Siva, Vishnu, Buddha and Mahabir, were almost like persons to be worshipped and given concrete shapes in form of idols -symbols before which spiritual yearning and worldly desires could be supplicated for spiritual solace and wordily props. Thus, worship before idols became extensive with more emphasis on ceremonial aspects than on spiritual contents. Tantricism was the common name given to the mode and form of worship of the deities and since rapport with deities by esoteric means was claimed, this form of worship came to be invested with miraculous and supernatural powers and effect in common mind. The Mahayan form of Buddhism specially came to be associated with Buddhistic Tantra. It was strong both in the north, north-eastern and north-western part of the country, and since these regions had large tribal population, many quaint practices got associated with Tantricism. Inevitably, charlatans and other unscrupulous persons, taking advantage of the esoteric form of Tantric worship introduced certain abominable practices for their own ignoble ends, and it degenerated into a series of antinomian cults and deadening rituals. Krishna Misra, of the court of Chandela king Kirtivarman, has drawn a picture of the religious practices in the 11th century in his drama "*Prabodh Chandrodaya*". He shows how the unholy alliance of corrupt and degraded Buddhist and Jain monks, depraved Charvaka materialists, unscrupulous Mimansakas and immoral Kapalikas, flourishing under a regime of falsehood and vice, oppressed truth and virtue and caused a truly spiritual crisis in the country.

Sankaracharya, the great philosopher and religious teacher, had tried to infuse new life in the orthodox Hindu practices in the eighth century of the Christian era, but ended only with founding a new ascetic order just like the Buddhists and the Jains. Moreover, his doctrine of Mayavad, extreme monism, denying the world of sense experience as a mere illusion bordering on something like philosophical nihilism,
was beyond the ken of common minds. He unwittingly gave a final blow to the old varnashram order where the householder Brahmin was made the repository of intellectual pursuits and spiritual speculations of the community and entrusted with the task of acting as advisers of the Kshatriyas in holding together social orders. He advocated the practice of entering into an ascetic order after finishing studies, relying on such texts as one whose concern is exploration of the self and reality, how can he have any business with begetting progeny? Establishment of four Mutts in four corners of the Aryavarta for ascetics and spiritual seekers was in the nature of a counterpoise to the Buddhistic bhikshu sanghas. This also heralded a new era of, what may we term, as apatheia in Hinduism, a blind faith in fatalism. Unconcerned with social progress or political stability, Hindu ascetics, shut-up in the ivory towers of spiritual bliss, looked upon with disdain on mundane affairs. The Kshatriyas, too, swerving from the established dharma, their path of duty, did not take governance

as a sacred trust on behalf of the community, but as an opportunity of personal enrichment and aggrandisement. Kingdoms were there, not for protection of the Vish, but to bolster the ego of individual kings. No wonder, the Vish, the common people, left to their own devices, strengthened the ramparts of caste and customs which they had built around themselves, and assigned their happiness to chance and fate. It was not the system that had failed; it was the ruling elite, the degenerate and the selfish who had abandoned the path of duty and brought down crumbling the whole edifice of social and political balance. There was indeed a vaccum, and destiny had willed that Islam should play a role in filling up this vaccum.

Six

Development of Literature and Art

Promotion of Indian Literature

With the advent of Islam, the classical culture began to decline and there came on the scene the numerous provincial languages of the present day, which, till then, had been looked upon merely as patois of the common people. Islamic rulers who were mostly men of the people, were profoundly interested in matters literary and artistic, and it is interesting to note that it was chiefly through the agency of the Arabs that some of the popular masterpieces of Sanskrit literature - folk-table in particular, were made known to the outside world. *Panchatantra* and *Hitopadesha* were through their Arabic and Persian renderings under the titles of Kalilah va Damnah, Ayar Danish, Anwari - Suheli, became popular throughout the western world. The language of the Arabs had with the rise of their political power become a medium of international learning and the learning of Hindustan in the fields of philosophy, mathematics, astronomy, medicine and other sciences was made available to the civilised world of Europe primarily by the labours of Arabian scholars. Their own special contribution to the Indian literatures and learning lay in a different direction. Sanskrit works were translated not only in Persian and Arabic and what is more important into the spoken languages of the people.

The epics and Purans were thus made available by the patronage of the Islamic rulers to the common people. The impulse that was first given by these princes reached its greatest development during the period of the Moghuls. Hindi literature had its golden era during the reign of Akbar and Jahangir. Royal patronage was not limited merely to appreciation and encouragement of literary talents. The Indian Muslims made important contributions to the literatures of the land. Amir Khusru is often referred to as one of the founders of modern Hindi. Religious diversity did not alter the fundamental fact that Islam had come to stay in India and that its Indian votaries were not to be denied their rightful share in the contribution to the common culture. While I could recite the names of scores of Muslim poets, each with his individual corner in the temple of fame, I must content myself with the mention of one who occupies a unique place in the entire realm of Hindi poetry and is undoubtedly one of the half-a-dozen of the greatest names of Hindi.

Muslim Poet in Hindi

Abdur Rahim Khan Khanan was the soldier-statesman—son of Bairam Khan—the guardian and tutor of Jalaluddin Akbar. Abdur Rahim—Hindus call him Rahim, was an accomplished scholar of Arabic, Persian, Turki and perhaps of Sanskrit, and a consummate master of Hindi. It was he who rendered the Turkish memories of Babar - *Waqiat-i-Babari* into Persian. His chaste and simple Dohas form even today the best introduction to Hindi poetry. The bulk of Rahim's poetry is now the current stock of popular wisdom and is no longer the prerogative or the pastime of the learned. Dohas of Rahim are to be heard from the untutored and the illiterate peasantry of the country and the only name which can be put by the side of the Khan Khana is that of his friend and contemporary - the immortal Tulsidas. And what about Kabir? He is claimed by both Hindus and Muslims and I must not attempt a communal adjudication. I am convinced that he belongs to those who even in part share his vision and delight in the company of his matchless verse.

Influence of Sufism

Sufism was the Persian contribution to the new Islamic culture which was forged as a result of a reorientation of cultural values. It had its own votaries among the tribe of poets. Malik Muhammad Jayasi wrote as early as 1510 A. D. the famous classic of Hindi literature - the *Padmawat*. Most manuscripts of this book are generally found written in the Persian script. Kutban, Usman, Qasim Shah, Nur Muhammad were poets who were inspired by the Sufi doctrines which they translated through the medium of the folk-table.

The cult of Krishna was also not without its Muslim adherents. The most famous name of course is that of Rasakhan who lived towards the end of the sixteenth century. Then there is Alam and his gifted wife Sheikh Rangrezin. These are all masters of the most melodious idiom of the Braja Bhasha. A whole work entitled "Hindi ka Musalman kavi" has been devoted to the study of Muslim poets in the Hindi literature.

Great People and Events

Another notable contribution of the Muslim must be mentioned in this place. The practical bias of the Muslims is responsible for a new branch of literature in the form of history and biography. Whatever the original motive may have been, it is true that before the Muslims came to this country, writing of history as at present understood was practically unknown. Compared to the paucity of materials for the pre-Muslim period of Indian history, the number of contemporary works available for the Muslim period is altogether remarkable. I must not pause in dealing with this branch of knowledge, for some of the great masterpieces of Muslim history are known all the world over. But a word must be said about the unique biographical literature produced chiefly by the Moghul princes. The memoirs of Babar and Jahangir are among the world's biographical literature. I only wish that Indian history could be made even partially as interesting as the fascinating pages written by Babar, Gulbadan Begam and Jahangir. The Mughals wrote chiefly in Persian, for Indian Muslims have always looked to Iran as the fountain source of Islamic culture.

Iranian Influence

A vast literature in Persian was produced in India which though may not find distinguished mention in the histories of Persian literature, is of considerable interest for the history of this country. Besides, it was a result of the widespread use of Persian, that a new patois was born which is known as the Urdu. It was primarily as a result of its contact with Persian that Urdu acquired its exquisite polish, its finesse and concise but effective expression. Though the framework of Urdu is Indian, the soul of it is undoubtedly Persian. Even the outworn mannerisms of the classical Persian were imitated by the Urdu writers of the eighteenth the nineteenth century, and the vogue has not yet disappeared altogether. The greatest handicap of Urdu however was not so much its want of living contact with the sources of its inspiration, but the use of a beautiful though difficult script - especially for purposes of a modern printing press.

The development of Urdu is but a phase of the Hindi literature and there can be but little doubt that a new and a more simple and powerful medium of expression will some day be born as a result of the amalgamation of the current Hindi and the prevailing Urdu.

A word may be said about the system of Mushairas - still so popular with the people. It brought the people in touch with the great poets and I am not sure whether the advantages were not mutual. Muslims were great bibliophiles and founded more libraries than they destroyed. Fine writing was appreciated as a separate art by itself and nowhere in the world were the calligraphists given so much importance as at the courts of Iran and India. Pages written by Yakut, Sultan Ali Abdur Rahman and Mir Ali were treasured as heirlooms in the royal libraries. As a result of this, some of the most beautifully written manuscripts in the world belong to the heyday of Islamic power. Finely illuminated Mss. of Koran beautifully written on fine hand-made paper are real works of art. The Arabic script was made an unsurpassed instrument of writing as well as of beautiful decoration. Excerpts from the Koran were woven into complicated patterns of architectural decoration and calligraphic panels were frequently used as mounts for the dainty miniatures that were painted - chiefly in the royal ateliers of the Moghuls.

Art and Architecture

Some of the Moghuls are undoubtedly among the most gifted of the rulers of the past. Within a few years' of their establishment in India they were busy, having the classics of India and Iran illustrated for the royal libraries. Thousands of lovely pictures were painted by artists who suddenly found themselves exalted from the ranks of poor craftsmen to the honoured position of court-officials basking in the sunshine of royal appreciation and patronage.

I cannot pause on the achievement of these artists who were said by Abul Fazal to have rivalled the masters of the West. They began under Iranian tutelage, but reverted to their own traditions in a short time. The Persian influence was however felt in the dazzling but subtle colour - schemes, and decorative compositions of superb workmanship. Sheer richness has also its attractions and nowhere was it so noticeable as in the master-pieces of Bihzad and Mirak, which furnished the patterns to the earlier painters of the Moghul court. It should also be noted that the services of these artists were requisitioned also to illustrate the pages of historical works which were compiled by the court - historians. We therefore possess an unrivalled picture - gallery of the principal actors and events of the Moghul period shown in their own natural setting. Mughul history with the help of these contemporary picture, passes as it were, in a vivid panorama of events and personages. But the traditional injunction against the representation of living beings circumscribed the imaginative flight of the artist. A highly sophisticated art dealing with the pleasures of the world was brought into being, but it lacked the inspiration of spiritual insight. Sculpture in any serious form or shape was of course impossible and the plastic art practically died out during the Moghul period.

While painting remained but a minor art - an occupation ancillary to the splendour of the court, fullest scope for the vision and imagination of the Islamic princes was furnished in the sphere of architecture. The Islamic faith had its own peculiar needs and the architectural standards of the country were consequently modified to meet them. Mosques, *magharas* and *sarais*-rest-houses in profusion all over the country, testify to the vigour wealth and good taste of the Islamic rulers of Hindustan. It was not only at the seat of the empire that magnificent buildings were constructed. In the provinces also elaborate construction of novel and singularly beautiful designs were brought into being. I known of few architectural building more beautiful than some of the exquisite mosques and mausoleums of the 14th and 15th century in part of Gujarat - especially in Ahmedabad.

And what about the gardens? I can but mention the Nishat, Shalimar, Chashma Shahi, Verinag in the valley of Kashmir, the Rambagh at Agra planted by Babar himself, the gardens of the Taj and the Itmad-ud - daulah and the palace gardens of Agra and Delhi, not to speak of the Shalimar at Lahore For a vivid description of these beautiful monuments of the past the reader must read the fascinating book by Mrs. Villiers Stuart on *Gardens of the Great Moghuls*. Babar had noted the absence of running water in Hindustan. His successors - specially Jahangir, found it in ample measure in the natural gardens of Kashmir. The stately Chenar, the gloomy Cypress, gorgeously tinted flowers, brimming reservoirs with lovely cascades and chutes (*baradaris*) are some of the outstanding features which came into prominence during the Moghul period.

Food, dress, furniture - especially Chinaware and carpets and manners too were greatly influenced by the Muslim love for the good things of life. The Islamic standpoint was essentially practical. It took the life as it found it and enjoined the Musalman to make the best of it. It imparted refinement, dignity and ease, wherever it went, for the life of a Muslim is essentially social and lived, as it were, in the open. This attitude of robust common sense was also reflected in the Muslim contribution of Indian music.

Musical Arts

Musicians from all over Asia found patronage at the court of Islamic rulers in India. The complicated Vina was made the starting points of a beautiful and simple solo instrument - the sitar. The sarod, the dilruba were some of the instruments which came into vogue during the Muslim period. The Muslim musician brought his essential gaiety and enjoyment of life to the contemplative mood of Hindus. The systems of Khyal associated with the name of Sultan Husain Sharqi of Jaunpur and Thumri lighter modes of singing came into fashion. The Arab has always appreciated vocal music more keenly than purely instrumental music. Qisida and ghazal or love song were the peculiar contribution of Western Asia to Indian music through the medium of Islam, as was also the case, if one were to judge from the linguistion form of the words, with such popular instruments as drums (Arabic *tabal*) reed-pipe or Shahnai (Arabic *Surnay*) trumpet (*nafiri*) kettledrum (*naqqara*) *tambura* - (Arabic tonbur) and cymbal (Kasa). Contrary to the general opinion, therefore, the Muslim contribution to Indian music has been important and farreaching especially as regard the musical technique and instrumental resources in North India under the rule of the Mughals, who patronized musicians and music from beyond the frontiers. Arabians, Persians and Turks all added something of their own to our common heritage. It has been said by a competent authority that "the cultivation of music by the Arabs in all its branches reduces to insignificance the recognition of the art in the history of any other country" (H G Farmer in the *Legacy of Islam*, p. 358, Oxford 1931). It is this addition and super-imposition of ideas from the Islamic countries of the west which differentiates to this day the musical art of Northern India from that of the South. It is to the lasting glory of the Muslim rulers of India that the stature of a supreme artist such as Tansen - a Muslim Hindu was accorded unexampled recognition at the court of Akbar. Never before or after in the history of India have the artists, poets painters, musicians and calligraphists received such generous appreciation as at the hands of these Mughal princes. Despite disfavour of Islamic theologians to the cultivation of music, a unique synthesis was achieved as a result of a common spiritual understanding. Differences of ritual and theological dogma were forgotten in the creation of a new symphony. The culture of Hinduism became the patrimony of all Indians irrespective of their creeds; for it is the genius of Islam to accept its surroundings and to mould them in accordance with its own unique qualities.

I have hitherto used the past tense in talking about the influence of Islam. What about the future ? It seems to me that the spiritual energy which transformed men of ordinary clay into redoubtable heroes, is still capable of great achievements in the modern world. The message of Islam is no longer the monopoly of any one particular community. Its patrimony is the common property of the world at large. The achievements of Islam in India are therefore not the sole concern of the Musalmans, but the proud heritage of the Indian people as a whole.

The world of Islam is again throbbing with life. Life would seem to be in the process of a new orientation. The sword of Islam was sheathed centuries ago; but the empire of Islam is greater than ever; for its real basic was laid for all eternity by the Prophet of the desert by his insistence on simplicity, charity, righteousness and equality between man and man.

Hinduism and Islam Together

The rise of Islam is one of the marvels of history. In the summer of A.D. 622, a Prophet without honour in his own country, left his native city to seek asylum in the town of Yathrib-since known as Madinat -un-Nabi, the city of the Prophet', more than two hundred miles north of Mecca, the town which had cast him out. Little more than a century later, the successors and the followers of the fugitive, were ruling an empire, which extended from the Atlantic to the Indus and from the Caspian to the cataracts of the Nile, and included Spain and Portugal, some of the most fertile regions of southern France, the whole of the northern coast of Africa, upper and lower Egypt, their own native Arabia, Syria, Mesopotamia, Armenia, Persia, Afghanistan, Baluchistan and Transoxania.

It was in A.D. 711 that the first Muslim invader, Muhammad bin-Qasim, crossed the sea, defeated Dahir, and laid the foundation of the first Muslim Kingdom in Sind. When the Arab commander reached Alor, the citizens resisted the invaders vigorously for several months. Then they sued for peace, insisting on two conditions: one, that no resident of the city be killed, and two, that there should be no interference with their places of worship. Muhammad bin Qasim in accepting these terms said : "The temples of Hindustan are like the churches of Christians, the synagogues of Jews and the fire-temples of the Magians."

Regarding the invasion of Sind two things may be noted: (i) that the oppression of the native rulers was the prominent cause of the success of the Arabs; and, (ii) that apart from the slaughter and plunder during the actual course of war, the moment victory was won and peace concluded, a most enlightened policy of administration was followed which stands in shining contrast to the deeds narrated in the contemporary European history. Here are some of the Qasim's orders :

"Muhammad Qasim ordered 12 dirhams weight of silver to be consigned to each men, because all their property had been plundered. He appointed people from among the villagers and the chief citizens to collect the fixed taxes from the cities and villages that there might be a feeling of strength and protection"

Muhammad bin Qasim maintained their (Brahmins') dignity and passed orders confirming their pre-eminence. They were protected against opposition and violence. Each of them was entrusted with an office.

Hajjaj, Governor of Iraq, the uncle of Qasim and his immediate superior, wrote to him as follows : As they ('Hindus) have made submission and have agreed to pay taxes to the Khalifa, nothing more can be properly required from them. They have been taken under our protection and we cannot in any way stretch our hands upon their lives or property. Permission is given to them to worship their gods. Nobody must be forbidden or prevented from following his own religion. They may live in their houses in whatever manner they like.

He (Muhammad-bin-Qasim) directed the nobles, the principal inhabitants, and the Brahmins to build their temples, traffic with the Muhammadens, live without fear and to strive to better themselves. He also enjoined them to maintain the indigent Brahmins with kindness, observe the rites and customs of their ancestors and give oblations and alms to the Brahmins according to former practice.

The invasions of the Ghaznavides were of the nature undertaken more for the sake of plunder than conquest. Mahmud, whom historians have invested with the character of a religious zealot, had in fact little ecclesiastical fervour. His chief aim was the establishment of an empire from the Punjab to the Euphrates, and his Indian adventures were mainly intended to provide him with the means for the fulfilment of his imperialistic designs, which embraced even the subordination of the Caliph to his will. This explains why he attacked one after another, the great centres of wealth in northern India and never seriously considered the problem of subjugating and ruling the country. Hindus were a aprt of his army. Mahmud's son Masud employed Servand Rao in his fight with his brother, and Tilak son of Jai Sen to bring to book Ahmad Nialtigin the rebel governor of the Indian province. Again he raised Hindu troops to fight against the Saljuk Turks, while his successor deputed the Kotwal of Ghazni to recall Bijai Rai a Hindu general to Ghazni from where he had fled on account of some political dissensions.

The conquests of Muhammad Ghauri and his general Qutubuddin Aibak were in the nature of a triumphant march made easy by the internecine quarrels of the Rajput princes who then controlled the destinies of northern India. Within the interval of less than a quarter of a century the whole of northern India had not only been overrun but brought under subjection. But the establishment of Muslim rule implied little more than the substitution of Hindu Rajas and Zamindars by Muslim chiefs. Sir Wolseley Haig in the Cambridge History of India points out:

"The rhapsodies of Muslim historians in their accounts of the suppression of a rising or the capture of a fortress, of towns and villages burnt, of whole districts laid waste, ...might delude us into the belief that the early Muslim conquest of Northern India was one prolonged holy war waged for the extirpation of idolatry and the propagation of Islam, had we not proof that this cannot have been the case ... . All Muslim rulers in India from Mahmud downwards, accepted, when it suited them to do so, the allegiance of Hindu rulers and landholders, and confirmed them as vassals in the possession of their hereditary lands."

And again, "on this (Hindu) population they (the Muslim rulers) relied not only for the means of support, but also to a great extent for the subordinate machinery of government; for there can be no doubt that practically all minor posts connected with the assessment and collection of the land revenue and with accounts of public and state finance generally made generations later, by Hindus were filled, as they were made generations later, by Hindus."

"Rebellion and overt disaffection were repressed with ruthless severity, and were doubtless made occasions of proselytism, but the sin was rebellion, not religious error, and there is no reason to believe that the position of the Hindu cultivator was worse under a Muslim than under a Hindu landlord."

"It was certainly possible for Hindus to obtain justice even against Muslims."

It may be conceded at once that the Arab conquest of Sind was an insignificant event in the history of Islam, from the political point of view. But the effects of this conquest upon Muslim culture were profound and farreaching. When the Arabs came to India, they were astonished, at the superiority of the civilization which they found here. The sublimity of Indian philosophical ideas and the richness of the Indian intellect were a strange revelation to them. The cardinal doctrine of Muslim theology, that there is one God, was already known to the Indian saints and philosophers. The Arabs found that, in the nobler arts which enhance the dignity of man, the Indians far excelled them. The Indian musician, the mason and the painter were as much admired by the Arabs as the philosopher and the man of learning.

Tabari records that Khalifa Harun once sent for an Indian physician to cure him of an obstinate and painful disease. The Arabs learnt from the Indians a great deal in the practical art of administration. The employment of Brahmin officials on a large scale was due to their better knowledge, experience and fitness for discharging efficiently the duties of administration. A great many of the elements of Arabian culture, which afterwards had such a marvellous effect upon European civilization, were borrowed from India. Arab scholars sat at the feet of Buddhist monks and Brahmin pandits to learn philosophy, astronomy, mathematics, medicine, chemistry and other subjects of study. The court at Baghdad extended its patronage to Indian scholarship. During the Khilafat of Mansur (A.D. 750-774) Arab scholars returned from India to Baghdad carrying with them two books, the *Brahma Siddhanta* of Brahmagupta and his *Khand Khadyaka*. These-works were translated by AI Fazari into Arabic with the help of Indian scholars. It was from these two works that the Arabs learnt the first principles of scientific astronomy. There is ample reason to endorse Havell's view that it was India, not Greece, that taught Islam in the impressionable years of its youth, formed its philosophy and esoteric religious ideals, and inspired its most characteristic expressions in literature, art and architecture.

Arab authors have accepted in unambiguous terms the superiority of. Indian achievements. Thus Al-Jahiz (A.D. 869) writes : "The Hindus excel in astrology and mathematics. They have a special Indian script. They excel in medicine and possess some wonderful secrets of that art, in particular those remedies that are of the greatest use in the most dangerous diseases. They have developed to a perfection their art like sculpture, painting, and architecture. They are the inventors of chess. They make good swords and know all the tricks of-fencing. They know charms that can remove poison and pain from the body. Their music is pleasant and they have all sorts of dances. From India we received that book called *Kalamallah-wa-Dimnh*. These people have judgement and are brave. In some virtues they surpass the Chinese."

Yaqubi (A.D. 895) observes: "The Hindus are superior to all other nations in intelligence and thoughtfulness. They are more exact in astronomy and astrology than any other people. The *Brahma Siddhanta* is a good proof of their intellectual powers; by this book the Greeks and the Persians have also agreed."

Al-Idrisi (A.D. 1154) speaking of the accomplishments of the Hindus, says : "The Hindus are by nature inclined to justice and never depart from it in their actions. Their good faith, honesty, and faithfulness to their promises are well known, and they are so famous for these qualities that people flock to their country from every side."

Another Arab historian, Quazi Said, observes : "The Hindus have always been considered by all other people as the custodians of learning and wisdom. Their knowledge of God ascertains His unity and purity. To kill or injure an animal is a sin with them."

Influence of Buddhism on Islam : Long before the Muslim scholars translated Hindu works into Arabic or Persian, and before the Muslim travellers brought news from India, the Muslim had some glimpses of India's religious conceptions through

Persian literature and also through the Buddhistic influence that still lingered in some of the most remote parts of Iran.

They knew the Buddhists as 'Samaniyah'. The word 'Bud' or 'But' had long ago degenerated into the sense of idol-worship and conveyed no other meaning. Buzasaf, that is, Budhisattva was known to them as the founder of Buddhism. Not long ago Buddhism had flourished in Balkh, Transoxiana, Khurasan, Turkistan and Persia, and to some extent also in Iraq, before the Muslims conquered them. After these countries were converted to Islam, the Buddhist priests did not at once stop their preaching. The rosary is one of the objects that Muslims inherited from the Buddhists. The Sufi doctrine of Fana is the Nirvana of the Buddhists. The whole Sufi system of spiritual Muqamat (stations) or chakras, that the seeker after illumination realizes on his way to 'extinction', is Buddhistic.

The inhabitants of Balkh and Bukhara had displayed a strong tendency to revert to their old Buddhist habits of thought. Abu Narshakhi (A.D. 943) relates in his history of Bukhara: "Every time the people of Bukhara were conquered, they accepted Islam, and no sooner than the Arabs retired, they gave it up again."

Twice a year there used to be held a bazar in which people sold Buddha's idols. On each market day the sale of idols used to amount to fifty thousand dirhams. Muhammad bin Jafar has recorded that "the bazar continued down to our times". (A.D. 940).

A good number of thinkers amongst Muslims, especially in the Abbasid reign, were more or less directly influenced by Buddhism. Ibn Muqaffa' (A.D. 760) translated the *Kalilah wa Dimnh* from Pahlavi into Arabic. In his introduction to the *Kalilah wa Dimnh* he describes an ascetic in the following words : "And I found that divine tranquillity comes over the ascetic when he is absorbed in meditation; for he is still contented, unambitious, satisfied, free from cares, has renounced the world, has escaped from evils, is devoid of greed, is pure, independent, protected against sorrow, above jealousy, manifests pure love does none any harm and remains himself unmolested"

Abul 'Ala-al-Ma'arri, the famous blind poet (A.D. 933-1058) was a veritable 'Buddhist', nay even a 'Jain'. Von Kramer considers him as one of the greatest moralists of all times whose profound genius anticipated much that is commonly attributed to the modern spirit of enlightenment.

Explaining the philosophical aspect of idol-worship, Abul Fazl says : "The inhabitants of this land are religious, affectionate, hospitable, genial and frank. They are fond of scientific pursuits, inclined to austerity of life, seekers after justice, contented, industrious, capable in affairs, loyal, truthful, and constant. The true worth of this people shines most in the day of adversity and its soldiers know no retreat from the field. They, one and all, believe in the unity of God; and as to the reverence they pay to the images of stones and wood and the like, which simpletons regard as idolatry; it is not so. The writer of these pages has exhaustively discussed the subject with many enlightened and upright men, and it became evident that these images of some chosen souls nearest in approach to the throne of God are fashioned as aids to fix the mind and keep the thoughts from wandering, while the worship of God alone is required as indispensable."

Long before Europe had learnt to enquire about religion in a scientific and detached spirit, many Muslim learned men had compiled books of comparative religion in which they displayed an amazingly free and rationalistic attitude of mind. Among them was that most eminent scholar Abu Raihan al-Biruni who compiled a comprehensive treatise on Hindus' religions and philosophies as early as the eleventh century.

Throughout the middle ages the Muslims took enormous pains to acquaint themselves with the religious literature of the Hindus. They translated almost all the important texts into Persian-the *Vedas*, the *Upanishads*, the *Mahabharat*, the *Ramayana*;

the *Dharma Shastra, Puranas,* the *Yoga Vasistha,* the *Yogashastra, Vedanta Shastra,* etc.

Among later writers may be mentioned the name of Mirza Jan Janan Mazhar (b. 1699). Mazhar wrote about the Hindu worship of Idols : "in idol worship, the process is similar to the Dhikr, contemplative ritual, which is prescribed for Muslim Sufis."

Mahmud Shabistari (A.D. 1317), the well-known writer of *Gulshan-i-Raz,* writing on the theme of idol worship, explains the difference and similarity between it and Islam : "The idol is the expression of love and unity in this world, and to wear the sacred thread is to take the resolve of service. As both faith and unfaith are founded in existence, unity of God is the essence of idol worship. They saw in the idol anything but external creation, and for this reason he became Kafir the eyes of the law. If thou too would not see that reality is hidden in the idol, thou wilt also be not known as a Muslim according to the law.

Islamic mysticism originated and grew in two regions of Muslim world, ancient Khorasan and Mesopotamia. In both these regions seekers of truth and enlightenment among the Muslims came into close contact with Indian mystics. The whole of Khorasan was studded with Buddhist monasteries and Hindu temples at the time of the Muslim conquest as is testified by Hiuen Tsang who had passed through these lands barely seventy years earlier. In Mesopotamia, Jundeshapur, Damascus, and Baghdad were centres of learning where Hindu scholars taught Indian science and Hindu ascetics (yogis; held debates with Muslim scholars. The Pramukhas of the Nava Vihara of Transoxiana became the prime ministers (Baramika) of the Abbasid Caliphs and they invited Hindu doctors, astronomers and scientists to Baghdad and encouraged the translation of Sanskrit treatises into Arabic. Thus, it was that the philosophy of pantheism and the practical discipline of Yoga passed into the Sufi circles of Middle East.

The mystic teachings of Vedanta, on the one hand, inspired Islamic mysticism and on the other, gave birth to the movement of Bhakti in India. Ramanuja was the pioneer of this Bhakti movement.

The Bhakti Movement : The spirit of Shakti moved across the country from one end to the other. As Priyadas points out in his *Bhaktirasabodhini*, The tree of Bhakti was once but a sapling; now it has climbed to the sky with its glory spread over the earth Once but a feeble thing, now contentedly sways the mighty elephants of the passions."

It was in schools of Rama Bhakti and Krishna Bhakti that the doctrines of mystic practices were developed, and the differentiation of the stages of progress towards unification with God, and of the emotions which accompanied them and the causes that excited and enhanced the emotional states and psychic conditions which followed them, expounded.

The process of training in devotion implied worship for the Adorable One, sorrow for one's sins, doubt of all objects other than He, celebration of His praise, living for His sake, assigning everything to Him, resignation to His will, seeking Him in all things, renouncing anger, envy, greed and impure thoughts.

The states of emotions and processes bear comparison with what the Muslim Sufis taught in regard to *hal* and *muqam* (states of rapture and stages of ecstasy). For instance, Abu Nasr al-Sarraj, the author of the oldest treatise on Sufism, recounts the seven stages, namely, (1) Repentance, (2) Abstinence, (3) Renunciation, (4) Poverty, (5) Patience, (6) Trust in God and, (7) Satisfaction; and the ten psychic states, namely, (1) Meditation, (2) Nearness to God, (3) Love, (4) Fear, (5) Hope, (6) Longing, (7) Intimacy, (8) Tranquillity, (9) Contemplation and (10) Certainty.

Apart from the founders of the four Sampradayas-Ramanuja, Madhava, Vishnuswami and Nimbaditya-who composed their religious treatises in Sanskrit and the propagators of Vaishnavite

Bhakti of the schools of Rama and Krishna, who appealed to the conservative-minded among the general public, there was a third group of mystics who employed the language of the people to preach their radical creeds. They mostly belonged to the lower castes and their movement represents the urge of the unprivileged masses to uplift themselves. Some of them were persecuted by government, some incurred social opprobrium, and others were not regarded as worthy of notice. But they were held in high esteem among the humbler classes who followed their simple teachings with eagerness and understanding. They laid stress upon the dignity of man, for they thought that every individual would reach the highest goal of human life by his own effort. They rejected the claim to special sanctity of priests (Pandits and Maulvis), of books (scriptures of Hindus and Muslims), of temples and pilgrimages, of rites and ceremonies, and encouraged the establishment of direct relation between man and God. The movement arose in the fifteenth century and continued till the middle of the seventeenth.

The leaders of this group hailed from all parts of India, but their teachings manifest the distinct influence of Islam on their beliefs. In the Hindi-speaking region, the most notable reformer was Sant Kabir, who was a powerful exponent of devotional faith centered on an impersonal, transcendental God, and a fearless denouncer of hypocritical and superstitious practices, Hindu or Muslim. Love of God and man was his religion, and he accepted whatever he, thought true in Hinduism and Islam. There were a number of, other teachers whose point of view was similar to that of Kabir and who founded their orders in different parts of the country.

In the *Punjab*, Guru Nanak founded the Sikh religion which was nourished by his nine successors. The last of them, Guru Govind Singh, transformed Sikhism into a military mission.

In *Maharashtra*, Namdeo, Eknath, Tukaram and Ramdas were noted saints who were hostile to idol worship, and indifferent towards external acts of religion such as vows, fasts, austerities, pilgrimages, etc. They worshipped Vitthal, the one God who conferred tranquillity, and prayed for release from the snares of the illusory world. They condemned caste distinctions and sought to reconcile Hindu and Muslim faiths.

Bengal had the good fortune to produce Chaitanya, who was a devotee of Krishna but at the same time opposed to the Brahminical system of ritualism and caste. Among his disciples was Thakur Haridas, a Muslim. But there were sects in Bengal which went far beyond Chaitanya in their criticism of Hindu orthodoxy, for example the Kartabhajas.

The Virasaivas or Lipgayats of the *Kannada* region were a sect which came into existence in the twelfth century and rapidly spread in Mysore and the neighbouring districts. Their belief in one God who cannot be represented by images or propitiated by sacrifices, and their rejection of caste, show their independence from the conservative religious ways. They did not approve of sacrifices, fasts and pilgrimages; nor did they recognize distinctions based on birth. A pariah and a Brahmin were equal as members of the sect.

In the deep South, the *Tamil* Sidhars rejected the theory of transmigration and the authority of the Shastras. They held that God and love are the same and desired mankind to live in peace, considering love as God.

Thus a powerful religious impulse which drew, its inspiration from Hindu as well as Muslim sources, spread all over India and sought to bring together the masses into a faith which transcended social, intellectual and communal barriers.

Islamic Mysticism: The' stirring in the Hindu society had its parallel in the Muslim community. We have seen that Sufism even before its arrival in India had absorbed the main features of Vedanta-for instance the philosophy of absolute monism. The Indian Advaita had become the Muslim Wahdat-al-Wujud.

Ibn al-Arabi, the great master of Islamic mysticism, affirms that God is one and the universe is His appearance. Creation is a process of emanation of which the three steps are: (1) the stage of absolute unity (*ahadiat*), (2) the stage of latent or potential multiplicity (*wshdat*), and (3) the stage of apparent or actual multiplicity (*wahidiat*). The multiplicity 'expresses itself in souls (*Ruh*), forms (*Mithal*) and bodies (*Jism*).

For both, there is a common discipline. It includes purification of self, mastering of passions and desires, filling of the mind exclusively with the thought of God, obtaining control over bodily functions and mental processes till the objective world ceases to distract consciousness, and till man passes away (*fana, nirvana*) from phenomenal existence and attains union with the divine. The soul stands self-enlightened and unperturbed by temptations and apprehensions.

The Muslim conquest of India was very slow. It took them six centuries to reach the southern confines of India. The invaders came to India in three stages. The first invasion took place in A.D. 712, the invaders being Arabs led by Muhammad bin Qasim. The second set of invasions occurred at the end of the tenth and the beginning of the eleventh century. These were fed by Subuktigin and Mahmud of Ghazni who belonged to a Turkish family. The final stage, which led to the establishment of Muslim rule in India, consisted of the invasions of Muhammad Ghori two hundred years later.

Muhammad bin Qasim maintained the dignity of Brahmins and passed orders confirming their pre-eminence. They were protected against opposition and violence. Each of them was entrusted with an office.

Dr. Ishwari Prasad in his *History of Medieval India* says: "It is not difficult to determine Mahmud's place in history. To the Musalmans of his day, he was Ghazi, a champion of faith, who tried to extirpate infidelity in heathen lands. To the Hindus, he is to this day an inhuman tyrant, a veritable Hu, who destroyed their most sacred shrines and wantonly wounded their religious susceptibilities. But the unbiased enquirer who keeps in mind the peculiar circumstances of the age must record a different verdict. In his estimate, Mahmud was a great leader of men, a just and upright ruler according to his own lights, an intrepid and gifted soldier, a dispenser of justice, a patron of letters, and deserves to be ranked amongst the greatest kings of the world."

After the Ghaznavis came the Ghoris. Their first exploit was the destruction of the city of Ghazni which Mahmud had converted into one of the most beautiful cities in the world. Alptgin followed up his victory and took the city of Ghazni by storm. The finest buildings of the city, exquisite memorials of greatness and splendour of Mahmud, were demolished, and during the seven days the Ghori chieftain remained in occupation of the town "the air from the blackness of the smoke continued as black as night, and these nights, from the flames rising in the burning city, were lighted up as bright as day. Raping and massacre were carried on with greatest pertinacity and vindictiveness, and men, women and children were either killed or made slaves. The dead bodies of all the Sultans of Ghazni except those of Mahmud and Ibrahim were dug out from their graves and treated with indignity and burnt."

The Ghoris next turned their attention to India. The victories of Shahabuddin Ghori are described by Persian chroniclers as victory of Islam, but when the actual facts are analysed, even historians who can in no way be described as partial to the Muslims, form the following estimate of Shahabuddin.

"It cannot be alleged that the religious fervour actuating Shahabuddin and his Mohammedens was stronger than that actuating the Rajputs. Although Mohammeden historians describe the former as making a religious war, Shahabuddin was fighting for conquest of territory and not for extending religion. Indeed we find that conversion of the people to Mohammedenism was not his motive; it was conquering Northern India".

After Shahabuddin the campaigns of Qutubuddin and Iltutmish are described in the self-same strains. But when we prune away the hyperbolic setting we find:

"Qutubuddin and Iltutmish were not fanatical Muslims and were wise rulers who saw the justice and even the wisdom of not interfering with the religion of the people".

Although in the medieval period the head of the State in India was a Muslim, the State was not Islamic. The State did not follow the injunctions of the holy scripture — the Quran, the Hadith, or the laws elaborated in the four schools of Sunni jurisprudence It is a mistake to call the medieval State of India theocratic, for it did not function under the guidance of the Muslim theologians.

Almost every one of the Muslim monarchs of India from the thirteenth century onwards expressed his inability and indicated the impossibility of conducting government in accordance with the Shariat. Iltutmish, Balban, Alauddin Khilji and Muhammad Tughlaq were among the pre-Mughal sovereigns of India who questioned the suitability of applying Muslim Law to India. Ziaud-Din Barni, the historian, in his *Fatawa Jahandari* says, "True religion consists in following in the footsteps of the Prophet . But royal government, on the contrary can only be carried on by following the policies of Khusrau Parvez and the great emperors of Iran." He admits that "between the traditions (Sunnat) of the Prophet Muhammad and his mode of life and living and the customs of the Iranian emperors and their mode of life and living there is complete contradiction, and total opposition." But he points out that the Shariat, which is the command of God, could be followed in State matters only in exceptional times. Muhammad succeeded in enforcing Shariat because he was directly inspired by God, and the first four Khalifas did so because they had been the associates of the Prophet. But their successors were faced with two irreconcilable alternatives : traditions of the Prophet and the policy of the Iranian emperors. But "Prophet-hood is the perfection of religion and kingship is the perfection of worldly fortune. These two perfections are opposed and contradictory to each other, and their combination is not within the bounds of possibility."

Iltutmish was approached by some Ulema with the request that as the Hindus were not the people of the Book (ahl-i-Kitab) who could be taken under Muslim protection as dhimmis, they should be asked to accept Islam and in case of refusal put to sword. Iltutmish asked his Wazir to give an answer, and he replied that the request was impossible of execution. So far as Balban is concerned, Nizam-ud-Din the historian observes : "He gave precedence to the affairs of the State (over religion): Barni states : "In the matter of punishment and exercise of royal authority he acted without fear of God, and whatever he regarded to be in the interest of government, irrespective of whether it was in accord with Sharia or not, he carried into action." Alauddin's discussion with Gazi Mughis-al-Din is well known. His parting reply to the Qazi was, "Whatever I consider to be in the interests of Government, and find to be the requirement of the time, I order. I do not know what the Exalted God will do to me on the Day of Resurrection."

Professor M. Habib says : "It is true that Muslim kings, mostly of-foreign extraction, sat on Indian thrones for some six or seven centuries. But they could only do so because their enthronement was not the enthronement of 'Muslim rule'; had it been otherwise, they could not have lasted for a single generation."

Among the Mughal emperors Babar, because he reigned for such a short period, and Humayun, because he was so beset with difficulties, had little opportunity to pay much attention to administrative matters. Akbar inaugurated a State policy which was not subordinated to the dictates of Islam. He treated all religions alike and regarded it his duty to make no difference between his subjects on the basis of religion. He threw open the highest appointments to non-Muslims. He married Hindu princesses and allowed them to retain their religion and perform Hindu rites in the palace. Their sons were successors to the Mughal throne. He eliminated the interference of the Ulema by assuming the authority to give final decisions on religious questions on which their might be conflicting opinions among the Mujtahids (Muslim divines). In many social and other matters he showed respect to the sentiments and traditions of his non Muslim subjects. Among these the most important was his abolition of Jazia (poll tax on the Hindus). Abul Fazl says, "Kingship is a gift of God And on coming to exalted dignity if he does not inaugurate universal peace (toleration) and if he does not regard all conditions of humanity, and all sects of religion with the single eye of favour and not be mother to some and be step-mother to others-he will not become fit for the exalted dignity." Again he adds, "Differences in religion must not withhold him from his duty of watching, and all classes of men must have repose, so that the shadow of God may confer glory. Thus, in the words of Ibn Hasan, "Both Islamic law and Hadith ceased to be the code of government."

The Muslims adopted many Hindu marriage customs, and followed a number of practices which were repugnant to Islamic law; for example, in the-matter of fixing the degree of kinship for eligibility in marriage, in prescribing limits of endogamy and exogamy based upon tribal and class divisions, in the observance of ceremonial accompanying the marriage contract. Laws of inheritance were supplanted by custom (urf) in many, parts of India. Widow marriage and divorce were frowned upon as among the Hindus.

The various Hindu and Muslim festivals were celebrated with impartial splendour. On the Dussehra, the anniversary of Rama's victory over the demons, the Imperial horses and elephants were arrayed in decorated canopy and paraded for inspection. On the Raksha-bandhan, the Hindu nobles and Brahmins fastened strings on the Emperors arm.-Diwali saw gambling in the palace, and Shivaratri was duly observed. Nor were the Muslim 'Id and shab-e-barAt neglected.

Marriages between Muslims and Hindus were rare, but those among the ruling families were well recognized. The Mughal emperors were not the pioneers of this policy. In Kashmir Hindu-Muslim marriages were of a long-standing. Zain-ul-Abedin (1420-70) married the two daughters of Raja Manakdeo of Jammu. Another daughter was married to Raja Jasrath, the Muslim Gakkhar chief.

The Bahmani kings of the Deccan allied themselves with Hindu families. Taj-ud-Din Firoz (1397-1422) married the daughters of Deva Raya of Vijayanagar and Narsingh Rao of Kherla. Ahmed Shah Wall, the ninth Bahmani ruler, wedded the daughter of the Raja of Sonkhed. Yusuf Adil Shah, the Sultan of Bijapur (died A.D. 1510), took as wife the sister of Mukund Rao, a Brahmin, and she became his chief queen. Amir Barid of Bidar (died A.D. 1539) followed the example.

Akbar, Jahangir, Farrukh Siyar, Suleman Shukoh and Sipihr Shukoh took Hindu princesses for their wives. The Hindu royal family of Kachh formed matrimonial alliances with the Muslims.

On the other side, the Hindu was far too ridden with caste inhibitions to receive a Muslim lady in the innermost sanctum of his palace. Yet such instances were not unknown, In Rajauri, Ladakh and Baltistan, Jahangir noticed inter-marriages between the two communities. The love affair of Peshwa Baji Rao I with Mastani is well, known. She was a dancing girl who became the Peshwa's constant companion and "accompanied Baji Rao in his campaigns and rode stirrup to stirrup with him."

In 1734 she bore the Peshwa a son, Shamsher Bahadur, who was brought up as a Muslim, the Brahmins having refused to allow him to enter the Hindu fold. He was killed at Panipat in 1761. He was succeeded in his jagir by his son Ali Bahadur. In 1787 when Mahadji Sindhia suffered reverses, reinforcements were despatched from the south under the command of Ali Bahadur as the representative of the Peshwa's house,

It was realized by the Muslim rulers on the whole that, in the conditions existing in India, the Islamic laws promulgated for the Arab society of Medina were not strictly applicable. The form of society which the Prophet of Islam envisaged and in which the State was the Church and the Church the State, did not last more than thirty years. The Umaiyads ceased to function as Imams and became merely heads of State. The Abbasids who came after them shed the simple Arab manners, surrounded themselves with pomp: and pelf, and introduced in their courts the etiquette, ceremony and splendour of ancient Iran.

In 1258 the Mongol conqueror destroyed the Caliphate, and a new era began in the Islamic civilization. The old concept of a single Muslim society with a single chief disappeared. It need not surprise us, therefore, if we find Muslim rulers and Muslim divines in India differing in their views concerning government and the people. From the time of Iltutmish, who expressed his inability to follow the advice of the Ulema in the matter of imposing Islam on the Hindus by force, to Balban, Ala-ud-din Khilji, Mohammad Tughlak and Sher Shah, most of them held the view that combination of religion and kingship was not possible. Similar opinions prevailed among provincial Sultans of Kashmir, Bengal and the Deccan."

Union of Two Faiths

The Mughals endeavoured to transmute this negative attitude into a positive policy. Babar, before his death, advised Humayun not to distinguish between a Muslim and a Hindu. Akbar's courageous efforts in this behalf are well known. Akbar found that there was no dearth of people in every religion who thought of themselves as perfect, who misinterpreted their religious belief and did not bring the standard work of their religion to the knowledge of the common people. Thus, the spirit of the faith remained concealed. Akbar found it essential to prevent the people from falling victims to the nefarious designs of such custodians of faith, and decided that if the standard works of different religions were translated into simple language, they will be able to know the truth for themselves. This would put an end to the monopoly of those who did not state the real spirit of their religion to their respective followers.

Akbar initiated a bold policy so that in his age -the pillars of blind following were demolished and a new era of research and enquiry in religious matters commenced.

The translations of Sanskrit works prepared in Akbar's reign were illustrated by the, court painters. One of the copies, of the *Mahabharat* made for the Imperial Library was in the possession of the Maharaja of Jaipur. Several independent translations of other Sanskrit works were made in the reign of Jahangir, Shahjahan and Aurangzeb, besides the works of Dara Shūkoh. Abdul Rehman Chishti (died 1683) gave an Islamizing explanation of the *Bhagawad Gita* in his *Mir, at-ul-haqaiq*.

Several original works on the fine arts, sciences and the philosophy of the Hindus were also written. The most noteworthy is the *tuhfat-al-hind* composed by Mirza Muhammad-ibn-Fakhr-al Din Muhammad, in the reign of Aurangzeb, at the request of Kukaltash Khan for the emperor's son, Prince Muhammad Mu'izzal-Din Jahandar Shah. Jahangir did not depart from the tolerant ways of his father and Shahjahan after some hesitation continued on the whole to follow the same lines.

Aurangzeb's Outlook: Unfortunately, Aurangzeb sought to turn back the hands of the clock. But he too realized ultimately the futility and undesirability of mixing religion with politics. In his *ahkAm* (precepts) collected by Hamid-ud-Din Khan, a favoured officer well known by his sobriquet "dagger of Alamgir" (*Nimcha-i Alamgir*), the following passages occur: "What have the worldly affairs to do with religion ? And why should bigotry intrude into matters of religion ? For you there is your religion, for me mine (*Lakum dinokum wa lie din-Quran*)." If the law were followed it would have been necessary to annihilate all the Rajas and their subjects. Another of his precepts was : "What concern have we with the religion of anybody ? Let Jesus follow his own religion and Moses his own."

Aurangzeb blamed his outlook. Bernier reports :

Aurangzeb asked Mulla Saleh : "But what was the knowledge I derived under your tuition?" and complained, "Was it not incumbent upon my preceptor to make me acquainted with the distinguishing features of every nation of the earth; its resources and strength; its mode of warfare; its manners, its religions, its form of government and wherein its interests principally consist; and by a regular course of historical reading to render me familiar with the origin of States; their progress and decline; the events, accidents, or errors, owing to which such great changes and mighty revolutions have been effected?" He added, "A familiarity with the language of surrounding nations may be indispensable in a king, but you would teach me to read and write only Arabic: Forgetting how many important subjects ought to be embraced in the education of a Prince, you acted as if it were chiefly necessary that he should possess great skill in grammar, and such knowledge of law and of the sciences only through the medium of Arabic? I have a perfect remembrance of your having, during several years, harassed my brain with idle and foolish propositions, the solution of which yield no satisfaction to the mind, propositions that seldom enter into the business of life. When I left you, I could boast of no greater attainment in the sciences than the use of many obscure and uncouth terms, calculated to discourage, confound, and appeal a youth of the most masculine understanding If you had taught me that philosophy which adapts the mind to reason, and will not suffer it to rest satisfied with anything short of the most solid arguments; if you had made me acquainted with the nature of man, accustomed me always to refer to first- principles and given me a sublime and adequate conception of the Universe, and of the order and regular motions of its parts. I should have been more indebted to you than Alexander was to Aristotle."

A New Form of Art

Most of the Mughal emperors were deeply interested in art. They were both patrons and critics, encouraging talent and guiding skill. They invited to their courts great masters of painting from Central Asia and Persia: They gathered the humble but competent practitioners of art of India. The two worked together and the one was influenced by the other. The result was a style of wondrous beauty. Whatever the subject, the picture is always bathed in clear light, every detail is rendered with immense care, the ground is carpeted with green and trees are in bloom. The mind of the human dwellers in these scenes is one of good cheer, the hearts are elated, heads are held high and the eyes look straight.

The style of painting at the Mughal courts became the prototype of the schools at the courts of provincial governors and of the Hindu Rajas of Rajasthan and the hill States in the Himalayas. Humayun brought with him two pupils of Bihzad, namely Mir Saiyid Ali and Khwaja Abdus Samad. Akbar invited Farrukh Qalmaq and Aqa Raza. But among his artists, there were many Hindu painters of great ability like Basavan, Daswant and Kesho. They were entrusted with the illustrations of works like *Shah Namah, Khamsa-i-Nizami, Babar Namah* and *Timur Namah*, as well as the *Mahabharat*, the *Ramayana, Nal Damyanti* and *Panchatantra*. Jahangir carried the art to perfection. He has stated in his *Tuzuk* that he could distinguish between the style of all living and dead painters and could say who the painter of a particular picture was. One of his painters was Mansur who was an expert in painting birds and flowers. Bishandas exalted in portrait painting and Murad and Manohar were unequalled in drawing. Shahajahan maintained the high traditions of his father. The great painters of his reign were Muhammad Nadir Samarquandi, Faquirullah Khan, Mir Hashim, Bishandas and Bichittar. Though the art continued under Aurangzeb, it began to decline rapidly after him.

Painting is the delicate plant and architecture the stately tree that adorns the arbour of culture. The Mughal emperors were endowed with an extremely refined taste in the arts, nurtured both with loving care. Babar laid out beautiful gardens with running water, cascading fountains and marble pavilions. Humayun erected a seven-chambered palace in which each hall was dedicated to one of the seven planets. Akbar created Fatehpur Sikri. Jahangir directed the completion of Akbar's tomb at Sikandra, and the Jahangiri Mahal in Agra. Shahajahan's contribution to India's architectural monuments is well known. The Red Fort in Delhi with its numerous halls, mansions and mosque, the Jama Masjid, and above all, the incomparable Taj Mahal, are immortal witnesses of his taste.

Sir Jadunath Sarkar says: "Two hundred years of Mughal rule, from the accession of Akbar to the death of Mohammed Shah (1556-1749), gave to the whole of Northern India, and much of the Deccan also, oneness of the official language, administrative system, coinage, and also a popular lingua Indica. Even outside the territory directly administered by the Mughal emperors, their administrative system, official nomenclature, court etiquette and monetary type were borrowed more or less by the neighbouring Hindu Rajas."

"All the twenty Indian Subhahs of the Mughal Empire were governed by means of exactly the same administrative machinery with exactly the same procedure and official titles. Persian was the one language used in all office records, farmans, sanads, land grants, passes, despatches and receipts. The same monetary standard prevailed throughout the Empire with coins having the same names and same purity and the same denomination, differing only in the name of mint town. Officials and soldiers were frequently transferred from one province to another. Thus, the native of one province felt himself almost at home in another province; traders and travellers passed most easily from city to city *subah* to *subah*, and all realized the imperial oneness of this vast country."

Seven

Mahatma Gandhi's Contribution

After completing his South African mission an experienced Gandhi returned to India in 1915 armed with a new technique of non-violent struggle, Satyagraha. At that time three towering personalities, Sir Phiroz Shah Mehta, Bal Gangadhar Tilak and Gopal Krishna Gokhale were dominatingly influencing the socio-political scenario of India. All the three had their own speciality. While paying tribute to them, Gandhi evaluates their personality in the following words: "Sir Phiroz Shah had seemed to me like the Himalaya, the Lokmanya like the ocean. But Gokhale was as the Ganges. The Himalaya was unscaleable and one could not easily launch forth on the sea, but the Ganges invited one to its bosom." Gokhale was most liberal among them and was heading a very respected public organisation, the Servants' of India Society. Gandhi found in him his guide of his requirement and, regarded him as his political Guru. Teachings of Tolstoy, Ruskin, Rai Chandra Bhai and Thoreau were the lights directing Gandhi to develop his personality on universal lines, and now Gokhale was here to give his personal touch in shaping the future multi-dimensional political guide of India having a universal outlook. Gokhale had visited S. Africa (1912) when Gandhi was engaged in his non-violent mission against the policy of apartheid and injustice meted to the Indian immigrants, and was much impressed by Gandhi's sincerity, innovative quality and ability of leadership. He had predicted that Gandhi would play an important role not only in India's emancipation from the British rule, but would provide by his guidance, the best path to do away with the age old superstitious bounds and reach its glorious destiny. After his return to India, Gokhale advised him to see India minutely before deciding his strategies to serve India in a suitable way. This, he did religiously and his extensive tour of India made him realize the complexity of Indian situation and got himself prepared to play a suitable role in the freedom movement. He attended the historic Lucknow Congress of 1916 for the first time as a delegate. In that Congress Bal Gangadhar Tilak, Pt. Madan Mohan Malviya on behalf of the Congress, and M. A. Jinnah on behalf of the Muslim League, had signed a pact to work for India's independence jointly and separate electorate was unanimously agreed upon as a constitutional strategy to accelerate the movement with the fullest satisfaction of the two major groups having a common goal. This Congress also prepared the grounds for Gandhi to launch his first ever Satyagraha on Indian soil, the Champaran Satyagraha in 1917. And thereafter, the steps he took, they like the mile-stones, became fascinating chapters of Indian history. After the Ahmedabad Mill Workers' and Kheda Kisan Satyagrahas, the first Non-cooperation joined with Khilafat movement was the first all India mass-movement which helped Gandhi to become the undisputed leader of India. This movement laid the foundation of a new era of our freedom movement also as its canvas got broadened beyond the boundaries of India and its echo was being heard in the streets of Morocco and Cairo. This was an unexpected development, which scared the imperialist forces, rather made them very panicky. They saw in Gandhi their enemy who had the capacity to mobilise not only the Indian masses but for Indian cause the world opinion also. They began to visualize the writing on the walls ... the dismemberment of the British rule in India soon.

Gandhi's commitment to the cause, urge for freedom, humane approach for solving the social and communal problems, simple but healthy principles of harmony and integration had made him very popular within a short time. In his broad ideals and conception of Swarajya, Indian masses as well as the intellegentia saw their future. And this Swarajya of Gandhi which guaranteed the fulfilment of aspirations of every section of the society, broadly speaking, was the goal of free India of his dreams. This happened to be the essence outcome also of Indian ethos, gradually developed through centuries as a result of its close contact with the outside world, specially with various ethnic and religious groups coming to India at stages. This base constituted of the best norms, became the features of his secular-democratic-political system, with a solid value-oriented humanitarian ground highly suited to India. He wanted this system not only to serve India having a plural and complex social fabric, but also to prove an ideal for the world of future. In this process Western civilization and conception of democracy and secularism least attracted him. Virtually, he discarded most of the Western approach. But till a foolproof system suited to the Indian ethos was evolved and concretised, he did not reject them outright but tried to draw the best out of it. And in this process his background of upbringing, close association of friends of various religious and ethnic groups, in India and abroad, helped him enormously.

Mahatma's Philosophy

Gandhi was a religious man but fanaticism and hypocrisy in the name of religion were alien to him. He has confessed unambiguously that he is a Sanatani Hindu and sincerely advocated the principle of equal respect for all religions - Sarva Dharma Sambhava. This, undoubtedly is a difficult proposition to believe and adhere to. Various arguments against it can be given in the light of the prevalent norms. But Gandhi was committed to this approach, and the circumstances in which he was assassinated confirm that till his death he did not compromise with his stand. Sanatani Hinduism inspired him to claim that he is a good Muslim, a good Christian or a good Sikh in the same way as he considered himself as a good Hindu. And this spiritual approach was the core principle of his views on national integration and harmony among different ethnic and religious groups. Since an "individual" is the pivot of his conception of value based socio-political structure ..., the `Oceanic Circle', his conception of independence, liberty and specially the "State" is also inspired by ethical norms. Therefore, modern conception of a

'Secular State' as floated by the West is not fully palatable to Gandhi as he believed in *"Juda ho deep Siyasat se to rahjati hai Changezi."*

Throughout the period of his leadership Gandhi played the role more of a Philosopher-guide than a power-oriented political leader. He wanted to mobilise a group of committed workers to shoulder responsibilities only to serve the people on solid grounds of values selflessly. He expected from them dedication of high standard so that under their safe leadership the newly independent country could stand in the fraternity of nations with full pride and self-reliant confidence. His call to boycott government schools, colleges, government services, give up legal practice, and burning of foreign cloths and as an alternative, establishment of national schools, preparing grounds for acceptance of Charkha and Khadi and his Constructive programmes and the last Testament to disband the Congress and organise Lok Sevaks, were the guiding spirit based on truth and non-violence to provide the required direction to kindle the spirit of nationalism among the Indians. Therefore, his conception of Society, Nation, State, State Power, Democracy, Secularism, etc, carries something special Indian with prime consideration of truth, non-violence and moral values. His humanitarian and universal approach made him fully acceptable among the renowned scientists and Western thinkers of his time and men like Eienstine, Romain Rolland, Sorokin, Louis Fischer, Holmes, Huxley, etc, recognised his brilliance and unhesitantly paid highest tributes to him.

The decentralized structure of power (Panchayati Raj) and economic establishment (Sarvodaya) is the foundation of Gandhian concept of State affairs and Swarajya in its totality is his ideal State in the form of Ramrajya. He says, "My Swaraj is to keep intact the genius of our civilization. I want to write many new things but they must all be written on Indian State" (*Young India*, 26.6.1924). His Swarajya was meant to civilise Indians and to purify and stabilize our civilization which give a paramount place to morality in all our affairs, public or private. Till Swarajya or Sarvodya of his ideal takes a final and concrete shape, Gandhi preferred unadulterated parliamentary system. In its ideal form Gandhi saw salvation of plural India to a great extent but for emancipation of the Indians of all shades Swarajya remained his final goal. In the preface of the reprint of *Hind Swaraj* in 1938, he is unambiguously clear in his concept of State, form of government and its functioning, when he says: "But today my corporate activity is undoubtedly devoted to the attainment of parliamentary Swarajya in accordance with the wishes of the people of India." In a parliamentary democracy a State plays a major role in the name of people. Gandhi is very much cautious in this regard also and to achieve his ideal state, he from the start wants to limit its powers, so that the process of its withering away starts from the very beginning. Emphasising his stand on state he clarifies : "I look upon an increase in the power of the state with the greatest fear because, although while apparently doing good by minimizing exploitation, it does the greatest harm to mankind by destroying individuality which lies at the root of all progress. The State represents a concentrated and organized form. The individual has a soul but as the State is a soulless machine, it can never be weaned from violence to which it owes its very existence." (*Modern Review*, 1935)

He was a religious man and was piloting the freedom struggle of a country which has a treasure of rich cultural heritage. He was a Hindu and majority of Indians profess Hinduism. But he never advocated a theocracy or supremacy of the Hinduism in state affairs and was clear in his stand that India will not be a Hindu State. He is also clear about functioning of State and emphasized : "I swear by religion. I will die for it. But it is my personal affair. The state has nothing to do with it ... ... The state would look after your secular welfare, health, communications, foreign relation, currency and so on, but not your or my religion. That is everybody's personal concern" (*Harijan*, 22.9.1946). For independent India, therefore, Gandhi advocated a secular State with a guarantee that every Indian should be entitled to profess his religion without any hindrance. He is clear also that State should not patronise any religion. The first Indian Governor General of Independent India, C. Rajgopalachari has very successfully elaborated Gandhiji's views in the following words : "The Mahatma taught that all religions are equally worthy of reverence; this teaching was not an invention of his for political ends, but was derived from common sense and Hindu religious texts of the highest authority. India today dare not forget religion in its quest for material prosperity. And if India's government is to be an institution integrated with her people's lives, it is to be true democracy and not a superimposed Western institution staged in Indian dress, religion must have an important and recognised place in it, with impartiality and equal reverence for all the creeds and denominations prevailing in India. This alone would be historically consistent with the peaceful revolution brought about by our Nation's Father." (C. Rajgopalachari, *The Place of Religion in Future India*, Vol. l, p. 83, 1959, quoted in D.E. Smith, *India as a Secular State*, p. 109).

There have been aberrations no doubt, but by and large this tradition of values have influenced our day to day life and every kind of faith, culture and mode of living flourish in its own way sharing the common glory. Concerned citizens of India within and outside the government have always considered casteism, communalism, linguism and regionalism as grave dangers for progress, integration and unity. Among them communalism deserves much condemnation, as it has created more problems, this has led to the partition of the country also and still this hidra-headed monster is creating problems in the sub-continent. In the light of historical experience 'Secularism' was found to be an antidote to check further deterioration and therefore, the Indian Constitution enshrines all those values which guarantee a civil society to function on healthy links.

With the demand of Pakistan on religious grounds in 1940, a terrible shock wave swept all over the sub-continent and the course of our freedom struggle changed. A sizeable number of Hindus and Muslims took antagonistic approach and ironically they tried to convince that both the communities, which have been living in India together since centuries, now cannot live together. The true religious segment of both the major communities were not carried away by the provocation of the power oriented leaders and tried their best to calm the situation by their compassionate healing touch. But in the presence of the Britishers, who had been playing a dubious game, full of sinister designs, and with whom lay the decision making power, the situation took its worst course and it became clear that partition of India was inevitable. And the fatal day came when on 14 and 15 August 1947 two independent countries, India and Pakistan, were carved out of a single motherland under unconceivable tragic circumstances. The pang of birth of two countries was experienced by millions of people. Human history had never witnessed such a horrifying state of affairs. Migration and massacre of human beings on an unimaginable scale was the price that we paid and still the wounds are oozing profusely. Gandhi had vehemently opposed the partition on religious grounds and believed that, partition of Indian meant a patent untruth. He says, "My whole soul rebels against the idea that Hinduism and Islam represent two antagonistic cultures and doctrines. To assent to such a doctrine is for me denial of God for I believe with my whole soul that the God of the Koran is also the God of the Gita, and that we are all, no matter by what name designated, children of the same God." (M.K.Gandhi, To the Hindus and Muslims, 415-16, 428). But his voice was unheeded in the situation created by the developments and with a bleeding heart he conceded that "If Muslims insisted for partition, nothing could prevent it."

Constitution of India

From December 1946 to December 1949 the Constituent Assembly consisting of several legal luminaries and freedom fighters devoted their time and energy for preparing a suitable Constitution of free India. This was the last but very significant act as the chapter of colonial rule was to end and an independent India was to emerge by throwing off the shackles of century old slavery. On 15 August 1947, it was in a position to plan for itself and execute it for its own betterment suited to its situation and if necessary by bringing fundamental changes in the existing socio-political structure. And in the words of Jawaharlal Nehru : 'Long years ago we made a tryst with destiny, and now the time comes when we shall redeem our pledge, not wholly or in full measure, but very substantially. At the stroke of the mid-night hour, when the world sleeps, India will awake to life and freedom.'

Gandhi had expressed earlier that Swarajya would not be the gift of the British Parliament, but must spring from the "wishes of the people of India expressed through their freely chosen representatives." And when the Constituent Assembly adopted the Constitution of India on 26 November 1949 and in its light on 26th of January, 1950 India, the biggest democracy of the world was born, the dream of the freedom fighters and Gandhi took shape. Participating in the Constituent Assembly debates Jawaharlal Nehru made it clear that, "the first task of this Assembly is to free India through a new constitution, to feed the starving people, and to clothe the naked masses, and to give every Indian the fullest opportunity to develop himself according to his capacity." (Constituent Assembly Debates 3, 316 quoted by Smith, op. cit.). K. Santhanam, another prominent member of the Constituent Assembly (who happened to be the Editor of *Hindustan Times*), considered the developments in the terms of "revolutions". He says, "the Political revolution would end with independence. The Social revolution meant to get India out of the medievalism based on birth, religion, custom and community and reconstruct her social structure on modern foundations of law, individual merit, and secular education. The third was an economic one; the transition from primitive rural economy to scientific and planned agriculture and industry" (*The Hindustan Times*, New Delhi, 8 Sept., 1946, quoted in Indian Constitution opt. cit., 26). "The choice for India, he says, is between rapid evolution and violent revolution ... because the Indian masses cannot and will not wait for long time to obtain the satisfaction of their minimum needs." (*Hindustan Times*, 17 August, 1947, ibid., 27). Sharing their anxiety Dr. S. Radha Krishnan stressed the need to guarantee socio-economic revolution, satisfaction of fundamental needs of common man and bring about fundamental change in the structure of Indian Society. (Ibid., p.27) Keeping all the factors in mind the Constituent Assembly drafted a Constitution of India on the western model. The West Minister

Parliamentary System with centralised liberal democratic structure of the State functioning also became the guiding feature for independent India.

The Drafting Committee of the Constitution consisted of the following members:

Dr. B.R. Ambedkar (Chairman)
Sri B.L. Mitter
Sri N.G. Ayyanger
Sri A.K. Ayyer
Sri K.M. Munshi
Sri Mohd. Saadullah
Sri N. Madhava Rau
Sri D.P. Khaitan (and after his death in 1948)
Sri T.T. Krishnamachari

In the light of the recommendations of different Committees and their concerted efforts, tireless point to point consideration of issues, a broad based and exhaustive Constitution was formally adopted by the Constituent Assembly on November 26, 1949. A day before its formal adoption Dr. B. R. Ambedkar in his last speech in the Constituent Assembly said : "On the 26th January 1950 we are going to enter into a life of contradictions. In politics we will have equality and in social and economic life we will have inequality. How long should we continue to deny equality in our social and economic life? If we continue it for long, we will do so only by putting our political democracy in peril. We must remove this contradiction at the earliest possible moment or else those who suffer from inequality will blow up the structure of political democracy which this Assembly has so laboriously built up."

Recently we have celebrated the Golden Jubilee of our independence and democracy, and thorough evaluations have been made at the highest levels, and most of the conclusions arrived at are not encouraging. We have been able to change the guard and have made significant progress in several fields no doubt, but the required basic change in our mentality, and age-old social structure is yet far away to be achieved. Criminalization and communalisation of politics, West domination in economic affairs, crumbling bureaucratic set-up and misinterpretation of the basics of democracy is creating havoc and the dream of a broad-hearted self-reliant India is yet an unfulfilled dream. As a matter of fact, present day India is at the cross-roads, its secular democratic structure is facing rough weathers. The dreams of the founding fathers of our Constitution is jeopradised by the power-oriented elements using emotional cards and postures denying the constitutional rights to the minorities by branding it to be 'appeasement' and 'vote bank' policy. On his way to attend the 2nd Round Table Conference as the sole representative of the Congress, Gandhi opened his mind on future Constitution of India in the following words : "I will strive for a constitution, which will release India from all thralldom and patronage, and give her, if need be, the right to sin. I shall work for an India in which the poorest shall feel that it is their country in whose making they have an effective voice, an India in which there shall be no high class and low class of people; an India in which all communities shall live in perfect harmony. There can be no room in such an India for the curse of untouchability or the curse of the intoxicating drinks and drugs. Women will enjoy the same rights as men." (*Young India*, 10 Sept., 1931).

But the situation in India, specially quick development after the decision of the British government to free India by vivisecting it, demanded immediate steps to plan the blue print to avoid confusion regarding the governance of the newly born free but turmoiled India. Nehru, his associates, and most of the members of the Constituent Assembly were not ready to go slow, and experiment decentralized alternative in isolation. Consequently, they in their liking, went for the best available model of Democratic Constitution with a Socialist bias. In this process Gandhian approach was bypassed, as it was not thought practical at the moment. Nehru emphatically held the view that, "any consideration of these questions must keep present facts, forces and human material we have today in view, otherwise it will be divorced from reality" (Nehru letter to Gandhi, 9 Oct., 1945, G. Austin, The Indian Constitution Corner Stone of a Nation, Oxford, 1966, p.43) Mahatma Gandhi was aware of the fact that his diagnosis of the social ills and his prescription for their remedy were not fully appreciated by his west-oriented ambitious lieutenants. On 28 July, 1946 he wrote in *Harijan*: "Congressmen themselves are not of one mind on the contents of independence. I do not know how many swear by non-violence or the charkha (spinning wheel) or, believing in decentralization, regard the village as a nucleus. I know on the contrary that many would have India become a first class military power and wish India to have a strong centre and build the whole structure round it."

The members who framed the Constitution had western orientation but were well aware of their rich heritage, plural socio-fabric and multi-religious and lingual set-up and its gross limitations. They wanted to enable India stand amidst the fraternity of nations with pride and confidence as quickly as possible and in their enthusiasm, to some extent, they forgot the bare reality of the existing Indian situation. In over confidence they decided as per their orientation, in favour of a democratic system which if practised judiciously, possesses the qualities guaranteeing the aspirations of the people. It also fulfils the needed qualifications of a Civil Society without prejudicing the interests of any component of the society. The preamble of the Constitution confirms this sentiments when it declares, "We the people of India, having solemnly resolved to constitute India into a Sovereign Socialist Secular Democratic Republic ... guaranteeing justice, liberty, equality, fraternity to all citizens irrespective of caste, creed, religion, sex or region ...". (Forty second Amendment 1976)

Democracy, theoretically means rule of the majority. But this rule enshrines the spirit of the rule of law and consensus, not merely the rule of numbers. (This pre-supposed number game ironically, scared the liberal constitutionalist and one time nationalist par-excellence Mr.Jinnah, who floated a theory, contrary to his mental set-up, that resulted in the vivisection of India). An ideal democracy guarantees unambiguously freedom to save life and full opportunity to every section of the society to blossom and prosper, specially the minorities, to lead a dignified life with full freedom to assert for its own welfare. The great poet-thinker Rabindranath Tagore advocates a more humane and holistic approach of democracy when he says : "It is for the majority community to uphold the nation's unity. It must never bargain by the minorities about how much of rights should it have and how much the others have to share. Every minority all the world over worries about being submerged or its identity being faced. This is not a political issue and it is only when the majority community wins and retains the confidence of the minorities in a country that it makes it possible for the nation to endure."

Conceptually, a 'Secular State' has nothing to do with religion; state and religions are separate identities. But the constitution of Secular Democratic India does not separate them into water-tight compartments. The State has no religion of its own no doubt, but has immense powers to interfere with the religious affairs of various religious groups. As a matter of fact in the complex social set-up of India, it is neither possible nor desirable to have a secular state as per the definition of the Western Secularism. In our context 'Secular State' means "its separation from religion and the consequent independence of religious bodies from the control and regulation by the State of their internal affairs." From the practical point of view we find interpretation of the person who controls the functioning of a unit of the State structure as the deciding factor. His approach towards an issue influences on the spot policy decision. Therefore, in state sponsored functions, such as foundation laying or inauguration ceremony, religious orientation is apparent. Here secularism is overlapped by personal whims, though not intentionally to damage secularism as a principle.

The Constitution of India is not only a prime legal document conferring the rights of citizenship and other obligations attached with it to all Indians irrespective of caste, creed, religion, sex or region but is also a guiding force that initiates and guarantees the social, political and judicial structure of the Secular Democratic

India to function in its holistic sense. Though it cannot be claimed 'Secular' in the strict sense of the term but at the same time it is difficult also to reject its secular credentials. We consider India not only a 'democracy' but the biggest in the world with all undemocratic features of its political-fabric and governance, misuse of parliamentary system and vulgarity practised in its name. In the same manner Secularism of Secular State of India with all its aberrations is an undeniable feature. After more than fifty years of independence and secular democratic constitution, in practice, India is faced with serious problems of communalism, religious fanaticism and nefarious politics in its name, casteism and several ifs and buts, its future is not yet totally bleak as Indian ethos guarantees that at the moment of crisis India knows well to overcome the adversaries. Of course vigil of the people is most needed.

With the opening remarks (quoting an American Jurist) of the Protem Chairman of the Constituent Assembly, Dr. Sachidanand Sinha on 9 December 1946, I conclude : "It has been reared for immortality if the work of man may justly aspire to such a title. It may perish in an hour by the folly or corruption or negligence of its only keeper, the people. Republics are created - by virtue, public spirit and intelligence of the people. They fall when wise are lavished from the public councils because they dare to be honest and the profligates are rewarded because they flatter the people in order to betray them." (Justice J . Story, 1779-1845).

Rise of Secularism

1. The main feature of secularism in our Constitution is its uniqueness, in that it is a kind of its own and is '*sui generis*'.

2. The philosophy of secularism under Indian Constitution has been best explained by Professor Dr. Radha Krishnan. While participating in the Constituent Assembly debates, Dr. Radha Krishnan explained the concept as follows:-

> "When India is said to be a secular State, it does not mean that we reject the reality of an unseen spirit or the relevance of religion to life or that we exalt irreligion. It does not mean that secularism itself becomes a positive religion or that the State assumes divine prerogatives. Though faith in the Supreme is the basic principle of the Indian tradition, the Indian State will not identify itself with or be controlled by any particular religion."

3. The learned professor elaborated it further by saying

> "The religious impartiality of the Indian State is not to be confused with secularism or atheism. Secularism as here defined is in accordance with the ancient religious tradition of India. It tries to build up a fellowship of believers, not by subordinating individual qualities to the group mind but by bringing them into harmony with each other."

4. The word secular is derived from the Latin word 'Saecula' which means worldly. So it is obvious that the concept of secularism in each country must be rooted in its history. And we must not forget that in history each period is an heir of the previous one and a testator of the future. Thus, when the Constitution was adopted in 1950, we started, as has been remarked by the eminent Jurist, Mr. Palkivalla, with 5000 years of Civilization behind us. The Indian tradition of religious tolerance "was born of the consciousness that truth can never be the monopoly of any sect or creed. The words of Rig Veda are world famous. "Let noble thoughts come to us from every side." (*India's Priceless Heritage*, by Palkivalla).

5. It is, therefore, obvious that Secularism is not entirely a gift of the Constitution. Rather it is inherent in our heritage and it is but natural that it would be given due importance and recognition in the Constitution.

6. Thousands of years before the Constitution, India had seen the reign of Emperor Ashoka. In the chequered history of world civilisation, we do not find any parallel to the edicts of Ashoka on which the principles of tolerance and comprehension of differing creeds are so eloquently inscribed. In his Rock Edict Twelve, Ashoka declared that he had reverence for men of all sects and he further adds that he who does reverence to his own sect, while disparaging the sects of others, actually inflicts the severest injury on his own sect. The edicts are vibrant with the most secular message "Concord is the supreme good."

7. Behind such serene and calm composure of the Emperor glows the sublime and ennobling presence of Buddha - the liberator of humans. His teachings are strikingly secular and do not even mention the existence of any God as its central theme. With its emphasis on problems of life and a compassion for the fellow being, Buddhism harps on the eternal spirit of Indian culture. The caste barrier which has been the bane of Indian Society through the ages and unfortunately defies even the Constitutional creed of equality could not cast its shadow on the teachings of Buddha. As the four streams that flow into the Ganges lose their names as soon as they mingle their waters in the holy river, so all who believe in Buddha tend to forget the caste to what they belong.

8. The high secular values of Indian culture have been acknowledged not only by Indian jurists but by western philosophers as well. Here if I may quote what Professor H.G.Wells said in *Outlines of History*.

> "In the third century B.C., when king Asoka was ruling India in light and gentleness, the Romans were reviving an Etruscan sport, the setting on of slaves to fight for their lives."

9. This organization of murder as a sport and show serves to measure the great gap in moral standards between the Roman community and our own culture.

10. Same is the view of Max-Muller, another great scholar and Indologist:

> "If I were asked under what sky the human mind has most fully developed some of its choicest gifts, has most deeply pondered over the greatest problems of life, and has found solutions of some of them which will deserve the attention even of those who have studied Plato and Kant - I should point to India."

11. This culture has not only produced Ashoka, but it has also thrown up the Great emperor Akbar who was the finest example of the blend of Islamic culture and Indian tradition. Justice Rama Jois, a great scholar Judge in his treatise on '*Legal and Constitutional History of India*' outlined the achievements of Akbar which are given below:

"(1) He repealed the discriminatory law regarding citizenship as also one unanimous system of justice for all.

(2) He abolished Hindu Pilgrims' tax as also Jizya (1564 A.D.).

(3) He permitted Hindus and Christians to build temples and churches, respectively.

(4) He permitted the buying back from servitude children who were sold to become slaves by their parents.

(5) He repealed the law which provided for imposition of death clause for criticising the religion of Islam or the conduct of Prophet Muhammad.

(6) He prohibited Sati unless the concerned Hindu widow wanted to do so voluntarily and without pressure by any one.

(7) He also modified personal law of the Muslims and provided that a Muslim should take only one wife, and could take another only if the first wife was barren."

12. So the seeds of secularism and freedom of religion of which we are so proud today were sown at least about four hundred years ago.

13. Islam came to India shortly after it was preached by the Prophet Muhammad. The mosaic of Indian culture has been substantially influenced and enriched by the advent of Islam.

14. Dr. Sayyed Waheed Akhtar, a noted Islamic scholar, described the historical importance and significance of Islam and its doctrine of equality and Justice in these words:

> "Before the advent of Islam the great Greek civilization had introduced a rudimentary form of democracy in the city states, and later the Romans also put up a semblance of democracy for a short time. But in Greek democracies only free men, not females, had a right to vote, and slaves were not considered of having any rights. The vast Roman empire was virtually a slave state, in which only the free ruling class enjoyed rights. The Byzantine empire that succeeded the Roman empire never practised the teachings of Christ and denied freedom of thought and enquiry to the Christians themselves. The Popes were equally intolerant of free enquiry. In the Christian theocracies and monarchies religious minorities were persecuted and discriminated against. The socio-political structure of the Persian empire was equally oppressive in which only the priests and noblemen enjoyed some rights. In this caste-ridden set-up common men could not even think of freedom. The Indian society and state were also caste-bound, where the lower castes, constituting the vast majority of people, were treated as non-human beings. In such an epoch, Islam emerged with a universal message

of human freedom that guaranteed equal rights for all human beings irrespective of their race, colour, nationality, faith and sex."

15. This is virtually echoing the freedom of religion guaranteed under the Constitution.

16. So it was but natural that our Constitution which is also the product of a struggle for human freedom, would be based on such principles. The framers of our Constitution were architects of and participants in our national struggle for freedom. So in the lofty ideas of our Constitution, if I may borrow, Nehru's phrase "the soul of a nation, long suppressed, found utterance."

17. Thus, the preamble to the Constitution understandably reads more like a declaration of Independence than a part of the Constitution. Of course, Supreme Court has held it to be a part of the Constitution. This preamble is based on the objective resolution drafted by Nehru which was moved by him in the Constituent Assembly on 13th December, 1946. In the preamble, as enacted by the founding fathers, the word secular was not there. But that did not, even in the remotest way, diminish secular credentials of the Constitution. This word has been subsequently inserted by the 42nd Amendment of the Constitution. I am of the view that by this insertion nothing, which was not there in the Constitution, has been added. The express and substantive provisions of the Constitution unmistakably point towards its secular features. Both Dr. D. Basu and Mr. Seevai, the two eminent jurists on Constitution, have also expressed similar views.

18. The anxiety to assuage the tension of the minorities that in free India they will not be persecuted for their religious belief and faith was uppermost in the minds of the framers of the Constitution much before our independence. In fact, this was one of the creed of our freedom movement. The Madras Congress resolution of May, 1928 established a Committee with Motilal Nehru as the Chairman. The Committee's report, known as Nehru

Report, contained justification for such provisions in the Draft Constitution providing for religious freedom.

19. From the report given by Mr. Motilal Nehru Committee which was set up in 1928 for draft Constitution, it appears that the founding fathers were aware of "the unfortunate existence of communal differences in the country. Therefore, they thought that certain safeguards are necessary "to create and establish a sense of security among those who look upon each other with distrust and suspicion." The report concluded by saying that it can be done best by securing "religious rights to all communities and by including them among the basic principles of the Constitution."

20. This protection was also considered necessary in order to prevent "one community domineering over another."

21. Unfortunately despite these efforts, the partition of India and the senseless killing and bloodshed of our innocent and mostly poor countrymen on so called religious divide could not be averted. In the backdrop of these events the relevance of Constitutional provisions can be best appreciated.

22. In establishing a secular state, the Constitution has maintained a very delicate balance between the rights of the individual and the regulatory powers of the State in the interest of the community at large. So the freedom given under the Constitution is regulated on well known grounds of public interest. In a way ,it is a facet of equality which is the most striking feature of the Constitution. That explains why secularism has also been pronounced by the Supreme Court as one of the basic features of the Constitution and also beyond the amending power of the Constitution.

23. The Constitutional provisions, relevant in this respect, can be divided into three broad categories : First, the provisions which ensure that religion is not at all relevant in matters of conferring rights and imposing liabilities on individuals; secondly,

the provisions which guarantee freedom in matters of religion to individuals, religious denomination or any section thereof; and lastly, the provisions which prohibit the political authority from promoting or propagating any religion.

24. Citizenship under the Constitution (Articles 5 to 8) is not dual as in USA but it is single citizenship and religion has nothing to do with acquisition of citizenship. This provision is totally secular in character. As soon as one becomes a citizen, various fundamental rights are granted to him under the Constitution.

25. The equality clauses in the Constitution embrace every one regardless of caste, race, religion or sex. Of these clauses, Article 14 is the genus and Article 15 and 16 are species of equality. Article 14 has two parts. The first part ensures "equality before law". Here law is used in a philosophical sense and as a generic term. The second part envisages `equal protection of the laws.' Here `law' is used in the sense of enacted and specific law. So the protection is very comprehensive and is the hallmark of our secular and democratic republic. It is significant to note that this article admits of no exception and reads as if it has been enacted to give effect to the promises in the preamble.

26. Similarly, Article 15(i) gives a guarantee of nondiscrimination on grounds of religion as also on other grounds. The same right is extended under Article 15(2)(a) and (b) to certain specific instances and benefits. Sub-Article (4) of Article 15 admits of exception to sub-articles (1) and (2) of Article 15.

27. Similarly, Articles 16(1) and 16(2) guarantee equality and non-discrimination on grounds of religion and other allied grounds in matters of appointment and employment under the State. Sub-Articles (4) and (4-A) admit of exception to the guarantee under Sub-Article (2) of Article 16 of the Constitution.

28. The provisions of Sub-Article (5) of Article 16 is in connection with the freedom of religion under Articles 25 and 26.

29. Article 17 of the Constitution abolishes untouchability in any form. This was one of the visions of Mahatma Gandhi in his *Ram Rajya*. This is like abolition of slavery by the 13th Amendment of the American Constitution. However, untouchability has not been defined either under the Constitution or even under the provisions of the Untouchability Offences Act, 1955. However, this provision has a very close nexus with the freedom of religion. Caste system under Hindu religion has a pernicious influence and persons belonging to lower caste were considered untouchables and were denied entry in various places of worship which are open to persons of higher castes of the same religion or even belonging to the same religious denominations. So this social custom of untouchability which has been abolished has a direct bearing on the freedom of religion granted under the Constitution, especially having regard to the provisions of Article 25(2)(b) of the Constitution under which the State can make law for throwing open all Hindu religious institutions of public character to all classes and sections of people.

30. The right to freedom of religion which has been granted under Articles 25 to 28 of the Constitution has been aptly called the 'Conscience of the Constitution' by Austin.

31. The right guaranteed by Article 25 is an individual right to choose any religion and the right to freely profess, practice and propagate religion. By this right the promise in the preamble to ensure liberty of thought, expression, belief, faith and worship has been translated in the shape of fundamental rights. This right also protects the freedom of religion even of an alien. But the right under Article 26 is a right of property given to every religious denomination or a section thereof.

32. However, both the rights conferred by Articles 25 and 26 are subject to public order, morality and health and other provisions of the Constitution.

33. Article 26 deals with the institutional right to property and its administration. But then Articles 26(c) and (d) would

authorise the State to regulate the right of a religious denomination in the administration of its property. But if any law is made which takes away the right of administration altogether from the religious denomination and vests it in any other authority that would violate the guarantee of Article 26(d) of the Constitution.

34. So the freedom of religion under Articles 25 and 26 of the Constitution includes a bundle of rights. Broadly stated guarantee under Article 25 would include (i) Right to profess and practice religion (ii) Right to propagate religion.

35. Rights under Article 26 would include (i) Right to manage affairs in matters of religion (ii) Right to establish and maintain religious and charitable institutions (iii) Right to own and acquire property and (iv) Right to administer property. But this right to manage religious and charitable institution is not a charter for a right to mismanage, squander and destroy property. In the event of such mismanagement, laws can be made for its proper administration and management in the interest of the religious institution.

36. In no other Constitution of the world, the right to propagate religion has been conferred. This is a right given to an individual and even to an alien. Even though this right is akin to the freedom of speech and expression given under Article 19, but there is a difference. Rights under Article 19 are confined to a citizen. But right under this Article 26(l)(a) is given to even an alien. The Constituent Assembly debates would show that this right to propagate was given keeping in view the doctrine of conversion in Christianity and conversion without force or fraud was included within the ambit of the right to propagate. But subsequently the Supreme Court held in 1977 in the case of Rev. Stainislaus that right of conversion is not included within this freedom to propagate one's religion.

37. Articles 27 and 28 have been enacted with the obvious intention of strengthening the secular fabric of the Constitution.

38. Article 27 prohibits the appropriation of the proceeds of any tax for paying the expenses for the promotion or maintenance of any particular religion or religious denomination. Being a secular State, where freedom of religion is guaranteed by the constitution both to individuals and to groups, it is against the policy of the Constitution to pay out of public funds any money for the promotion or maintenance of any particular religion or religious denomination.

39. Article 28 contains the guarantee that no religious instructions shall be provided in an educational institution which is wholly maintained by State fund. But exception has been made in favour of an educational institution which may be run by the State but established under any endowment or trust which requires imparting of religious instruction. It further guarantees the right of non-participation by a person without his consent in any religious instruction and worship given in an educational institution if it is funded by the State or receives any aid from the State. A conjoint reading of these two articles show that there is no state religion.

40. Another important provision is Article 51-A(e) which imposes a fundamental duty on every citizen "to promote harmony and the spirit of common brotherhood amongst all the people in India transcending religious, linguistic and regional or sectional diversities."

41. The sure test of the secular character of constitutional provisions is to be found in the manner in which the Government is formed to rule the country. In India, government is formed on the basis of general election. Such general election to the House of the People and the Legislative Assemblies of the State is held on the basis of adult suffrage. This is provided under Article 326 of the Constitution. Under the said provision adult suffrage has been defined to mean "every person who is the citizen of India and who is not less than 18 years of age on the date fixed by the appropriate Legislature and is not otherwise disqualified under

the Constitution or any law made in this behalf shall be entitled to be registered as a voter." The disqualifications mentioned in the Constitution are neither on grounds of religion, caste, race or sex but such disqualification rests on secular grounds like non-residence, unsoundness of mind, crime, corrupt or illegal practices. Therefore, the formation of the Government is based on purely secular principles. There is also no disqualification based on grounds of religion for occupying such highest elected post like that of the President, the Vice-President, Prime Minister, Chief Minister and any other Ministers of Cabinet rank. Nor is religion a ground of disqualification for being appointed to the post of High Court Judge or the Supreme Court Judge nor does religion disqualify any one for appointment to the post of highest Law Officers of the country, namely, Attorney General, Solicitor General and Advocate general. Religion is not again a bar for appointment to the post of Chief of Army Staff or Comptroller and Auditor General of India.

42. While mentioning these secular provisions, I may point out certain other provisions which atleast, to my mind, appear to be slightly at variance with the basic secular character of the Constitution. Here I will refer to those provisions.

Under Article 26(c) religious denomination or any section thereof has been given the right to own and acquire movable and immovable property and under sub-article (d) has given the right to administer such property in accordance with law.

43. Obviously this right under Article 26 is a fundamental right being in Part III of the Constitution. But the fundamental right to property under Article 19(1)(f) has been abolished by the 44th Amendment of the Constitution with a great deal of fan fare and it has been proclaimed that under the Constitution property right has ceased to be fundamental. A religious denomination would mean a religious body or sect having common faith and its own organisation and which is known by a distinctive name. Of course a religious denomination cannot be said to be a citizen, however, it certainly consists of citizens. But suppose, a group of

citizens form an educational trust with very noble objects but in that case, the said trust, just because it is not a religious denomination, does not have the fundamental right to own and acquire movable and immovable property even though they want to acquire it for a very laudable cause. So here difference is created mainly on the ground of religion. But under Article 15 of the Constitution the State has declared that it will not discriminate against any citizen on the ground only of religion. Here the discrimination which is made on the ground of religion may not be against an individual citizen but discrimination is certainly made against a group of citizens. So the guarantee under Article 15 is a little whittled down.

44. It may also be mentioned here that fundamental right under Article 26(c) is not subject to Article 300-A of the Constitution. Therefore, for acquisition of any property of a religious denomination the compensation that has to be paid will not be the amount fixed by any law but compensation has to be the just market value of the property taken whereas the property of any citizen can be acquired under any law relating to acquisition of property without payment of market value as compensation.

45. Article 48 is a part of directive principles of State policy and may not be enforceable. Under this Article it has been provided that the State shall endeavour to organise Agriculture and Animal Husbandry on Modern and Scientific lines and shall, in particular, take steps for preserving and improving the breeds and prohibiting the slaughter of cows and calves and other milch and draught cattle.

46. The objects set forth under Article 48 of the Constitution are a little overlapping. There can be no dispute about the necessity of re-organisation and modernisation of agriculture but to combine it with the protection for cow, strictly speaking, is not very logical.

47. This Article, however, shows the predominance of Hindu sentiments in the Constitution. It is well known that cow is a very sacred animal according to Hindu religion. So this special

provision for the protection of the cows and prohibition of slaughter of cows promotes the said sentiment. Commenting on this provision Mr. Graneville Austin in his book *The Indian Constitution* has observed that as various provisions of the Irish Constitution show that Ireland is a Roman Catholic Nation, so Article 48 shows that the Hindu sentiment prevailed in the Constituent Assembly. Austin also pointed out that there is evidence to show that Nehru was opposed to this provision.

48. Article 290-A is not a very well known Article in the Constitution. The Article is set out below:

> "A sum of forty six lakhs and fifty thousand rupees shall be charged on, and paid out of, the Consolidated Fund of the State of Kerala every year to the Travancore Devaswom Fund; and a sum of thirteen lakhs and fifty thousand rupees shall be charged on, and paid out of the Consolidated Fund of the State of Tamil Nadu every year to the Devaswom Fund established in that State for the maintenance of Hindu temples and shrines in the territories transferred to that State on the 1st day of November, 1956, from the State of Travancore Cochin."

49. This provision was made in view of Article VIII of the covenant entered into between the rulers of Travancore and Cochin in May, 1949 on the belief that the State belongs to God and the ruler is merely a representative of the God. Under this provision a sum of rupees forty six lakhs fifty thousand is charged on the consolidated fund of Kerala every year to Travancore Dewaswom fund and a sum of rupees thirteen lakhs and fifty thousand is charged on the consolidated fund of the State of Tamil Nadu every year to the Dewaswom Fund established in that State for the maintenance of Hindu temples and shrines in the territories transferred to that State on 1st November, 1956 from the State of Travancore-Cochin. It is well known that the Consolidated fund of the State is a fund created out of public revenue. Therefore, as a result of this provision the aforesaid amount from public revenue are to be paid every year for maintenance of Hindu temples and

shrines whereas Article 27 carries the injunction of fundamental right to the contrary. It is difficult to reconcile this provision with the secular character of the State under the Constitution.

Constitutional Principle

Now while commenting on practice of the Constitutional principle of secularism one has to accept that normally there is some difference between the ideal and the real between the principles and its practice. So in this case also there is some difference between the high secular principles enshrined in the Constitution and its practice in its actual reality. To my mind the reasons for this disparity can be traced back to the all round degeneration of values in public life. The framers of our Constitution were men of high calibre and talent and were drawn to public life with a mission, namely, to liberate our country from the foreign rule. But today not necessarily the best talents in the society are drawn to public life nor do they have before them any mission of a similar nature. Change of perception and character among persons drawn to public life is reflected in the quality of governance. There is no dispute that by proper governance only the high ideas of secularism can be translated in actual life.

It is, however, true that under the democratic system the people get the Government they deserve. If our representatives chosen on the basis of popular vote do not show strict adherence to Constitutional principles, then the fault lies with us that we have not been vigilant about our own rights and have chosen such persons as our representatives who may trample on our rights. The freedom of religion which has been given under the Constitution is a very noble and precious right but it can be preserved by its keepers, if only they act with a sense of discipline and restrain. Freedom of Religion can be only enjoyed if we respect the freedom of the person who follows a different religion. Without mutual respect for each other's freedom, this freedom becomes fragile and is at peril. All cases of religious bigotry and fanaticism thrive on this lack of mutual respect for the freedom of the fellow citizen who has a similar freedom to follow a different religion.

As soon as a person starts despising the freedom of his fellow being, he undermines his own freedom and drains it of its vitality and strength.

As has been rightly observed, freedom is not to be inherited in one's blood stream. But every generation has to fight for its freedom and once freedom is achieved it has to be defended not by might alone but by 'eternal vigilance' and proper restrain and only then it can be passed on to the next generation. Journey towards freedom and its reach is always an unremitting endeavour and is never a final achievement. It may be remembered that the freedom enshrined in our Constitution especially the freedom of religion is not strictly based on legal or formal principles but they are based on moral principles. Moral principles for their survival are to be lived in life, both in private and certainly in public life. In this connection, if I may quote Joseph Story a great American Judge. The words are almost prophetic:

> "The structure has been erected by architects of consummate skill and fidelity; its foundations are solid; its compartments are beautiful as well as useful; its arrangements are full of wisdom and order; and its defences are impregnable from without. It has been reared for immortality, if the work of man may justly aspire to such a title. It may, nevertheless, perish in an hour by the folly, or corruption, or negligence of its only keepers, The People Republics are created - these are the words which I commend to you for your consideration - by the virtue, public spirit and intelligence of the citizens. They fall, when the wise are banished from the public councils, because they dare to be honest, and the profligate are rewarded, because they flatter the people, in order to betray them."

But I do not want to conclude with a note of despair, even though the present scenario is not exactly encouraging. Let us all hope this to be a temporary phase. So may all of us find solace in the robust optimism sounded by Swami Vivekananda, one of the greatest secular souls India has produced. Swami Vivekananda said:

> "There have been periods of decay and degradation; I do not attach much importance to them; we all know that. A mighty tree produces a beautiful ripe fruit. That fruit falls on the ground, it decays and rots and out of that decay springs the root and the future tree, perhaps mightier than the first one. This period of decay through which we have passed was all the more necessary. Out of this decay is coming the India of the future. It is sprouting; the first leaves are already out; and a mighty gigantic tree is here, already beginning to appear."

Let us hope that the next millennium will see the emergence of 'India of the future'.

Eight

A New Life for Dalits

One of the great enigmas of Indian history has been the almost total extinction of Buddhism in the land of its birth, while it remained flourishing in the land of its adoption like Ceylon, Burma, Tibet, China, Mongolia and Japan. The reason is its ultimate absorption within the fold of Hinduism. As Radhakrishnan said, "Hinduism killed Buddhism by a fraternal embrace." Unkind foreign scholars have described this as the `omnivorous capacity of Hinduism', the octopus of Hinduism spreading its tentacles and finally absorbing all shades of thought and reconciling divergent faiths by owning them. The fact, however, is that Buddhism was never a separate religion; it was just a part of the ancient Aryan thought and culture. Under the wide Indian canopy all shades of philosophical speculations and the subtlest dialectics had flourished, one never crossing the path of the other by hatred, antagonism and persecution. Sankar in his commentary on the Gita calls the Charvakas (atheists), the Jains, the Buddhists, and the followers of Sankhya philosophy as only `misguided', incapable of understanding the true import of Braham Vidya or knowledge of the Divine. He, however, does not term them as non-Hindu or anti-Hindu. What Buddhism did in relation to Vedic religion was to disown the Griha Sutras, the Householders' Duties which comprised rituals and ceremonies, and laid down its own ethical code of duties, which sometimes coincided in part with the ancient code. Thus the schism between the orthodox and the reformist was never complete; at many points, both touched each other. Man cannot also live for long without leaning on some idealised superhuman power, and, thus, in course of time, Buddha the man, became Buddha, the divine, admitted ultimately even to the pantheon of Hindu gods. The Mahayan Tantricism and Hindu or Brahminical Tantricism, (the rituals associated with the worship of deities) converged, ultimately almost obliterating the distinction between Hindu and Buddhist. With the decline and destruction of Buddhist monasteries and seats of learning like Nalanda and Vikramshila, the separate identity of Buddhism in India came almost to be forgotten, the laity merging with the common mass of Hindus - in many cases as distinct castes or groups, and the Bhikshus who could escape the swords of the invaders getting sanctuary within the folds of Hindu ascetic orders.

The influence of Mahayan Tantricism was greatest in Bengal, Bihar and Eastern part of modern UP In the turmoil that followed the conquest of these regions by the Muslims, the Nath Yogis, as ascetics as well as spiritual guides to the common people, became prominent. Adi Nath, the founder of the sect was a Vajrayan Buddhist, who aimed at making the human body fit for attaining divine unity through Yogic postures. As many as 84 Siddhas or Perfect Yogis are recalled in contemporary literature. Later on this sect turned Hindu in the sense that Siva became the presiding deity instead of Buddha. There have been 84 Naths also. Yogi Matsyendra Nath and Yogi Gorakh Nath being the most prominently known. This sect got divided in course of time, each developing its own philosophical nuances; but the prime concern of all shades of Nath-Yogis remained the perfection of bodies by Yogic feats. This naturally evoked admiration among the masses, for the weak, whether of body or mind, are always attracted by the strong. However, among the orthodox sections of the Hindus, the lay followers of Nath Yogis were looked down upon as degenerates. The Sen rulers of the south who followed the Palas in Bengal practised and encouraged social discrimination against them. In such a situation, the arrival of Sufi saints on the scene was significant. They laid stress on the need for making the body fit to receive divine grace, and spoke of -fana (extinction) as something like nirvana; but there was no social discrimination or inequality amongs their followers. Such egalitarianism as a way of life brought new hope for these bewildered mass of people and a very large number of them accepted Islam. The enthusiasm was so great that they conceived of the Prophet as Dharm Thakur, a new messiah and an embodiment of righteousness. These people were mostly of occupational classes, and the very large number of Muslim population of Bengal and parts of Bihar and Eastern UP may be traced back to these conversions.

However, though they accepted Islam they were not cut asunder from their old moorings. For, it must be understood that the Sufis were not missionaries in the strict sense of the term. They were not concerned with popularising the normal rites and rituals of Islam, but with spreading the gospel of love: for the Divine and for the common brotherhood of mankind. This aspect of their life and teachings attracted even those who did not formally accept Islam. They did much to restore social equilibrium in a society which had got unhinged due to prolonged sectarian differences and by Muslim domination. They also helped in restoring the spiritual confidence of the people, and showed that paths may be many, but the goal was one. The Sufis lent to Islam in India a mellow humanism which was exactly what the Indian society needed at that time. The result was a spurt in the cultural and literary activities of those who followed them. Mention may be made of *Gyansagar* of Ali Raza, *Gyan Pradip* and *Gyan Chowtisha* of Syed Sultan, *Sur Kandil* of Muhammad Shafi, *Bara Masa,* Yog Kalandar, and *Satya Gyan Pradip* of Murshid. All these works are a fine amalgam of Sufi mystical thoughts and the Nath Yogis practices. A magnificent blend of the two was witnessed in the poems and the teachings of Kabir. Among the followers of Gorakh Nath there were many such Muslims; Gorakh Vijay, recounting the many feats of Guru Gorakh Nath is ascribed to one Faizullah. In the same vein is Abdus Shakoor Niahmud's writing in *Gopi Chand Sanyas.*

With the conquest of the Indus-Gangetic Valley by Muslims, the Hindu society as a whole had turned defensive, and, as a consequence, the orthodoxies became more pronounced and rigid.

Any deviation entailed ex-communication. The Kshatriyas having been routed, the Brahmins took upon themselves the task of protecting Dharma, which instead of being righteousness in the broadest sense as originally conceived, became something dogmatic anti ritualistic. There is nothing strange about this. When the sword is broken, it is the defensive apparatus of the mind that works. The nearest example that comes to mind is that of the Jews whose integrity and distinctiveness were saved by the Rabbis when the Temple was destroyed and the Jews dispersed by the Romans. Johanan ben Zakhai, the leading Jewish Rabbi, established the great Jewish Academy at Jebneh in the heart of Roman Palestine itself to guard and propagate zealously the doctrines of Judaism. However, the situation in India was different. Here, though the Muslims dominated, the Hindu social system was allowed to remain intact and the Hindu chieftains still ruled the roost; the economic apparatus continued to be largely in the hands of the Hindus, and above all the people lived as self-sufficient village communities. Besides, a very large part of India south to the Gangetic valley did not owe permanent allegiance to the central Muslim authority, and several strong Hindu principalities continued to flourish.

The challenge of Islam was both political and spiritual: the scimitar of the crescent Islam not only cut physically but also made a deep dent spiritually. While its egalitarianism made it socially attractive, the spiritual heights of the great Sufi saints were bound to make a deep impression on an essentially spiritual people like the Hindus. Fortunately for the Hindus, the great Bhakti movement of the south, deeply spiritual in content and humanistic in approach, was then sweeping over and making its impact on the north as well. While religious life in northern India had assumed all the characteristics of decadance, society in the south was intellectually vigorous and emotionally vibrant. Unlike the north, there were no Kshatriyas proper in the south though the Reddys of the Andhra Des, the Vellat as of Tamil Nadu and the Nayyers of Malabar, claimed to be as such, and the so-called Sudras or non-Brahmins produced a large number of royal families. But, nevertheless, the non-Brahmins in the south suffered a kind of social stigma unknown in the north. On this account, worship of God in his personal aspect to whom one could lay bare one's heart outpourings became very popular among the Sudras of the South. Tamil Nadu had a long tradition of religious singers, called Alwars, who were mostly Sudras, the chief of them, Sathkop being a pariah. Their moving compositions in praise of Vishnu are offerings of complete surrender to the will of the deity, who is made a sharer of the joys and sorrows of the singers. The Saivas had similarly their Saiva singers, and some of the compositions of Saivite Mannika Watchk Gar are of indescribable beauty. The original home of Mahayan Buddhism which elevated Lord Buddha to a Personal God presiding over the welfare of the devotees was also in the south, Sail Parbatam to be precise. However, Sir George Grierson in the old *Imperial Gazeteer* (Vol. II, p.418) would like us to believe that the concept of the Deity as "able to sympathise with our infirmities" was peculiarly Christian, and an inspiration from its Nestorian sect, and this was the principle adopted by the Bhakti cult in India. Now, Nestorius, to whom the Nestorian sect of Christianity is ascribed, was the patriarch of Constantipole from 428 A.D. to his condemnation and deposition at the General Council of Ephesus in 431 A.D. He upheld the divinity and humanity of Christ, but denied their union in a single self-conscious personality, that union being merely moral or sympathetic. The personality was thus broken into a duality. He preached that the Lord was to be worshipped in His human aspect, and His help was necessary in overcoming frailties of human nature. It has to be remembered that in its early days, true Christianity followed what was decided by consensus at Christian councils and a lot of polemics was involved, resulting in proclamation of the faith and heresies to be condemned. For example, Apollinaris, the Younger, Bishop of Laodicea in Syria (died 390 A.D.) held the doctrine that logos or divine nature of Christ took the place of the rational human soul or mind and that the body of Christ was a spiritualized and glorified form of humanity. He was, however, condemned for denying the true human nature of Christ took the second oecumenical Council at Constantipole in 381 A.D. These episodes would go to show that there was a good deal of controversy and clash of opinions in regard to the essential humanity and transcendental divinity of the personality of Lord Christ as had happened with Lord Buddha in latter times. Buddhism was a living religion in the Middle East and in Central Asia when such controversies were coming up and it is more than probable that the Nestorians borrowed the doctrine of "deity sympathasing with the infirmities of devotees" from Mahayan Buddhists who had raised the essentially human personality of Lord Buddha to that of occupying a transcendental divinity.

The genesis of the idea of Bhakti is to be found in Swetashwatar Upanishad: "He, who dwells in our heart is to be worshipped and attained."

If the Lord is in every human heart how can there be discrimination between the Lord dwelling in one heart and the: Lord dwelling in another? This is the crux of the doctrine of equality, acceptable to both the Vaishnavas and the Sufis who also hold that God dwells in every human heart. Service to humanity thus became the greatest worship, and a pariah devotee had as much right to equal treatment as a Brahmin. Ramanuj, the great Vaishnava saint of the south, treated all devotees-Sudras, Brahmins or non-Hindus-equally and all the great masters followed him in this respect. The Vaishnavas were against all caste barriers; once one became a servant of the Lord - a true Vaishnava, he was beyond all social classifications. Of course, their code of conduct - *achar* - was strict in respect of food, but in other respects, they were liberal. The Saivas, likewise, abhorred caste classifications and their food restrictions were also not so rigid. The Vir Saivas or Lingayats who came into existence in the 12th century in Kannad Desh, spreading far wide in the neighbouring regions, were against image worship and propitiating sacrifices and firmly rejected the caste system; they made no distinction between a Brahmin Vir Saiva, and a pariah Vir Saiva. "All men are holy in proportion as they are temples of the great spirit", declares firmly Uttappalcharya, the saint in deep south in Tamil Nadu, the Siddhars rejected the authority of the Shastras, and did not believe in transmigration of the soul - a commonly held belief among the Hindus. To them God and Love were the same.

It is interesting to reflect how far these movements in the orthodox south were inspired by Islamic gale of Wahadat (oneness of divinity) and Ummat (brotherhood of man) that was then raging in the intellectual firmament. There was already a constant relationship between the Arabs and the people on the Indian West Coast on account of the vigorous commerce being carried on between them from time immemorial. The Arabs were intrepid sailors and India was then famous for its excellent ship-building industry (this situation having 'lasted till the beginning of nineteenth century). Arab Muslim scholars and saints visited the Malabar region, where even now a sizeable Muslim population of Arab origin exists. Thus, Islam having influenced the growth of Hindu movements in the south against image worship and caste restrictions, preaching equality amongst men, is an assertion not to be lightly put aside. The wind from the south blew to the north and did much to invigorate further the liberal humanistic movement that was growing due to the impact of the teachings and practices of the Sufi saints. Kabir was one of its greatest exponents and he stands among the world-class teachers as an emancipator of the human mind from the narrowness of religion or sect.

Kabir stands for a universal humanism where no man made distinctions of sect, caste or nationality, would stand between man and man. His is a religion of love, of devotion to a universal power of pristine might and glory. It is said that he was a Muslim who had become a disciple of Ramanand, a Brahmin saint hailing from Allahabad and living at Benares to which city Kabir belonged. But this is open to grave doubt. Kabir has left a vast literature of his sayings in form of Dohas, Sakhis, Ramainis and aphorisms. It is significant that nowhere he has called himself a Muslim, although this may be due to his belief that there are no separate religions. He calls himself a Jolaha, a servant of Rain who stands for Divinity. Now this caste of Jolaha or Jola finds mention in 'Brahainauarta Puran' (10th Chapter) according to which a Zola is one begotten of a Mlechha, wife of a Kabind, a caste engaged in the occupation of weaving. The caste of Kabinds in turn, according to the same Purana, is said to have originated from the Sudra wife of the legendary Vishwakarma - the divine architect and engineer of Hindu mythology. It appears therefore, that the Jolaha caste to which Kabir belonged was a sub-caste of the occupational caste Kabind, a Sahajyani house-holder variety of Mahayani Buddhist Nath Panthis. Apparently, they had embraced Islam but not shed their original philosophical leanings. Kabir, therefore, calls himself neither a Hindu nor a Muslim, but a Xolaha. That the family of Kabir followed the customs and traditions of Nath Panthis is also proved by the fact that Kabir was first cremated and then buried which was the custom amongst Nath Panthis even now followed amongst them in Tripura. Kabir's writings themselves bear enough testimony to the fact that philosophically he belonged to the Sunnyavadi School of Buddhistic thought. He says:

"Shorn of all doubts and fancies about self, I am submerged in the ocean of nothingness - a state of ultimate sojourn denied even to the wisest."

His conception of the state of Samadhi is that of the Sunnyavadi, a state where dissolving oneself in nothingness is not a denial of existence, but the ultimate refuge, the journey's end of innumerable births and deaths from which there is no coming back. How to attain this state? In formulating his teachings, Kabir borrowed from the Buddhistic and Hindu Tantricism, and built a superstructure of his own with many bricks taken from Islamic mysticism. According to Tantra, Nad or vibration has been identified as the primordial energy, in itself in a state of quiescence, without attribute, but once endowed with divine will, it assumes the aspect of Bindu, both the first cause and the final cause. Kabir calls Nad, the attribute less or Nirgun Siva as Sate;: Punish, and Bindu, the active Sagun Siva as Niranjan Punish. Like the followers of Tantra, he assumes, that it is divine Shakti or power which is capable of translating Nad into, Bindu and vice versa. In one of his enigmatic poems of indescribable lyrical beauty, Kabir raises the eternal question: "Which comes first ? Cause or effect; sky or earth; wind or rain; sun or moon: life or death; male or female; seed or bud; night or day; good or evil?; and whether there is anything positive ultimately?"

Characteristically, he answers in one pithy sentence:

"The whole world is one He: He is the world, and the world is in Him; Existence and He are identical."

Now this conception of ultimate reality is the same as the Sufi concept of human ast. Abu Hasan Khurkani, the great Sufi saint, has explained this lucidly in the following words:

"I don't say that heaven and hell have no existence, but I do affirm that for me they have no separate existence; for, both have been created by Him, and for me only He is real and not his creations."

The identification of the creator with the created sends Kabir in flights of ecstasy for God and His creations, and in the process he discards all rites and rituals. When the flood of Love flows in the heart, it sweeps away all embankments created by man - caste, creed, and particular modes of worship. For Kabir that path is the true and easy path which leads to God: cf:

"Everyone says that his path (of religion) is the true path, but only that path is true which leads to God."

Kabir is an iconoclast, in the company of the truly great who shun all formalism and hypocrisy, and he comes down heavily on both Hindu and Muslim practices which are devoid of dedication to God. Kabir declares himself to be neither Hindu nor Muslim; no human or artificial label can cling to him, for he lives in and for his Beloved:

"I am drunk with love, what have I to do with sobriety? Whether I live in society or snap its bond, the world cannot allure me. My beloved is neither far off from me for a moment nor am I ever separate from my dearest. My Love for the Beloved is ever flowing; why should I pine for him?"

Kabir's life and teachings represent the great synthesis of Bhakti and Yoga on the one hand and the Hindu pantheism and Islamic mysticism on the other. Kabir's philosophy was a force behind the composite outlook on life which came to be shared by people of all religions and all classes in India, as the essence of Indianness. Kabir has a long list of illustrious successors in thought and deeds down to the present age. Rabidas, a fellow disciple of Ramanand, Sundar Dass, Sahjo Bai, Shaikh Razzab and host of others, too numerous to mention. Their influence on Indian thought and action cannot be minimised.

Another preacher of almost the same class, but of a different persuasion was the great Vaishnava saint of Bengal, Mahaprabhu Chaitanya. Born in an orthodox Brahmin family, a profound scholar of the Hindu scriptures, a logician of unrivalled intellectual calibre (whose friend and disciple, Raghunandan, founded a new school of logic, Nava Nayaya) he was yet against all bonds of caste and rituals. Under his inspiration, his two disciples, Rup Goswami, and Jiva Goswami, themselves scholars of Persian and Sanskrit who were once employed in high administrative posts under Sultan Husain Shah of Bengal, propounded a new school of philosophical thought, comparable to the mono-dualistic school of Vaisnawanism. What distinguished Chaitanya most, however, is not his school of thought (Abhed-a-Bhed) or soul being similar in kind to Divine, but functionally distinct, but the way to salvation he showed for the common mass of people. It was the gospel of love which he preached - love expressed by way of chanting the name of the Lord which suited everyone, high or low and to which everyone was entitled without any distinction of caste or creed or sex. This chanting of the Lord's name came to be called Sankirtan, a congregational singing of Lord's name which cleansed the mind and made the soul pure, and fit for receiving God's grace.' It was just like the sessions of singing and ecstatical fervour which the Sufi saints aroused by purifying the minds and hearts of the people, which had then flooded north India and Bengal countryside for long, casting a profound spell over the common people. It is true that devotional music was and remains a part of Hindu ritual, but it was a passive affair so far as the congregation of listeners was concerned. Chaitanya made every member of the congregation an active participant; the distinction between the singer and the listener did not hold good any longer; one was both a singer and a listener. Chaithanya also popularised anew the Krishna cult, his Krishna being the Krishna of Srimad Bhagwat, a god of Love, of fun and frolic, not the Krishna of the Gita of stern visage calling Arjun (symbolising mankind) to duty and to the battle of life. Chaitanya's Krishna is beyond the ken of human intellect, being Mayapati or the Lord of Illusion, but the moment one opens one's heart to the Lord by pure devotion and love and surrenders to His will, the web of illusion is shattered, the magic is broken, and one can feel the presence of the Lord within one self, as real and as concrete as one's own personality. This is the experience of Baqa or real existence of the Sufi conception. No wonder, the Krishna cult caught the imagination of many Muslims as well and Brajbhasha, the language of the region where Krishna was born, was adopted by many Muslim writers and poets. Raskhan's poems describing the childhood pranks of Lord Krishna are well known.

Thus, within two to three hundred years of the establishment of Muslim domination, Islam, and Sufism became a part of the Indian psyche and Gujarat, Maharashtra, and far South had come under its charm. In Maharashtra particularly, Eknath, Tukaram and Ram Dass, not only spread the Bhakti cult, but preached equality of mankind irrespective of caste and creed. Thus, even though there might have been political rivalry between Hindu and Muslim rulers, so far as the masses were concerned, they had come to recognise one's religion as the worship of the same divine power, whatever the form. Tulsidas, the great saint, poet and preacher appears as a messenger of hope, a poet not of defeat and despair, but of ultimate victory of truth over falsehood, of the rule of righteousness over evil. Tulsidas restates and synthesizes the fundamentals of Hindu faith in the new environment of Indo-Islamic renaissance. He believed that only a true Kshatriya - the symbol of wisdom in action-could establish the rule of justice in human affairs, and in doing so partake of the signs and symbols of divinity. Thus Ram, the hero of *Valmiki Ramayan*, is elevated by Tulsidas to the position of Supreme Godhead. But in the human form as the son of king of Ajodhya, Ram has to undergo trial and tribulations engineered by man and decreed so by an unkind fate. However, by dint of his valour and exemplary character he is able to destroy his enemies. His is a triumph of wisdom over mere skill, of eternal values over mere worldly expediency. It is this wisdom as guiding star of the true destiny of man, which represents the universally accepted code of life for Indian society as a whole.

In Semitic religions like Judaism, Christianity and Islam, the concept of the supreme deity is that of not only a Master and Protector, but also of a Judge. According to Islamic tenets, benevolence of God is available to man, but strictly on terms of right conduct to be followed as revealed to the holy Prophet and propagated by him. It is more in the nature of a covenant between man and his creator. For every deviation from the right path as laid in the scripture, and for indulgence in temptations of the Satan, punishment is to be visited upon the sinner; though if he abjures vices sincerely, there is hope of mercy or of being judged rightly; but all have to bow before the supreme will of God. Verily there is a day of judgment, and it will come. This is in contrast to the Aryan conception of the inevitability of the Law of Karma, the veil of Maya which engulfs the reality, the cycle of births and deaths denoting the permanence of reality but change of form ever changing shadows, as it were, of the same permanent object. Man, after all, is not an automation caught on the wheels of Maya for ever, since he partakes of the essence of Reality itself, and once he comes to recognise his true self, the veil of Maya will stand pierced and shredded. But for this man requires both Purusharth, determined will, which comes by pursuing the path of Dharma as also Kripa (grace), which comes only if sincere invocations are made for the same. Both are necessary for social and spiritual success.

It is interesting to note that Islam also lays stress both on Jihad (effort) and Karam (grace) as the twin paths of attaining salvation. Tulsidas in *Ramcharitmanas* lends much charm and beauty to these soul-stirring truths in the background of mythologically alive tales and philosophically eternal varieties. Tulsidas has put the duty of man in pithy and succinct words:

"It is the duty of man to conceive God as without any appellation (Nirgun), but at the same time, to be aware of the presence of an Ever Present God all around oneself (Saqun), and to remember Him continuously by chanting the sweet name of Lord Ram."

The efflorescence of Hindu-Muslim composite ideology finds perfect expression in Guru Nanak, the great saint, preacher and reformer of Punjab. He presents essentially Hindu musings in Islamic idiom. His whole life bears testimony to his search for a universal brotherhood. His wanderings-for spiritual solace and inspiration took him not only to all parts of the country, but also to the Islamic holy shrines of Mecca, and Baghdad. His concept of the Eternal Reality, though essentially Vedantic, is in a Suffistic mood which he expresses in the following words:

"He is invisible, unbounded, beyond the ken of mind and intellect; incapable of being grasped by the senses; neither bound by time nor by action; incapable of being differentiated, unborn; and beyond comprehension and delusion." (Mahala-1, Sabd-7, First two lines).

Now, if God is such a Being, how can man, who is negation of all that He is two hypners i.e., he is visible, bounded, governed by mind and senses, he can feel and be felt by senses, bound by both time and action, classified and differentiated from one another, subject to births and deaths, both conscious two hypners and deluded ever experience Him? Guru Nanak furnishes the typically Vedantic answer to this question. He says that Sabd, the primordial vibrations consisting of indestructible elements, Achhar, are the cause and effect of the phenomenal world:

"Sabd is the seed of creation (Pran-sangli II-8) echoing upanashidic" "Salid Achhar are the true manifestations of one Almighty; when all are destroyed, one and only one remains." (Brahm Bindu Upanishad-16).

Baba Farid, the great Sufi saint of Punjab, in one of his compositions, calls Allah as Alif, the first word, the Ism -e-Azam (the great name) as the Sufis call him, the Primum, as it were, comprising and carrying all with it. This may be compared to Gospel according to St John:

"In the beginning was the word (logos) and the word (logos) was with God and the word (logos) was God" (St John-1).

Logos the Greek word, is perhaps nearest to Sabd. Now Sabd is made of Achhar, literally incapable of destruction. These indestructible are the primordial vibrations, the basic wave-lengths of which the phenomenal and noumenal words are made of, and Sabd is the coherent combination of Achhar in shape of concepts, the sheet-anchor of all our cogitations, whether conscious or unconscious. When one takes the name of Allah or Ram, conceiving of Him in his being as premium mobile, that is, the sphere round which the entire creation moves, a link is formed with the primordial vibration - subject and object merge, as it were. This is the secret behind Jaap or Zikr . The intensity of Jaap or Zikra results in Muraqbah or Dhyan. When the vibrations are so intense that the whole being is lightened by vibrations, as it were. It is for this reason that to Guru Nanak the name is 'nectar' in the heart as well as in the mouth, and what is this name?

"It is the name of Ram; by taking this name one drinks the sweet nectar, the easiest way to salvation by the grace of Guru." - Mahla: 4, Sabd: 2 (Satguru Prasadi).

Guru Nanak was God's own wandering minstrel with one Muslim and one Hindu companion, Mardana and Bala, rousing people to the ways of the Lord, asking them to be specimen of humanity and not of any caste, creed or community. Sumaran or remembrance of the Lord's name, he preached, was the sure way to cleanse and ennoble them. However, the organization of his followers which he left behind was modelled on Islamic principle of equality, simplicity and brotherhood of man. Sangat, the brotherhood of his followers, like Ummat in Islam was supreme; the Guru, just like the Caliph or Imam, was the symbol of inspiration, and in the absence of the physical presence of the Guru, his seat was to be venerated just like the physical presence of the Guru. Guru Angad, whom Guru Nanak nominated to succeed him in preference to his equally versatile and spiritually gifted son, Sri Chand, started the practice of venerating the seat of the Guru, even in his absence, as Guru himself. Guru Nanak shunned all rituals and dispensed with all ceremonials and worship of symbol or image in any form. Not only did he advocate a casteless society, but practised one; there was interdining and inter-marriage, as if his followers were one congregation. To put stress on this he started the practice of *langar* or community dining. Guru Nanak did not establish any ascetic or monastic order: all the Gurus were ordinary householders, the institution of Guru becoming hereditary with the successor of Guru Ram Das, the fourth Guru, Guru Arjundev, who started compilation of Guru Granth Saheb with the compositions of Hindu and Muslim saints. However, parallel to the organization of Guru Nanak's followers with their simple social practices and habits, was the ascetic order founded by the son of Guru Nanak, Sri Chand, called Udasins, and sometimes the two intermingled. Later, the followers of Guru Nanak got embroiled in political conflicts with Mughal Emperors, the result being the birth of a militant community of Khalsa (Pure) who took upon themselves the task of defending the Hindus and Hindu practices. Thus, what Guru Nanak preached was pure Vedantic monism, employing even Vedic idiom to stress the attainment of salvation by practising *sabd-yoga* or attuning one self to the primordial waves creating and sustaining the universe; but his organisational set up, though upanishidic in inspiration, appears to have adopted Islamic organisational media to bind his followers together for social equilibrium and spiritual solace, and his ways are, perhaps, the finest specimen of an Aryan-Islamic fusion.

In a way, the period of about three centuries of Indian history, fifteenth to seventeenth, was one of comparative political stability, economic prosperity, religious bonhomie and cultural blossoming. The period be considered to be one of the brightest chapters in the long history of this land; an appraisal of the same follows in subsequent pages.

Muslim Mystics

The symmetrical thoughts of Islam, with a clear vision of the Absolute Being and a definite code of life came into contact with the neo-platonic and mystical conceptions evolved in Egypt and Persia, when these lands were conquered. In Egypt there was a large flourishing Hindu colony. There was a constant contact between Indian saints and mystics and their counterparts in Egypt. This colony was destroyed in the beginning of the third century A.D. by Caracalla, the Roman Emperor, but he could not destroy the Indian influence on the intellectual plane, the evidence of which we have in plenty, in the writings of Plotinus, Parphyry and Philostratus. For example, Plotinus wanted to go to Persia and India to study philosophy which he could not do, but his writings show how deeply he had imbibed the Indian philosophical thought. It has been said that he directed all his effort towards a fusion of Pythagoras and Plato, but his doctrines, in essence, are of purely Indian character. Thus, according to him, all actions and thoughts count, The purified and the detached are not reborn into the corporeal; they remain in the world of the mind and of bliss, without reason, remembrance or speech; their liberty is absolute; they are made one with the perfect and absorbed into it without losing themselves in it. Such bliss can be obtained in the present by ecstasy.

This line of thought is pure monism of the qualified variety of the Hindu philosophical tradition. We have already noted the existence of large numbers of Hindu monasteries and temples in Khorasan and presence of Yogis and spiritual teachers in Syria and Mesopotamia who exercised influence even in the courts of

Abbasid Caliphs. The Magis of Persia were also greatly influenced by the Hindu mystics and Yogis and their spiritual discipline was not unknown among mystics of Perisa, Syria, Egypt and Mesopotamia. It may be noted in passing that for achieving purity of thought and action, spiritual discipline of Yoga is common to all the denominations of Indian religion, and the Hindus have carried this thought and practice wherever they have gone. Islam too was confronted with mystical thoughts and practices prevailing in Persia, Egypt and Middle East and its votaries could not but be influenced by these. However, so far as Islam itself was concerned, it stood against extreme asceticism. The Prophet was against absolute celibacy for which he had advanced very cogent reasons. Man's duty was, he taught, to be ever vigilant against forces of evil (shaitaniat). It was his duty and privilege to struggle (Jihad) against blasphemy (kufr) and all evils. For this asceticism was not congenial; rather one had to follow the Quranic injunctions to live a perfect married life.

In course of time, certain ascetic orders came into existence in the Islamic brotherhood, but their asceticism was more of spirit than of form, as the votaries all lived married lives. (1)The Marjais believed in purity of action, love of' God; and strict ethical conduct as the gateway to heaven; (2) the Qadris, however, claimed that they had already achieved this goal by following the above path; (3) the Jabris denied that man was responsible for his deeds, as, according to them, everything was ordained by God; (4) the Motazal is, sought to examine the sacred texts on the touchstone of logic and denied the inevitability of fate as against the concept of a just universal order; and finally (5) the Asharis were exponents of the view that a Muslim's life should be ordained strictly according to Kitab and Sunnah. The last represented the orthodox school and most of the Ulema and divines were of this order; but among them, too, those belonging to more liberal persuasions were quite a few. All the schools of thought sought to derive their authority from some Aayat of the holy Quran, including the Sufis, a special class of ascetics, who based their teachings on love of mankind. The Sufis represented a broad spectrum of spiritual yearnings within Islamic ideology and appear to have been pioneers of mysticism in the Islamic world. We find traces of both monistic and pantheistic thoughts in the utterances of Sufi saints and poets. While the "Wajudia" creed "Hama ust" (every thing is Him) is purely monistic and theistic, the "Shahudiya" school holds "Hama az ust" (every thing from Him), and is inclined to be pantheistic and dualistic. However, this difference is more apparent than real, since He is what He is, and man has to travel a lot spiritually before he can enter into the world of Reality which is one and the unity, the goal of all human endeavours. Ibnal Arabi, a great master of Islamic mysticism, explains and affirms that God is one and the Universe is His appearance. Creation is a process of emanation of which the three steps are: (1) the stage of absolute unity (ahdiat); (2) the stage of latent or potential multiplicity (wahdat) and; (3) the stage of apparent or actual multiplicity (wahidat). The multiplicity expresses itself in souls (Ruh), forms (Mithal) and bodies (Jism). It would be interesting to compare this with the Hindu conception of the Reality as undifferentiated (abhisome) like the conception of ahdiat, all-pervading (sarvatrayastha) like the conception of wahidat, and (shuddha), known to man in the immediacy of the experience of self (alma) giving it the appearance of multiplicity, and it would appear that there is no basic difference between the two conceptions.

There may be found traces of mysticism in the Holy Quran itself, and in the utterances and actions of the Prophet, and of the four 'Righteous Caliphs' According to ancient tradition prevalent in Sufi circles. Baba Rattan, a Hindu saint of Punjab, had met personally the Holy Prophet, but it is difficult to say how far this is historically correct, though there is nothing improbable about it. Quran has conceived Allah as "the source of light of the earth and the sky", this divine light was near as well as far, high as well as low, both outside and inside one's being. According to Hadith, Prophet Muhammad (P.B.U.H.) enjoined on one of his followers to hark to his inner self as Allah dwelleth therein. According to another Hadith, the Prophet used to pray Allah might illumine his eyes and ears with divine light, and used to conclude his prayers with this benediction "Let Allah fill my whole being with divine light." It is this divine light that permeates a lacing when, in course of his meditations, he passes from the world of senses into the realm of higher consciousness; this is really the state of an ideal existence (Ehsan). The authoritative command of the Prophet is to pray God as if you are in His presence, and it is in this way that one can attain the state of "Ehsan". As Shibli says "I never saw anything except God".

The teaching of the sufistic doctrine of "Fana" (annihilation) calls for cessation of all mental activities. When one is not aware of even the fact of this cessation it is `Fana-ul-Fanaah' (annihilation of annihilation) and when the very `consciousness of unconsciousness', a state of pure metaphysical conception is attained, it is 'Baqa', the real life. As Baba Kohi Shirazi says:

"I melted into nothingness, and lo! and behold! I attained eternal life, as I saw nothing else than God!"

Thus for the Sufis, God is not a far off, separate entity. It is that Reality which is all-pervading, irrespective of space and time. Nevertheless, this kingdom of God is within us and can be obtained by any one. The holy Quran declares, "Whosoever will try for me, I shall guide his steps" (24:69). It is said that Sufi mysticism originated with Caliph Ali, but Sufis of Bistamia, Bektashia and Naqshbandia consider Caliph Abu Bakr to be the originator. The Suharwardia order was founded by Ziauddin Najib Suhrawardi of the Junaidi clan. Another well-known order was that of the Qadiriyas. The Chishtiya order originated in India and was established by Muin-al-Din Chishti, and counted amongst its luminaries such personalities as Qutbal Din Bakhtiar Kaki, Feridal Din Ganjshakar, Nizam-al-Din Aulia, Shaikh Nasiral Din Chiragh, Saiyid Banda Nawaz Gesu Daraz and Shaikh Salim Chishti. The mystics of the Chishtiya order were upholders of the philosophy of absolute monism. They refused to accept any favour from kings and potentates and treated both the Hindus and the Muslims alike, giving them love and extending friendship and spiritual guidance without distinction.

The Sufi saints were men of great piety, determination and personal valour, and were imbued with missionary zeal to spread the Islamic message of peace and amity for all. They arrived in large numbers in the wake of Muslim invasions and the occupation of a large part of the country, specially in northern India which was undergoing a kind of spiritual crisis. Buddhism of the Mahayan variety, cloistered in monastic establishments, had lost touch with the masses and had failed in ministering to the spiritual needs of the people, being engaged in endless sectarian dialectic disputations on the nature of Nirvana, which was a state of pure nothingness (Sunyabacn, according to most of them, leading to a state of *apaiheia* among the people, a sign of the death-wish of the community. The death-knell of Buddhism in India was sounded after Hindu teachers like Sankar were able to show how the Hindu philosophy could fully contain whatever was taught by Buddha, and when the Buddhist seats of learning started declining and some of them got destroyed by invading armies. The end of the Magadhan empire of the Palas saw the last of the Indian kings professing Buddhism. Princes from the south like the Senas, and Rajput clans from the west and central India like the Chauhans, Gaikvads, etc, established small principalities in northern India and were no match to the deluge of invasions coming from across the west, and they finally went under, leaving behind utter confusion not only politically, but also in religious and social life. The Buddhist Palas were liberal in patronising both Buddhism and Saivism, which was then the rising Brahminical sect under which the rigours of social inequalities were not severe. The Brahminical orthodoxy which the Karnatak Princes from the south and the Rajput chiefs from the western India brought with themselves was socially iniquitous, the scales being heavily tilted against people belonging to the so-called lower order who were mostly of the occupational classes practising a mixed type of Hindu-Buddhistic beleifs. After defeat at the hands of the Muslims, orthodox Hindus, specially the Brahamins and Kshatriyas became all the more rigid and unbending, and caste rules became all the more severe; those who did not practise the rituals strictly, came to be looked down upon. Kulnism, that is, the ranking of Brahmins according to lineage, or pedigree, developed in Bengal and Mithila. Brahmins and people of even other higher castes were brought in from the south or from predominantly orthodox areas. Those ranking lower in the social or religious scale among the Hindus were now defenceless. Those not conforming to the orthodox Hindu practices were tolerated, but they were still discriminated against and the greatest sufferers were the erstwhile Buddhistic laity who had lost their social and spiritual moorings. There was a vacuum in their lives, and the Sufi saints of those days played the part of providing spiritual solace and succour.

The democratic spirit of Islam does not admit of any class distinction. The Sufis who were essentially men of peace, amity and toleration took special care to treat all alike, and did not practise any social discrimination against the Hindus, even of the lower order. This created a profoundly favourable impression specially on the erstwhile Buddhistic laity, who found in the Sufi practices an echo of their own philosophical beliefs. Adhering strictly to the obligatory duties and practices of his faith, the Sufi saint always kept the central vision of one Eternal Reality in view and the path he traversed was aimed at union with this Ultimate. The journey he undertook was essentially in the region of the heart, though intellect was not neglected, the traveller (Ravindgan) undergoing a rigorous discipline in pursuit of his objective of attaining unity with the Divine Reality. Nafskushi (control of senses) and Tawakkul (reliance on God) were essential aids. According to Abu Nasr al Sarraj, the seven stages through which a Sufi had to pass were (1) repentenee, (2) abstinence, (3) renunciation, (4) vow of poverty, (5) patience, (6) trust in God, and (7) satisfaction. It was difficult to go on such a path alone and unaided. A guide or Murshid was essential, like the Hindu Guru or Buddhistic Kalyanmitra. The veneration in which the Wali as Insan-i-Kamil or a perfect man was held in Sufi circles was something unique. The Hindus, however, had different categories of Gurus, the spiritual guide being only one of them. For the Sufis, the spiritual guide was the be-all and end-all of their existence, and thus arose the institutionalization of the seat of Walis as 'Khankahs', or monasteries, and the practice of veneration of shrines created on the tombs of Walis, and of pilgrimage and holding of annual Urs, etc, at these sites, For, even after death, the Wali was supposed to guide his followers. Just as in Hindu and Buddhistic ascetic orders, so in Sufism also stress is laid on the virtues of *rata* or resignation or quietism, *zuhd* or continence ill habits of life, *tajarrud* or observance of celibacy even in married life. The do's and don'ts of some of the Sufis' practice read more like the *vidhi* and *nishedh*, observance and prohibition amongst the Hindu ascetic orders.

The Sufis go far in emulating the yogic practices, the physiological and psychological practices prescribed for not only controlling the senses but also for attaining spiritual purity so as to make one deserving of attaining the supreme reality. Thus, Nabs-i-anfas, is nothing but the practice of *pranayarna*, - the basis for all physiological and psychological controls in Hindu and Buddhistic orders. It is believed that in the pursuit of the goal of divine union, the soul has to rest a while on the path of beatitude to renew strength for further pursuit; these resting places are called *chakras* in yogic literature. Six out of these chakras are recognised, but Buddhism finally recognises only four chakras, namely, Manipur (at the site of the navel), *anhat* (heart) *visuddh* (throat), and *sahasrarar* (crown of the head). The Sufis call these *mokams*. According to them, concentration or meditation on these mokams evoke certain spiritual conditions when the soul lays off its physical garments one by one and catches reflections of the Divine light. For correct appreciation of these states of self realization, the guidance of a spiritual teacher is considered necessary, rather compulsory.

However, for spiritual audition, the Sufis depend to a large extent on *zikr* or *jaap*, that is, chanting the name of Allah like '*La-ialha-ill-Allah*' which can be uttered all the time, in addition to salat i.e. namaz at the five fixed hours of the day. This was not an innovation, as *zikr* is enjoined in Islamic teachings. Besides individual zikr using rosary, the Sufis made congregational chanting of names , with accompaniment of music much popular as a means of cleansing the mind of evil thoughts, and filling it with remembrance of and 'gratitude to the Almighty'. Many Sufis started the practice of ceremonial piety, standing in a circle and then moving in circles, all the while chanting the name of Allah. Now, Islam, as such, is against instrumental music, and this was frowned upon by the orthodox. In the ninth century, Ibu Abit Dunya, wrote a treatise which linked musical audition with gambling, drunkenness, and fornication, as among the forbidden pleasures. However, this was stoutly opposed, amongst others, by the celebrated mystic and philosopher, Al-Ghazzali, who opined that music was fitting for the Muslims on seven distinct occasions; i.e., pilgrimage, war-songs, in the battle, lamentations for having committed sins, marriages and feasts, on occasions of love, and lastly, more importantly, to arouse longing for God. Others came to support this .view, particularly, Abd Rabbehi who wrote a scholarly treatise dealing with the origin of singing and argued cleverly from the Holy Quran, and the Hadith that it has had approval of the Prophet. Thus, the Sufis did not consider music to be un-Islamic, and their congregational chanting of names was a practice which caught on and made Islam popular amongst Indians.

Zikr was a step towards the ultimate object of filling the void in the heart with constant remembrance of Allah, which the Sufis called muraqaba or "Dhyan" However, Islam does not admit of any form in worship. God may be formless, but He is all-pervading, and man's heart is the nearest approach to his perception. The Holy Quran declares Allah to be the light of the earth and sky (*Allaho Nurassamvati wal Ard-Quran*). When Hazrat Ali was asked: "Can you see God?" the reply was: "How could one worship if one could not see the object of worship?" It is this faith in the inner light which is the key to realizing the divine being. A passage in the Holy Quran which says that the sun can be seen by its own light is the authority for the assertion that it is only by perceiving the inner light one can be conscious of the divine light. This process has been called firasat by the Sufis. It is this inner light which is the object of *zikr* and *muraqaba*. Then the whole being of the devotee is filled with divine light, When everything but the divine light is obliterated it is *fana;* and when even the consciousness of this obliteration ceases, it is *fana-ul-fana*. Oblivion of even the consciousness of oblivion is the real existence, *baqa* and then man becomes one with his Maker.

Thus, *muraqaba* or samadhi is a positive concept with the Sufis; there is nothing negative in this as in *sunyabad* of Buddhistic nirvan, or in 'ascension into eternity' of Sankar's monism. It is an emergence into altogether a new life divine, as the great Arabic Sufi poet, Shams-i-Tabriz has so eloquently expressed:

> "Lo! for I to myself am unknown - now in God's Name what must I do?
> I adore not the cross nor the crescent, I am not a Giour or a Jew.
> East nor West, Land or Sea is my home, I have kin nor with angel nor gnome
> I am wrought not of fire, nor of foam, I am shaped not of dust nor of dew,
> I was born not in China afar, not in Spain and not in Bulghar,
> Not in India where the five rivers are, nor Iraq nor Khorasan I grew.
> Not from Eden and Rizwan I fell, nor from Adam my lineage I drew
> In a place beyond uttermost place, in a tract without shadow of tree,
> Soul and body transcending, I live in the soul of my Loved one anew".

The Sufi lives in the soul of his Loved one anew, and drinks the nactar of eternal life of love. He has passed the four stages, namely, *jayrata* (waking), *swapna* (sleep), *sushupti* (dreamless sleep), and *turiya* (fourth state). The Vedantis refer them as *vaisvanara*, *tayasa*, *prajna* and *chaturtha*. In Sufi literature these are termed *nasut*, *jabrut*, *malakut*, and *lohut*. The discipline for reaching such state in both Hindu and Sufi meditative contemplation is similar, but the Sufi's ways are essentially those of the heart. When everything sensual and selfish has gone away what else can remain except love? This love in Sufi's heart is over abundant and ever flowing for the entire creation. When everything is His handiwork, how can a Sufi make distinction between man and man or even between man and beast? This love for God remains quiescent in the heart of the Sufi, but whenever by any external sight or sound he is reminded of God, he gets into a state of ecstasy. Music and poetry sung in praise of God were great stimulants, and it was a practice of Sufi saints to hold music sessions to create spiritual awakening among the people. They themselves became ecstatic in listening to the praise of God. According to Abu Nasal Sarraj, the Sufi had had to undergo much travail before being certain of the Love of Allah. The ten psychic states enumerated by him are: (1) meditation, which required constant *muraqbat*; (2) *muraqbat* automatically brought, in time, the feeling of being near to God; His presence became constant and unmediate to the Sufi; (3) feeling of nearness engendered love; (4) the attainment of the long sought feeling of love for God also sometime produced the feeling of fear that one may lose Him; (5) but then realising that mercy of Allah was immense, hope ever remained kindled in the heart; (6) this feeling of hope gave rise to longing for God; (7) constant longing made one intimate with the Divine presence; (8) once this intimacy was gained, one attained tranquillity; (9) tranquillity made the whole being of the Sufi contemplative: (10) and lastly he was certain of having attained the desired goal. These varying moods of the Sufi found tremendous expression in the writings and discourses of the Sufi saints, in prose and in verse, and we have one of the finest devotional literatures of the world in Sufi writings.

Though transmigration, that is *tanasukh*, does not form part of the teachings of Islam, we find a faint echo of this in the Sufi writings. Pythogoras of Egypt, under the influence of Hindu thought, was a believer in metempsychosis, the Persian Magi had adopted this doctrine, and the Sufi saints were sympathetic, but they did not develop it as a part of their essential teaching. A line from the *masnaui* of Maulana Rumi, the great Sufi saint-poet of Persia is generally quoted in this connection

"Haft sad Haftaad Qalib Dida am,
Hamchun sabza Barha Ruida am."

"I have witnessed seven hundred and seventy forms, I have grown so many times like vegetable plants."

However, the following full quotation from Rumi will show that he was more a believer in Irtiqa or evolution than in transmigration or metempsychosis:

"I died as an inanimate matter and arose as a plant; I died as a plant and arose again as an animal. I died as an animal, and arose as a man. Why should I fear to become less by dying? I shall die once again as a man to arise as an angel perfect from head to foot. I shall become what passes the conception of man. Let me then become non-existent. To Him shall I return."

Now this sentiment of returning to Him finally in a new life is not very different from what the Sufi call baqa or life divine. What Rumi is very definite and explicit about is the process of evolution of the soul. The above lines may be compared to the process of evolution as explained in the scripture of the Hindus, the Aitareya Brahmana:

"He who knows the atma as Him in manifestation, he most enjoys that manifestation. Herbs and trees and all that bear life, he knows as the self in manifestation. In herbs and trees, rasa (sap, life) is seen, and mind in them that have prana. In them that have prana, the atma is (more) manifest. In them rasa also is seen, while mind is not seen in the others. In man, the atma is (most) manifest, he is most supplied with knowledge; he speaks that which he knows the visible and the invisible; being mortal he desires the immortal. Thus supplied is he. But of the other animals, hunger and thirst are the only knowledge. They speak not the known; they see not the known; they know not what belongs to yesterday, nor the visible and the invisible; only this much have they. According to the knowledge are the births."

According to Hindu belief, the wandering of the seif from birth to birth stops only when the self considers itself one with the Maker. "United with Him he obtains immortality", as the Upanishad says. This is what the Sufi practices aim at. Thus both in respect of the destination as well as the wherewithals for attaining the same, the Hindu and Sufi meditative practices are almost the same. In such a situation the Sufis could not but wield enormous influence on Hindu thought and practices when they came to India to preach and spread their gospel. Islam shorn of ritual was then no more an alien philosophy for India. The Sufis by their humanitarian approach, examples of personal piety and probity, equal treatment to all high and low, co-religionists as well as those professing religion other than Islam made a profound impression on the Hindu psyche, and they did much to temper and lighten the stigma of Islam being the religion of invading marauders who sometimes thoughtlessly wounded Hindu religious susceptibilities in their flush of victory. With the extinction of Buddhism and the near chaotic position obtaining in Hindu religious ideas, specially in north India, a kind of bewilderment had overtaken both the elite and the masses of the region. The depopulation on account of constant warfare and the feeling of insecurity and helplessness engendered on account of easy victories of Turko-Afghan invaders had shaken their faith in Puranic legends and empty rituals ordained by the priests. As happens with live communities, the Hindus tightened their social defences more securely in these moments of despair and disaster: their rituals became all the more rigid, the taboos were enforced strictly, and views became more orthodox. The situation was, however, saved on account of two happy factors: one was the reformative breeze of *bhakti* and *samarpan* that was blowing from the south to the north but the other, and perhaps more important, was the broad humanitarian, democratic and electric beliefs and practices of the great Sufi saints whose advent in north India brought in waves of ennobling and elevating thought which could move the hearts of common people. This was happening during the Turko-Afghan as well as the Mughal periods.

Some of the Sufis were most remarkable personalities, saints in the true sense with great spiritual powers who could cast a spell on all those who came even casually into contact with them. Mention may particularly be made of Baba Farid of Punjab, Shaikh Ismail of purely Indian descent, again of Punjab, Syed Jalal Bukhari of Sindh, Mohammad Ghaus of Gawaliar, Nizamuddin Aulia of Delhi, Khawaja Chishti of Ajmer, Makhdoom Srarfuddin of Bihar, Shah Jalal of Sylhet and several others too numerous to mention. 'Their main contribution was to bridge the gulf between Hinduism and Islam, and to develop a common heritage for the Indian people, Hindus and Muslims. While not departing from Quranic injunctions, so far their own code of conduct was concerned, they showed that the spirit of Islamic teachings was universally applicable and no distinction need be made between man and man on account of his creed. As poet Saib has so eloquently expressed:

> *"Guftgu-i-Kufr-o-Din Akhir Ba Yakja mikashad - Khwab yak khwab Ast Amma Mukhtalif Taabirha"*.

> "All talks about faith and infidelity at last converge on one point - Dream is one but interpretations are many."

Thus, the Sufis believed that whatever the form, it was God who was worshipped in all religions and for authority relied on: *"Ainama Tuwallu Fa-samma Wajhullah."*

> "Whichever direction you turn your face, it is the face of Allah."

The Sufis, therefore, emerged as the best specimen of Islamic humanism. As against the Mullas who insisted on the letter of the tenets of Islam, the Sufis represented the spirit of the faith. A Sufi measured himself not by his knowledge but by his faith and devotion. He considered service to humanity without any distinction to be an essential duty for the discipline, its gains being superior to those of formal worship. He put aside his own desires to render himself agreeable to all, irrespective of caste and creed and was free from all complexes and shackles of colour and race. He believed in gentle persuasion and infectious examples and devotion rather than in mere dialectics and arguments to win others on his side.

They became, therefore, potent and effective propagators of Islamic faith in India. They could not but win the hearts of the simple folks of the country. They also promoted a spirit of love and liberalism among the Hindus and the Muslims. Mutual tolerance and respect for each other's faith permeated the general atmosphere of the country.

To sum up, their catholicity and fervent devotion to Reality, immanent in all things and to be known through divine illumination and grace; their exalted sense of moral duty and unblemished personal life; their ascetic practices similar to the yogis discipline of *pranayyam* and *samadhi*; their inspiring spiritual sessions for the masses through devotional music, all these strands of Sufism found an intimate echo in Hindu hearts and brought Islam in the broad spectrum of Indian ethos, liberating it from the vested interests of professional Mullas. Thus began the great reformation movement which was pioneered by seers like Kabir, Nanak, Tulsidas and Chaitanya, changing the tone and temper of the religious life of the Indian masses for the better.

Rights for Downtrodden

The concepts of secularisation as a process and secularism as an ideology and value system have been understood differently by different people. These concepts originated in the West. They are embedded in the Western cultural experience and religious traditions. In the West secular ideologies were often presented as antithetical to religious traditions and established order. They projected a just future based on rational principles. They also indicated certain definite changes that came about in the perspective and understanding of specific meaning systems of these cultures and religions, all of which had far-reaching consequences for the rest of the world. (Werblowsky, 1976:6)

Secularisation is part of a wider phenomenon which we may call globalisation. We do not live in fixed tents on an unmoving flat surface. We are part of an ever moving and ever changing universe in which social relations, social institutions and political structures are continually being transformed. Some of the changing social situations have been pluralism, especially, religious pluralism or rather the awareness of it, population growth, technological revolution, mass media, urbanisation, unequal power relations and inequalities between social groups. Globalisation can be understood as the process in which social groups, cultures, religions, political ideologies and nations are brought together and made more and more inter-dependent on one another. Secularisation can be understood as the process in which peoples and nations are challenged to take note of these social realities and to develop increasingly reflective self-awareness, critical understanding and scientific analysis of the historical process and the ability to transcend themselves and their meaning systems in order to be relevant in the new global village. However, instead of liberating and transforming peoples and nations, the process of globalisation and secularisation have often become instruments of exploitation in the hands of the powerful. In the following discussion we shall briefly look at the experience of the Dalit community in India's response to secularism.

The word "Dalit" also needs some explanation. Substantively, the word Dalit means "crushed", "broken", and refers to the social groups who, in the Hindu caste system, were called by various names such as the *panchamas* (the fifth born), the *anlyajas* (the last born), the *ashrishya* (the untouchable). The British referred to them as the Depressed Classes, or the Exterior Castes. Gandhiji called them Harijans (the people of God), which was not accepted by most Dalits. The Government of India Act 1935 gave them a new name, the Scheduled Castes, referring to the schedule prepared by the Government to list them, thus already suggesting a secular connotation. This term is still used in the Government documents. Finally, the term Dalit was introduced and was popularised by the Dalit Panthers at around 1970. This term, invented by the Dalits themselves, has become popular and is widely used today, gradually replacing all other terms. In recent years the term Dalit has been used not only to refer to those who were formerly called Untouchables but also the tribals and some of the most Backward Classes. Some have begun to use the term to refer to all those who are oppressed thus giving the term a more secular and class based meaning.

Backward People in Mainstream

The story of the Dalit struggle for equality can be traced back to the Aryan conquest of India. Our knowledge of the Aryan life and institutions is based on the Rigvedic hymns composed prior to 1000 B.C. From this literature it appears that the Aryans entered India in numerous small tribal groups at different times. They were mainly a cattle breeding people, but gradually took to agriculture, and settled in Ganga-Yamuna region (Basham, 1975). There were intense conflicts among the Aryan tribes as can be seen from the battle of Ten Kings, in which the King of the Bharat tribe defeated the confederacy of the ten tribes formed by Vishwamitra, and later the famous struggle at the Kurukshetra between the Kauravas and the Pandavas. But the main struggle was between the Aryans and the non-Aryans. Among the earliest Aryan tribes with whom the Aryans had to deal were the Panis and the Dasas also known as Dasyus. The Aryans, according to Thapar (1978) used iron and light spoke wheeled chariots. This seems to have given the Aryans a definite advantage over the indigenous people. From the later use of the word *dasa* to mean "slave" we know that the Aryans conquered and subjugated their first enemies.

In this historical process there was no secularisation or transcending narrow cultural boundaries but only a further tightening of a rigid caste system. An important distinction between the Aryans and the non-Aryan Dasas was their colour. The Dasas were of darker colour and flat features. The Aryans had fair skin and clear cut features. To add to this, the possession of a superior technology might have made the Aryans conscious of a superior power. The fear of losing their tribal identity, social customs, and religious practices might have heightened their sense of ritual purity, cultural superiority and political power. Society was thus divided into two main groups: the Arya varna and the Dasa varna. The Arya varna consisted of three social groups - the Brahmins, the Kshatriyas, and the Vaisyas. The Dasa varna consisted of the non-Aryans and were called Shudra.

As the Aryan tribes moved eastward along the Gangetic plain, they encountered other non-Aryan tribes, some of whom possessed powerful kingdoms (Magadha Andha, Vanga and Kalinga). The non-Aryans were now called *mlechchas* (the barbarians) and the region where they lived was called *mlechcha desha* in opposition to Aryavarth where the Aryans lived. The *mlechcha desha* became forbidden land. Those Aryans who ventured to associate themselves with the *mlechchas* lost their Aryahood and were treated as *mlechchas*.

A number of transformations took place in the Aryan society during this period. There was an increase in the agricultural activity. The increase in agriculture also brought an increase in trade. Many of the Shudras moved up on the social ladder and became cultivators. There was a gradual cultural fusion between the Aryan tribes and the powerful non Aryan tribes. A number of ruling non-Aryan tribes came to be accepted into the Aryan social system at various levels. "The degree of assimilation can be seen in the fact that the accepted lexicon, the Amarkosha, in its definition of *mlechchas* merely lists the three tribes - the Kirata, Pulinda, and Sabara" (Thapar, 1978:178)

The Shudra class itself gradually became divided into two groups - the clean Shudras and the ritually impure Shudras. The latter were identified as the fifth class (*panchamas*) and were relegated to do meanly jobs in society. The whole tribes - some of them were Nishadas, the (Ahandal, the Doms and the Ballas) became economically powerless, ritually polluting and social outcastes. For centuries they were condemned to live at the outskirts of the villages as untouchables exploited by the rest of the society. The process seems to have spread to South India integrating strong and powerful ruling groups into the Hindu caste system and relegating weaker groups to the status of social outcastes. The spread of Aryan power and culture in India was a process of globalisation in the sense that different peoples were put in contact with one another. At the same time it was a process which controlled and subjugated the non-Aryan peoples.

Dalits Mustering Courage

For centuries the Hindu religion and society kept the Dalits in the dustbin of the caste system. The Dalits themselves could not bring about a social and cultural revolution.

Hinduism underwent powerful anti-Brahman revolts in the form of Buddhism and Jainism. Buddhism, at least in principle, rejected caste distinctions and gave a better deal for the lower castes. The Bhakti movement in the fourteenth and fifteenth centuries gave rise to the poet Saints of Maharashtra among whom was Chokamela, an untouchable Mahar from Pandharpur (Zelliot, 1969).

The Muslim rule in India too was somewhat beneficial to the Dalits in so far as Islam professed an egalitarian philosophy (Mujeeb, 1967). Large number of untouchables embraced Islam hoping to overcome the social disabilities they suffered in Hinduism. However, the influence of Islam and of the Bhakti movement was limited. Bose (1959) suggests that neither Islam nor the Bhakti movement could seriously affect the existing social system because neither of them was able to initiate a new economic order. According to him, it was the economic changes which came about during the British period which initiated the social change that followed. The British social and political institutions were built on different foundations than those of Hinduism and gave rise to different consequences.

The first general condition which became beneficial to the Dalits during the British rule was the fact that the British did not practise untouchability. As a consequence, when new employment and educational opportunities became available in India, the Dalits were able to take advantage of the situation.

Some got employment in the households of Europeans, others got jobs in the railway or in the mills. Some of them got recruited into the army. Dr. Bhim Rao Ambedkar (1946) speaks of "a new vision and a new value" which, the opportunity of military service and education - made available to the soldiers and their families - gave to the untouchables. Some of the important leaders - Dr. B.R. Ambedkar, Dr. M.C. Raja from Madras, Babu Jagjeevan Ram - came from families which served in the army.

While the service in the army provided employment opportunities to the Dalits, the educational policy of the Government opened up a new chapter in their lives. In 1858, the government of Bombay announced that the government schools would be open to all classes. Very few Dalits were able to take advantage of the policy immediately, but it did give them a right which they had never possessed before and which they would increasingly take advantage of.

Another factor which deeply affected the future of the Dalits was the new legal system initiated by the British in India. The equality principle of the British legal system set in motion a social revolution among the Dalits. Although, for various reasons, its awareness and affirmation among the Dalits was slow to manifest themselves, the new law provided them with a new symbolic world view and a new self-image. It also offered them "a new prestigious alternative to the traditional values of caste." (Galanter, 1972)

While the British legal system laid the foundation of equality before the law for the Dalits, the Christian missionaries contributed in a significant way to move the principle of equality from the realm of theory to that of practice. It is generally agreed that it was the Christian missionaries who first started social work among the Dalits in India, and that the work of the Indian Reformers for the uplift of the Dalits (Brahma Samaj, Prarthana Samaj, Arya Samaj) came as a response to the missionary challenge. (Sondhi, 1977) The widespread social and educational institutions and activities of the Christian missionaries were primarily directed to the advancement of the Dalits. These initiatives for which they had often to fight with the British Government both in India and back at home in England went a long way to build up critical self-awareness, self-image and self-identity among the Dalits.

The external factors - the British policies, the Christian missionaries and the nationalist reform movements - had widespread effects on the Dalits. The effects can be seen in their renewed attempts of social mobilisation, manifestations of social protest, political mobilisation and their more and more articulate claims to be part of the nation-building process. The earliest expressions of this can be seen in their attempts to improve their status within the existing social order. M.N. Srinivas (1952) has described this process as Sanskritisation. Soon, status seeking was replaced by various forms of mobilisation and political action. The social movements which appeared among the Dalit communities announced a new era of social mobility for them. Some of these movements were the Satnami movement in the Chattisgarh area of Madhya Pradesh, the Mahar Conference of Maharashtra, the Jatva Vir Maha Sabha of Agra, the Adi Dravida Mahajana Sabha of Madras, the All Bengal Namasudra Association, the Depressed India Association of Bombay, and the Paraya Mahajana Sabha of Madras. The social awakening and protest movements among the Dalits were resulted from the British colonial rule. The British left the Hindu religion and society more or less untouched, but controlled the economic, political and legal systems and replaced them by the British system. This was bad for India, for it brought India under the colonial rule. It was good for the Dalits, for, it weakened the hold of internal colonialism of Hindu religion and society over them. In the case of the Dalits, the British system unwittingly challenged the Hindu religious value systems and opened up new secular vistas for the Dalits which were beyond the control of the traditional Hindu value system.

Awareness for Political Rights

On August 20, 1917, Edwin Montagu, then Secretary of State for India announced in the House of Commons a new policy of His Majesty's Government towards India. The policy envisaged "increasing association of Indians in every branch of the administration and the gradual development of self governing institutions with a view to progressive realisation of responsible government." (Ambedkar, 1946: 16)

Recognising the ongoing political awakening, the Gaekwad of Baroda said: "In the political world a struggle has commenced for wider self-government and greater social equality. The same principles which impel us to ask for political justices for ourselves, should actuate on to show social justice to each other... By the sincerity of our efforts to uplift the depressed classes we shall be judged fit to achieve the objects of our national desire." (*The Indian Review*, December 1909)

After his announcement, Montagu with the Viceroy of India, Lord Chelmsford, made an all-India tour hearing testimonies from Indian groups on their wishes for the forthcoming reforms. Out of 21 representations made by low caste groups, at least eleven represented the depressed classes. As a result of this and other pressures from the depressed classes groups, a number of depressed class members were nominated to the Legislative Councils and in 1927 M.C.Raja of Madras was also nominated to the Central Legislative Council. These events had an electrifying effect on the Dalit community.

In 1928, the Indian Statutory Commission was appointed with Sir John Allsebrook Simon as the Chairman to evaluate the parliamentary reforms of the previous ten years. The Simon Commission toured India and received representations from various groups. The Congress Party boycotted the Commission but the Dalit communities everywhere came forward to make their representations.

During the Simon Commission, ,the Government had announced that, after the work of the Commission was over., the Indian representations would be assembled for a discussion on the future Constitution of India. Accordingly, three Round Table Conferences were held in London from the fall of 1930. Two Dalits, Dr. B. R. Ambedkar from Bombay and Rao Bahadur R.Sriniwasan from Madras, were chosen to represent the Dalit community at the Round Table Conference. Recalling this event with pride, Ambedkar later commented: "For the Untouchables, it was a landmark in their history. For, the Untouchables were for the first time, allowed to be represented separately by two delegates in the framing of the Constitution of India." (Ambedkar, 1946:40)

Special Status

On January 24, 1947, the Constituent Assembly appointed an Advisory Committee on Minorities with Sardar Vallabh Bhai Patel as the Chairman. This Committee prepared a list of seven minority communities (Anglo Indians, Parsees, Plain Tribesmen in Assam, Indian Christians, Sikhs, Muslims and Scheduled Castes). Commenting on the problem of the minorities Sardar Patel clarified the view of the Committee. "We wish to make it clear, however, that one general approach to the whole problem of minorities is that the State would be so run that they would stop feeling oppressed by the mere fact that they are minorities and that, on the contrary, they should feel that they have as honourable a part to play in the national life as any other section of the Community. In particular, we think it is a fundamental duty of the State to take special steps to bring up these minorities which are backward to the level of the general community (Kananaikil, 1982:15). The committee after "exhaustive discussion," on August 8, 1947, recommended reservation of seats in the legislatures for the minorities on the basis of their population. Commenting on the recommendation of the Advisory Committee on Minorities, Mr. V.I. Muniswami Pillai from Madras, who represented the Scheduled Caste, stated that "the Untouchables who form one sixth of the population of this sub-continent are a minority community, because their social, political and educational advancement is in a very low state." (Kananaikil, 1982:15)

The Outcastes

The Government of India Act, 1935, replaced the term Depressed Classes by "Scheduled Castes" and defined it in terms of castes, races and tribes. It did not include religion as a defining feature of the Scheduled Castes. However, the accompanying Government of India (Scheduled Castes) Order, 1936, introduced a new clause: "Notwithstanding anything contained in the last preceding para (a) no Indian Christian shall be deemed to be a member of a Scheduled Caste." Thus, for the first time, a religious criterion was introduced into a Government document to define the Scheduled Castes.

The consequence of introducing a religious criterion into the definition of the Scheduled Castes was not immediately felt since all the religious groups were given political representation. The situation changed drastically after Independence.

The communal riots, large population movement and the partition of the country that took place at the dawn of India's Independence, made the Advisory Committee on Minorities, and the members of the minority communities themselves to recommend dropping all reservations for minorities.

It was at this stage that Mr. K.M. Munshi from Bombay introduced an amendment calling for the deletion of number seven of the Schedule which enumerated the Scheduled Castes as a minority and asked for the inclusion of a new clause making the Scheduled Castes a section of the Hindu community. The amendment also asked for the extension of the benefits of reservation for them for ten years. The amendment was passed without much discussion. Neither Dr. Ambedkar nor the minority communities seemed to be aware of the consequences of this amendment.

Article 341 of the Constitution empowered the President of India to identify the castes, races or tribes which shall for the purpose of the Constitution be deemed to be Scheduled Castes. Exercising this power, the President of India, issued the Constitution (Scheduled Castes) Order 1950. Para 3 of this order stated: "Notwithstanding anything contained in para 2, no person who professes a religion different from Hinduism shall be deemed to be a member of a Scheduled Caste."

In 1956, due to pressure from the Sikh community, the Presidential Order was amended to include Scheduled Castes converted to Sikhism as Scheduled Castes. In 1991, the Order was again amended to include Scheduled Castes converts to Buddhism as Scheduled Castes. The demands from other minority communities to recognise Scheduled Castes converted to other religions as Scheduled Castes have been ignored so far.

The historical events narrated above indicate that the Aryan invasions of India controlled and subjugated the Dalits. The powerful social and cultural institutions built up by the Aryan society reduced the Dalits to the status of untouchables. Subsequent interventions on the Indian society by outside forces can be seen as a process of secularisation in the sense that such interventions weakened and, in some cases, replaced the hold of the Aryan (Hindu) social, cultural and religious institutions on the Dalits and paved the way for more rational laws and institutions. Each time, however, the new laws were manipulated or re-interpreted by the powerful groups to suit their own self-interests.

The Safeguards

The Constitution of India declares: "We the people of India, having solemnly resolved to constitute India into a Sovereign, Socialist, Secular, Democratic, people and to secure to all its citizens:

> Justice, social, economic and political
> Liberty of thought, expression, belief, faith and worship
> Equality of status and of opportunity and to promote among them all
> Fraternity assuring the dignity of the individual and the unity and integrity of the nation... we do hereby adopt, enact and give to ourselves this constitution.

This resolve has been further articulated in various Articles of the Constitution. Clarifying the issue of reservation in the Constituent Assembly Dr. Ambedkar had pointed out that there were two principles which they were trying to reconcile. These were the principle of equality and merit, on the one hand, and the principle that those who belong to backward communities would not be able to get justice by themselves without some state protection. Reservation, therefore, can be looked upon as a form of distributive justice made necessary for the weaker sections to claim justice before the law. However, for many in the Constituent Assembly reservation meant privileges granted to the Dalits which should be discontinued at the earliest time.

A number of provisions have been included in the Constitution for the Dalits. These provisions can be divided into (a) General provisions (b) Directive principles (c) Specific provisions for the Dalits. Some of the specific provisions are Articles 15(4) which empowers the Government to make special provisions for the advancement of the Dalits.

1. Article 17 which abolishes the practice of untouchability. Article 46 which directs the state to promote the interests of the Dalits.

2. Article 330 to 332 which provide for reservation for the Dalits in the Parliament and in the Legislative Assemblies.

3. Article 335 which provides for reservation of services and posts.

4. Article 338 which provides appointment of special officer for the Dalits.

5. Article 341 which empowers the President of India to specify the Dalits.

What are the results of all this? No one can deny that some good has been done. The Constitution of India was a gigantic step in the process of secularisation for the Dalits. In whatever way the Hindu society looks at them, the Dalits today are citizens of India with equality with all others. The abolition of the practice of untouchability has restored their dignity at least in principle.

The reservation of seats in the Parliament and in the Legislative Assembly has given them representation even if in practice they are not yet able to raise their voice effectively for the community they represent. The reservation of jobs and seats in the educational institutions has given them a semblance of representation although they have still a long way to go. The Government programme for the benefit of the Dalits have done some good, but for the most part the resources have been eaten up by the middlemen leaving the community far behind in literacy and education, in poverty alleviation, and economic development.

However, the future of the Dalits will be largely decided by the Dalits themselves - by their ability to organize themselves and to build up their power in order to effectively intervene in the globalisation and secularisation process. Dr. Ambedkar was fully aware of this. He knew that it was not by the upper castes people doing penance for their sins that the lot of the Dalits will change but by the Dalits organising themselves into a viable force.

Dr. Ambedkar realized the importance of Dalits becoming a political force. He felt that separate electorate for the Dalits would have been the best way to build up their political power, but he did not succeed in this. Gandhiji undertook a fast unto death in order to oppose separate electorate for the Dalits.

Dr. Ambedkar realized that caste and the practice of untouchability were basic to Hinduism and hence he felt that no good can come about for the Dalits from Hinduism. Dr. Ambedkar was a religiously liberated man. His religion was a secular religion. He said that he was born a Hindu but it was not his fault. However, he said that he would not die a Hindu, because it was in his power. He exhorted his followers to renounce Hinduism and to choose a religion of their choice, a religion that was liberal and secular.

Ultimately, as the spirit of globalisation and secularisation envelopes the peoples and nations of the world stage. With the big players and the small players in the arena, it is those who stand and watch, who can make the difference. All of us who are in some way the fence sitters are challenged to take a stand for the Dalits in their struggle to make their voice heard.

Nine

Evil from the West

No alien rule can continue unless it acquires some sort of legitimacy in the eyes of the ruled. The concept of legitimacy is complex and involves many diverse factors - both ponderables and imponderables. Fortunately for the British, history in the eighteenth century was being shaped by contending peers who were all adventurers themselves, Alivardi in Bengal, Sa'adat and Safdar Jung of Oudh, Saifuddulah in the Punjab, and the Nizamu-ul-Mulk, Hyder Ali and Tipu Sultan in the south. The English merchant adventurers from 'across the seven seas' alongwith merchant adventurers from other European nations, also entered the fray, and were accepted as amongst the contending forces. All these native adventurers sought or pretend to seek and derive authority from the Mughal Emperor at Delhi - a phantom of former entity, but still a figure which represented legitimacy to rule over the country. Hence when the English, after defeating the combined armies of Emperor Shah Alam, Nawab of Oudh and Mir Kasim of Bengal, at Buxar in 1764 A.D., forced Shah Alam to grant them the Diwani of Bengal in 1765 A.D., their claim to rule over India, or a part of India acquired legitimacy in the eyes of the people of this country.

However, legitimacy is one thing, and acceptability is another. It is astounding how, in spite of impoverishing and wrecking the economy of Bengal — both agricultural and industrial—resulting in widespread misery, recurring famines, large-scale unemployment and virtual serfdom of a large part of the population, English rule in Bengal came to be hailed as dawn of a new era, the image being promoted by British historians, and their adherents amongst Indian writers, including many from Bengal itself. The image was cherished, supported and made an accepted reality by the new middle class, of landowners, lawyers and civil servants, who gained under the new dispensation, while the masses of Indian people sank under poverty and degradation. The rationale of this assertion is not difficult to fathom. Bengal has had a history of acting independently of the rest of India since long. Nestled in the far eastern corner of the country, a land of rivers, rivulets and swamps, where the bounties of nature are generous and plentiful, giving life a romantic halo of ease and luxury and where people are endowed with a refined taste which expresses itself in weaving magic webs of incomparable beauty and grace on the loom as well as in patterns of thought, Bengal has always behaved and acted as if it was a self-sufficient unit of the country. Most of the time it remained independent of the authority at Delhi; even when it acknowledged its authority formally it had had its own identity, duly recognised by the central authority. While the rulers were always Muslims except for a brief period, soldiering was left to the Muslims and Bihari Hindus as can be witnessed by a large number of Hindu 'Majumdars' (Zamindars), Brahmin 'Khans', 'Mustafis', 'Biswas', 'Buxi', Mullicks', etc. While the farmers were mostly Muslims, majority of rent-collectors (Zamindars) under the Muslam Nawabs were Hindus; so also, while the artisans were mostly Muslims, the trade was in the hands of the Hindus. While the different avocations were shaped largely by fixed social groups, the society was on the whole harmonious. However, the British administration, tried its best to disturb this social and economic equilibrium, bringing ruin and destitution to a large number of people but benefiting a few; this minority could hail the English rule as a civilizing and a modernizing influence.

In the Indian economic system, land was considered to be a gift of God, and only right of possession was recognised, this possession being regulated by custom and in certain cases by governmental authority. The State was entitled to a share of the produce for its regulatory and peace-keeping functions. The 'Khas' land of the rulers were as much a part of this system as that of a farmer; the title of the ruler to land was not recognised as such, as even for 'Khas' land, right of possession could be claimed if it remained in possession of a farmer for a long or stipulated period. In the feudal and manorial and later on squarichal system in England, the situation was totally different. In theory the land belonged to the Lord of the Manor or of the Squire who leased land on rental basis, rent being increased or decreased according to circumstances, the only exception being the Yeomen, who possessed right to land on a fixed basis or held land even freehold for historical reasons. The English in India by one stroke changed the customary land tenure in Bengal and introduced a system which was in essence the old English manorial system, with local variations and modifications. The old rent collecting agents called Zamindars as well as the new entrants were declared tenure-holders on stipulated payment of a fixed permanent revenue. They became owners of the land, in theory and in fact. The actual farmers became tenants at will, who could be ejected from possession of land for non-payment of rent and in many cases, at the sweet will of the Zamindar. Later, Government tried to regulate the rights of the Zamindars and the tenants, but these were tilted largely in favour of the Zamindars. The old village communal system based on custom and usage was given a complete go-by and the peasants were reduced to quasi-serfdom. The governmental rent collecting authority created by the English was also vested with magisterial and judicial powers and the whole purpose of governmental machinery was geared towards collection of revenue peacefully and with minimum of effort and in this the active help of the zamindars was expected, who became strong pillars of the new government. This was the colonial pattern of administration which the English had borrowed from the Dutch, in this case from the Dutch colonial system of administration in the Spice Islands - with such modifications and variations as appeared to them to be warranted by local conditions.

Legal Niceties

The English, unlike the Dutch, however, were great sticklers for form and legal niceties. The boast of the Englishman is that he is governed by law and law alone, and it is law that determines ultimately social and economic relationship. The rentier system of rural economy in England had given rise to a great amount of litigation - litigation between landlord and landlord, between landlord and peasants and between peasants and peasants, for rights, title and sometimes for rent only. The common law being a law of right, usage, and practice, unless modified by statutory law, required judicial interpretation, had judge-made law based on precedents and re-interpretation became a complicated and technical affair, par excellence, requiring expert knowledge. Since both the judges and the lawyers - mostly younger sons of the nobility - came from the same class, lawyers in England came to acquire great prestige and command handsome remuneration. Law, diplomacy, and administration became the preserve of the governing class in England. The English by introducing the tenure-holding system and later on in rest of the territories they conquered in its modified form, called the Ryotwari System, gave rise to a distinct class in India too. Lawyers became the de facto interpreters of the Indian's needs, sentiments and aspirations to the alien Government and purveyors of English institutions and English ideas to the Indian people. Law and politics became synonymous and the legal profession became the E1 Dorado of every educated Indian. The English encouraged this class by enacting the Earnings by Learning Act which ensured possession of one's own earnings irrespective of anything contrary in the personal law. The lawyers, in course of time, came to be the most affluent professional class, the better among them earning and building up large fortunes. It is not surprising that the English rule was the dawn of a new era for them.

Interests of the English

The main interest of the English in India had been trade and commerce, but in spite of being the clothiers of Europe, they could not sell their heavy and coarse cloth, both cotton and woollen, in India for which there was virtually no demand. Thus, the main interest of the English commercial class was "to purchase cheaply in India and to sell dearly abroad." But the English manufactures at home in England were so jealous of Indian goods that by Parliamentary legislation in 1700 and 1720 cotton and silk goods imported from India "could not be worn or otherwise used in England." However, even in 1832, the parliamentary Committee discussing the renewal of East India Company's Charter noted that: "our stately fops admire themselves better in an Indian dressing gown than in one made at Spitalfields." When the English came to acquire power, first in Bengal and gradually in rest of the country, they utilised their authority in forcing the artisans to sell their exquisite products below the cost price, sometimes as low as one-fifth of the manufacturing by entering into unequal forward contracts for supplying manufactured articles, and in case of failure to subject them even to bodily punishments like flogging. The Indian merchants were forced to act as their brokers, and to borrow from the Company and its servants at usurious rate of interest. The Zamindars, many of them showy, extravagant and profligate, also used to borrow money from the English, mortgaging their estates. The mortgagers ultimately owned the estates and the English forced the peasants to grow commercial crops like cotton, indigo, coffee, rubber and tea and then purchased the commodities at throw-away prices and paid poor wages to the labourers working on such plantations. The whole industrial pattern of the country thus lay in ruin being geared to the profit-making ends of the new mercantile masters; the result was that artisans became labourers, and the prosperous Indian merchants became the agents and brokers of the English merchants. The new land-holding class became almost parasitical, the old communal accountability having gone out of the system. They were given to a life of ease and indolence in the capital town of Calcutta and other provincial towns. Land improvement ceased to receive any attention, methods of cultivation were not modernised, farmers were reduced to be peasants, and peasants became seasonal labourers. The Indian peasant became something like the *jacquerie* of the pre-revolutionary France. Unemployment became a regular feature of the economy. Such widespread misery of the rural population had never been known in the long history of India, not even when it had been subjected to periodical attacks by marauders from outside.

In the meantime, England in reverse proportion was ascending to new heights of prosperity. The Englishman, then, and perhaps even now, is a country-loving creature; he pines for the sights, sounds and the smells, the scent and peculiar odours of the country side. The English aristocracy, unlike that in France and other continental countries, was not confined to those born in it; its portals could open for those who could acquire riches and prestige enough in any walk of life. Thus, many English adventures, returning from India, gorged with ill-gotten wealth and called 'Nabobs' invested freely in the countryside and "raised the price of fresh eggs of rotten boroughs." This gave a fillip to the 'agricultural revolution' of the eighteenth century, which preceded and supplemented the Industrial Revolution. Vast improvements were made in methods of cultivation. The 'enclosure' movement made capital investment in agriculture possible, leading to modernization of techniques and large scale farming. Lands were enclosed, drained, manured, and cultivation of turnip and clover and grass and herbs for flattening cattle and sheep was developed. There was now no starving of cattle in winter and it was no longer a case of "from Christmas to May, old cattle decay". The change has been rightly called an Agricultural Revolution. New methods of improved cultivation like Arthur Young's rotational method of cropping, use of horses instead of oxen for ploughing, introduction of multipurpose 'drill' for sowing by a Botanist, Jethro Tull, were some of the methods employed and agriculture became completely capital-intensive, bringing in its train new prosperity in the countryside and opening way to an Industrial Revolution in which a large number of labourers released from intensive farms could be employed gainfully. A series of inventions had set England to an Industrial Revolution, almost a century ahead of its continental competitors, and with Indian industries ruined, now cloth came to be imported in India from Lancashire, and cotton— its price in India artificially depressed— was exported out of India. British ascendancy was complete, both politically and economically.

However, it was in the field of intellectual subjection of India that England seems to have scored a remarkable victory. The turmoil in which the country had been plunged due to the weakening of the central authority at Delhi, which was inexplicable to the common mind, the easy victories which the alien merchant-adventurers secured against the numerically superior native forces, the predatory nature of force employed by the native princes against each other, the cultural degradation of the contending elite of the country — each of these in itself and collectively — had a profound effect on the minds of the Indian and raised doubts about the adequacy of their own age long beliefs and institutions.

In Bengal, and in many parts of the country, with the beginning of English rule the nightmare of Maratha raids was, however, over, and people heaved a sigh of relief. The uneasy calm of the British rule was thus preferable to the turbulence of the native rule in the common mind yearning for peace. Indian masses are not afraid of want and poverty, as these have been considered badges of a spiritual life; what they want is peace and tranquillity to pursue the avocations which fate has willed them. This feeling, no doubt is universal in character; but more so in India where spiritual life is valued more than mere existential life. During the times India was passing into the hands of the British, the masses looked inward to the mirage of a golden past, which, perhaps, existed more in imagination than in reality. On the other hand, the new elite - the tenure-holders, the lawyers, the neo-merchants and above all the native service-holders - who were being increasingly employed by the alien rulers due to exigencies of ever-expanding administration and English trade and commerce, after passing out from English medium schools and colleges, were exposed to western thought and institutions and the methods of administration, and civil and military organization. They became unduly conscious of inadequacies of their own social and institutional life, as victims of the stagnation of their thought processes.

England, in the previous two three centuries had been fortunate in producing great men in every walk of life, in literature, politics, administration, science and practical philosophy of life. The array of luminaries was indeed impressive for any age or any country. The highest products of the human mind have been said to be the outcome of chance, and sometimes, of needs, but chance perhaps favours those whom it intends to make great and also those who deserve. England was favoured by chance no doubt, but England at this period of time also deserved the pre-eminence she attained in many fields of life. She had both freedom and variety; she had liberty and authority co-existing; she had rule of law but also national discipline to observe its parameters; she had a privileged class but this class did not close its doors against outsiders who too deserved the privileges; and masses and classes of society respected and accommodated each other. The happy fusion of local autonomy with national authority as well as of individual liberties with social responsibility, or individual initiative and enterprise within bounds of collective good, had given her a vitality not only to garner wealth from the four corners of the world, but also made the minds of her sons to soar high in realms of thought and invention. The new emerging Indian elite, both Hindu and Muslim, could not but be impressed. At the same time, however, it engendered in them a feeling of inferiority vis-a-vis their rulers. The English tried their best to cultivate an aura of their own innate superiority and invincibility, debunking in the process the Indians, and their institutions. A romantic aloofness, both personal and social, was deliberately cultivated by the English administrators as if the very presence of the inferior race of Indians would defile the lily white of their skin, specially after the 1857 events which had exposed their feet of clay. However, it must be said to their credit that even most of the riff-raff who came out to India began to act as models of bravery and chivalry, east of Suez, trying to keep back their knavery and depravity, west of Suez. The apparent looked real to the Indians, stamping on their minds the feeling of racial superiority of the English. In commercial transactions, too, honesty became their best policy.

Ethos of a Race

The ethos of a race or a nation is a continuum: it is rooted in the past, it shapes the present, and is an inspiration for the future. The sure way to subjugate a race is to shatter its pride in its ethos, or, at least, to raise a question mark over it. One of the ways is to distort history. In the phrase of Matthew Arnold, history then tends to be 'Mississipi of falsehoods'. The British undertook the task of reconstruction of Indian history, and they led the educated with their own fables and myths in regard to events in India. Having been engaged in mutual religious strife and in ruthlessly eliminating their religious adversaries over the centuries, they could never conceive it as true that in the long history of India there had not been any religious wars as such. The tribals from Central Asia who poured into the country through north-west from time to time came in to settle down and were absorbed in the mainstream in course of time. That in the last few hundred years they had turned into Muslims had not altered the character of their raids, settlement and absorption which was a picture unacceptable to the British. Thus, in Indian history, according to British historians, there was a "Hindu period" and "a Muslim period". By the same analogy the British Raj should have been termed as a 'Christian period'. The English were not unaware of the great contribution Islam had made to the march of human civilization, its glory and power, its democratic spirit, its enunciation of principles of equality, its catholicity and spirit of accommodation. Yet they tried to suggest subtly that Islam stood for intolerance and violence, by painting the Muslim kings and potentates as so many blood-thirsty tyrants bent upon oppressing and decimating non-believers, and showing the average Muslim as overzealous and fanatical, always at logger heads with his Hindu neighbours. The Hindus were painted as ignorant, superstitious, meek, mild and weak, whose lot was enslavement still the English had so generously come and liberated them by enslaving both the Hindus and the Muslims and by restoring hence an order in the country and separating the warring Hindus and Muslims. Not that they were not aware of the glories of India. For example, we find Lord Hastings, declaring in 1786, "the writers of the Indian philosophies will survive, when the British dominion in India shall long have ceased to exist, and the sources which it yielded of wealth and power are lost to remembrance." But this knowledge was thrown outside the wind when they tried to rewrite for us the history of India.

The westerners first became aware of the depth, subtlety, and sublimity of Vedantic thought through the excellent Persian translation of 50 Upanishads by Dara Shikoh, that prince among scholars and scholar among princes, who had translated them with the help of his Sufi mentor, Mulla Shah Mohammad of Badakshan, himself a great scholar of Sanskrit and Persian. Since then interest in India had become widespread in England and on the continent and scholars armed with study of antiquities and with new and improved methodology poured into the country to discover for themselves her past glories and present plight. No doubt this engendered a new awareness and confidence among the Indians, but one pernicious effect was that they began to look for enlightenment and guidance from the Westerners with a sneaking admiration for the western institutions exclusively. The European observers tried their best to imply that the genius of Hindu enlightenment and culture had got stilled, if not destroyed by the Muslims. This was one of the premises on which they tried to build up the myth of Hindu and Muslims as being two mutually distinct and hostile religious groups inhabiting the country.

Another of the myths carefully fostered was that India was never one entity in its long history, the picture of a perpetually war-torn, mutually hostile kingdom. This was partly true in the sense that there were many political divisions in the country, but it was false in the sense that these political divisions were in any way, distinct racial, ethnic or even religious groups. As we have been emphasising, the political arrangements in India were considered accidental to fortunes of war and peace; they had never interfered with the feeling of living in one country, in spite of immense diversities in language, belief, and social groupings of the people. From the Himalayas to the seas, from the borders of Afghanistan or even part of the modern Afghanistan to the eastern part of the country on the Bay of Bengal, *"a sang ta bahere sangin"* (from the Himalayas to the great sea beyond), as one Persian writer has beautifully put it—India, was one. Even in the political field the theory of Chakrauartiya or Jehangiri was prevalent. The idea was something like Paramountcy which the English claimed to have in exercise of their sovereign power in India even when a good part of the country was not under their direct rule. Besides every inch of the land was sacred to the Hindus and the Muslims alike, being dotted with sacred places, monuments, *dargahs* and *khankahs*. Political division was a nuisance but never a hinderance for visitors from one part of the country to another part. For example, Chaitanyadev, who was a subject of Husain Shah of Bengal in conflict with the Hindu king of Orissa - the traffic between the two being strictly prohibited - did, nevertheless, travel without hindrance to and from Bengal and Orissa and later on into Southern India then under different political regimes. Similarly, Guru Nanakdev travelled to every nook and corner of the country, and wrote his devotional poems "Pran Sangli' in Ceylon which was brought to India at the instance of Guru Arjandev, the fifth Guru. According to tradition, the Tamilian Alwar devotional singers got their inspiration initially on a visit to far-away Ayodhya on pilgrimage. The cultural unity of India was obvious.

As we have explained in some detail, India was one unit economically and commercially also, during the sixteenth and seventeenth centuries in spite of political divisions. This was not the case on the continent of Europe where there were trade barriers, and restriction on travel; in many cases, even between cities under the same kingdom - the whole of Europe being divided into so many kingdoms, principalities, dukedoms, etc, - England and Scotland were not united till the beginning of the eighteenth century, and even when united, the English sneered at the quaint and queer ways and parsimonious habits of the Highlanders, the latter registering their protest in sullen resentment and holding more strongly to their own 'quaint and queer' ways. It was the prosperity which England earned (through her Colonies) and shared with Scotland which could keep the union going. Ireland, on the other hand, has been treated more like a colony than a real part of the British Isles. As for Wales, though it is fully integrated now, but the word 'Welsh' as a verb still means for, 'to run off from a race-course without settling or paying for one's bets perhaps is allusion to the alleged bad faith of Welshmen and shows in what contempt the English held the people of Wales initially. Strong parochial feelings exist in Scotland and Ireland even now against England's dominant position.

It must however, be conceded that in India, the intelligentsia in the nineteenth century was profoundly influenced by the movements for national unification going on in Europe at that time, and specially the Italian unification movement under Mazzini and Garibaldi. This gave to the Indian people the vision of a strong, national state one unified political authority, and in course of time this was to became a national obsession. The wind of liberalism and humanism then blowing in England in the wake of her unprecedented prosperity gave to India new concepts in social and political organization. The fiery speeches of Burke, the anti-slavery movement of Wilberforce, the evangelical spirit of Dissenters in England preaching human values, the enshrinement of personal liberty and freedom through judicial pronouncements, the passionate advocacy of rule of law by Coke and others - all these combined to create the ideals of liberal democracy which became a desirable goal to be cherished by English educated Indians. This was re-inforced by the publication of John Stuart Mill's *Liberty* (1859) and *Subjection of Women* (1869) attacking the bondage of convention, and proclaiming the rights of individual men and women. Mill's ideas have ever remained in the minds of western educated Indians, germane to the issues of personal liberty and specially the social emancipation of women. Thus, by the beginning of twentieth century, parliamentary democracy based on adult franchise came to be recognised as the most desirable form of government - the goal for which the Indians were urged to strive.

In their enthusiasm, the nationalist forces which had come largely to be dominated by educated Hindus, overlooked or neglected to consider certain stark realities. The Muslims, as a religious group, were an important segment in Indian body politic. They had exercised dominant political power specially in the north for the last few centuries, and the crown of India, however titular or symbolic, had passed from the head of a Muslim Emperor to the British king. The Muslims as a class had suffered most from occupation of the country by the English. The ruin of Indian village industries meant the ruin of majority of Muslim artisans, whose traditional occupations were destroyed. The recruitment in the British army was selective and discriminatory and the Muslims, being looked upon with suspicion, were ignored. In agriculture, too, the lower class Muslims had their share in the cup of woes under the tenure-holder system introduced and implemented by the English. The economic and social condition of the upper class Muslims also worsened. Being mostly a land-owning aristocratic class, of both indigenous and foreign extraction, given to soldiering, administration or diplomacy, they lost their pre-eminence in all the fields in which they had excelled so far. In Bengal, as we have already seen, the lower echelon of civil service under the Muslim Nawabs was occupied by Hindus of certain castes. As the British rule expanded, Brahmins, Kayasthyas, Vaidyas and Khatris in the north, and Brahmins, Nayyars, Reddys, Deshmukhs and Methas in the south, took to English education in a big way, occupied lower positions in service and began to clamour for higher posts. The Muslim upper class, fitted by aptitude and training only for higher positions found their entry almost barred since these were not available to Indians. Sullen and resentful at having lost their former pre-eminence and proud of their traditions and heritage, they could not bring themselves easily to the apposition of hewers of wood and drawers of water, and they simply neglected to take advantage of the English system of education to the extent the Hindus had done. However, when towards the close of the nineteenth century, it became clear that due to the new spirit of liberalism that was prevailing in England, the rulers wanted to associate Indians in Government increasingly through elected representatives and to open to them gradually even higher posts of administration, the disadvantage of the Muslims as a class became clear. Not only they were numerically weaker but also backward educationally in relation to the Hindus. A feeling of insecurity was engendered amongst them. The British civil authorities in India played upon these fears to teach a lesson to "the seditious Hindus", and Lord Minto encouraged the Muslim leadership to seek separate electorate. They now sought representation on the basis of separate electorate with weightage, which was conceded to them by the Britishers in 1909 and later on sealed by a pact between Hindu and Muslim leaders in 1916 at Lucknow. But the spectrum of a permanent minority status in any political arrangement based on election now began to haunt and plague the minds of the Muslim intelligentsia.

British Domination

The British domination produced still another kind of reaction amongst the Muslim elite. Brooding over lost glory and pre-eminence vintage had now begun. The Wahabi movement had, no doubt, petered out, but the quest was not over. The *coup de grace* was the abolition of the Turkish Khilafat at the end of the First World War. The Indian Muslims were stirred to a man, as nothing had so stirred them collectively in their long history. The reaction even amongst other pre-eminently Muslim nations had not been as acute as amongst the Muslims of India. The Congress party under the leadership of Gandhiji dovetailed its own non-cooperation movement launched against the British government with the Khilafat movement of the Muslims. But the aims were divergent. In the restoration of the symbolic Khilafat, the Muslims were seeking their own recognition in the body politic of India, whereas the Congress was fighting for the nebulous idea of self-government. Muslim fundamental ideas of adapting and propagating the ancient mores of the faith got a fillip during the movement Tabligi Anumans, or proselytizing societies were formed during this period. Customs as had grown in India were being considered "un-Islamic" from the orthodox point of view and were frowned upon and the Muslims masses were advised to eschew them. Maulana Abul Kalam Azad gave a call for setting up theological courts for the Muslims under an Amir in each province and district, with an elected All-India Amir-i-Hind. Interestingly, even during Muslim rule such a call had never gone forth and was never thought of by Muslim rulers. It was in this context that Maulana Hasrat Mohani, a Muslim divine, mooted the idea of a separate holy-land, Dar-ul-Din for the Muslims, a romantic idea indeed where the Muslims would practise the tenets of the faith strictly. It, however, did not catch the imagination of the Muslim masses as it was considered too idealistic. Moreover, the enlightened Muslims along with Hindu liberals were against any mass agitation. The history of French Revolution had shown that mass hysteria was easy to generate but difficult to control and in the long run it strengthened the very forces it sought to destroy. After the collapse of the Khilafat movement due to Turkey being declared a secular State by Kamal Ata-Turk in 1924, the British civilian authorities actively played at Hindu-Muslim differences. The era of Hindu-Muslim strife began thereafter.

The Hindu leaders were also to be blamed for this sorry development. Apart from pinpricks like the Suddhi movement started by Arya Samaj to match against the Muslim proselytizing zeal, they failed to assure enlightened Muslim opinion of equal partnership in any future political arrangement.

A powerful unitary State of Roman-Teutonic mould on parliamentary pattern had taken such a hold on Indian mind that they could not envisage any other political system. Later on, the more radical amongst them began to mouth socialistic shibboleths without spelling out what they meant by these. Their talk of abolishing all intermediaries in land-tenure system further alarmed the Muslim landed aristocracy who thought it to be primarily directed against their economic interests. Had a truly federal polity with small viable States and with plenary and residuary powers freely federating into a unity with overriding powers for purposes like defence or foreign affairs, been enunciated, the fears of Muslims of being in a permanent minority status would have been largely allayed. For, then, in many of the states, the Muslims would have been in majority, being able to fashion their lives according to their choice. To buttress this arrangement, perhaps, a high-powered- council something like the privy council of England or simply an upper chamber of legislature-elected on the basis of an economic collegium, i.e., representatives of associations of economic interests like farmers, labourers, entrepreneurs, professionals, etc., could have been envisaged. The idea is not at all novel. Modern thinkers seized with problems of international strife, recurring wars, and minority trouble have on many occasions contributed ideas for solution of the same. Aristocracies and oligarchies are bad but democracy of the western pattern is also full of pitfalls. Its capacity to bring sunshine in the life of the common man has proved more illusory than real. Perhaps a mixture of collective will and practical wisdom - what Santayana calls, "Timocracy" and Dewy "Pluralism" -would be the true answer. At least the idea could have been floated for a national debate, but Indian leadership, consisting mainly of lawyers nurtured in British traditions of rule of law and constitutional rigidities, could not have an experimental attitude towards meeting the problem and evolving new solutions. The result was that a fair and just solution, suited to the conditions of Indian polity which would have the effect of reconciling the realities with Muslim aspirations remained elusive.

Not that ideas other than those of a pure parliamentary democracy as the goal of constitutional reforms were unknown. For instance, in 1925, Dr. Annie Besant, in consultation with other eminent Indians, formulated constitutional proposals in the shape of "The Commonwealth of India Bill", in which she upheld the ideal of the ancient village panchayat system. This did not, however, carry mach conviction or commendation. In 1928 was published the Report of the All Parties Conference, popularly known as Nehru Report, which advocated a pure western parliamentary model and it held the field. None of these proposals, however, measured up to the expectation of vocal Muslim intelligentsia. In 1933, Rehmat Ali, a Punjabi graduate from Cambridge, floated the idea of a separate Muslim state in India to be called `Pakistan', formed out of the Punjab, Afghanistan, Kashmir, Sind and Baluchistan. There was a howl of protest, but the more the idea was resisted the more it increased its appeal to the Muslim elite. If the Hindus were so vehemently opposed to the idea, there must be some good in it - so ran the argument in the Muslims minds. "We always resist prohibitions, and yearn for what is denied us", said Spinoza not long ago. It proved true in this case. The British civilian authorities in India were there to play their part in this great divide, not only communally but also emotionally.

The partition of the country came in 1947, not with good grace and goodwill, but accompanied with the worst holocaust in history and exhibition of extreme bestial passions, to the utter shame and sorrow of every Indian. This was the culmination of the 'western cultural trap' in which India had fallen in the nineteenth century, when she was not only conquered militarily, but also emasculated ideologically. She had then accepted the superiority of western ideas and western institutions in political and economic fields unreservedly in preference to her own heritage of institutions. Judged in the western political framework, the Partition might have appeared 'desirable' to the Muslims and 'disastrous' to the Hindus, but in the context of the Indian historical process, this kind of Partition went against the well-established Indian ethos which had prevailed right since the advent of Muslims in India. The Indian sub-continent had not been a stranger to political divisions, but was traditionally used to a meeting of minds and the unity of hearts amongst the different communities inhabiting this land. The political developments culminating in the partition of country in 1947 thus sought to drive a wedge between two parts of the same organic unity, not only politically, but also socially and culturally.

It has to be clearly understood that, in the historical context, India has never been a nation-State of the Western type; the whole concept is alien to its thought processes. To explain this further: in the Indian traditions of thought. Hindu as well as Muslim, man is the measure of things. His freedom is never in question, as he is already free. He partakes of the divine essence. In Muslim theology, he is Asliraf-ul-Makhlukat, the best of God's creation. But since his is a material existence with higher and lower appetites, he must also live a corporate life, a life of discipline and restraint for his own good, as the well-being of all is his own well-being. Social norms are thus forged so that he may not misuse his freedom. For the Indian law-givers, therefore the problem was not of individual freedom for that was self-evident and assured; the problem was of restraint and restriction on possible waywardness and evil propensities that may surface in an atmosphere of unrestrained freedom. In both Hindu and Islamic thinking, therefore, a universal, immutable, moral law, prescribing a code of conduct for the individuals, both for the ruled and the ruling, is most important. This had nothing to do with the chimera of the state, that absolutist institutional monstrosity of Graeco-Roman conception, controlling corporate life in its entirety, apportioning reward and punishment through the coercive apparatus of government, whether operated by an individual or by a class. This was purely a macrocosmic view of social and political organization, and the individual, had little place in it. Therefore, the whole history of western political thought is centered round the struggle for securing individual liberty, and equality in treatment of the ruled by the ruling. When Christianity was accepted by the paganistic Romans, the belief that man was born in sin and had to be redeemed, was adopted and the Church became co-terminus with the state, coalescing and coagulating in its coercive operation.

Historical Materialism

According to Marx, the forces of historical materialism worked for social change, from stage to stage, feudalism, mercantilism and, finally, industrial capitalism. According to Spengler, Toynbee and other Western thinkers, the development occurred in a natural cyclic order. However, both the systems of thought are agreed on one point: the quest of individual freedom has been the goal. According to Spengler, society moves in the vicious circle of rise, apex and decline, and since capitalism is the stage of apex, its decline will mean descending into barbarism again. On the other hand, the Marxists assert that the state cannot wither away and human freedom assured, unless the means of production and coercive apparatus of the state are completely in the hands of the actual producers. However, by 'producers' Marx does not mean the peasants whom he saw as so many potatoes in a sack, incapable of political organization. Marx saw British mission in India as of destruction and regeneration of old Asiatic social order and the creation of a materialistic society for the Asian people by atomization of the old communal and corporate social life, provoking class consciousness and leading ultimately to a voluntary- corporate structure of communism. Whichever way we look - whether in the Marxian or a non-Marxian direction, the transformation of the old social structure of the East on Western pattern seems to lead to the emergence of fragmentary groups based on creed, language, race, or merely the memories of old racial and historical animosities, all seeking absolutist power of the Nation State, as an index of freedom and of self-development on the western institutional model. It is in this vow of the matter that the situation may be characterised historically as the Easterners falling in 'Western cultural trap'. This has meant an intellectual subjugation of the East to the West. The Western model had been the product of the peculiar socio-religious milieu of these societies. Its blind imitation could be no solution of the problems of organization and power structure in the Asian societies.

India, though in size and population equal to Europe, is different from Europe in the sense that, in spite of its political divisions, and diversities of race, creed and language, it is a unity, verily a commonalty with an outlook on life, all its own. Its social division into castes and communities might be rigid and irreversible, but within the given social group, it does not admit of social inequality based on riches and power, as these are considered to be ephemeral and individual peculiarities which do not influence the corporate life. In Ginsberg's phrase, it is 'the consciousness of kind' and it is this which brings together the individuals of a group into ties of fellowship. Since such social groups cannot function in isolation in economic and political fields, they have to enter into mutual relationship with other groups, and build up a federal polity. In this scheme of things, political and economic power have to become functional, as a means and not an end in themselves. On the other hand, western societies, since the medieval times, functioned on the basis of Estates - the nobility, the Church, and the commoners - all mutually exclusive, the first two being repositories of state power and of wealth, the third Estate, whenever the first Estate, the general mass of the commoners, being nothing but the means to such power and riches. The history of modern Europe is thus a history of the struggle for ending the servile state of the commoners, and of capturing or at least sharing the state power monopolised by the first two Estate, the nobility, has been accommodating as in England, wherever the stranglehold of the organized Church has been broken or at least loosened as in the Teutonic countries (including England where the Church was nationalized) the transition to democratic equality has not been so bloody and bitter as in France where the nobility and the Church refused to give up their privileges. This led to deist and even atheist movements, enthroning reason in place of faith, and raising equality to be the very principle of life. It was this struggle for state power the key to economic prosperity and social advancement - that gave rise to various Nation States in Europe, each developing according to its own instincts and character. Thus, in England, the long struggle for securing the right of 'being judged by ones' peers', and of 'being governed not by men but laws' - the twin pillars of individual liberty - was the peculiar expression of the English national character of reconciling two extremes by balance and harmony reconciling the despotism of the Roman system with conception of individual liberty as enshrined in the Common Law. However, rule of law can operate only among those people who habitually respect law and are obedient to it. In 1836, monarchical England appeared "much more republican than the Helvetic Republic" of Switzerland to Tocqueville, that discerning French observer.

This does not, however, mean that other democratic countries have had no rule of law. This only means that other peoples have not had that peculiarly legalistic approach in their institutional framework which comes so naturally to the English people. Those who imitate the English without acquiring this trait of theirs are bound to come to grief sooner or later: without respecting and abiding by law habitually means turning such an empty rule of law into a rule of lawlessness. That national character persists in spite of changes in political framework - can best be illustrated by the example of France. The French people in their revolutionary zeal tried to smash all the old idols of the French polity, but they could not still change their own nature which asserted in the personality of Napolean, at once the restorer of ancient regime as well as the preserver of the Revolution. His conseil revived the Conseil du Roi of the monarchy, and his prefects were true copies of royal Intendants. The Code de Napolean fuses together strong elements of monarchical despotism with the creed of Jacobinism. Yet, France is as much a democratic country where individual liberties are valued as in England, even though the means by which these liberties are obtained and preserved are not the same as those of the English.

European Concept

The Indian tradition defies the feature of European concept of a nation-State or a conglomeration of nation-States. Yet it is a nation with well-defined geographical boundaries, and the nostalgia of a common historical past, a common legacy of social corporate life and above all a common outlook on life where the same values are cherished in one part of the country as in another. As we have already shown. India can appropriately be described as a federal social polity, being multilingual, multi-racial and multi-religious with a common outlook on life, the characteristics which, on the analogy of what is termed by Trevelyan as "Englishry" we can term as "Indianry". The various religious, racial and linguistic groups are the warp and woof of the Indian texture, and one cannot cut them asunder without damaging the rampant. The Hindus cannot wish away the Muslims, their own blood brothers; and the Muslims cannot but be haunted by their common ancestors. Memories of the past cannot be obliterated by a political brush, nor can future be built up on sands of unrealities and with imported bricks. No political, social or economic framework in Indian sub-continent can be enduring unless erected according to the genius, instincts, and character of the people inhabiting herein.

Teachings of Islam : The Answer

The teachings and glories of Islam belong to the entire mankind; they are no longer the exclusive preserve of those who profess Islam formally. Islam, in its wisdom meditates not on death but on life and seems to do away with that supine passivity which, had become the hallmark of the typical oriental mind. Its meteoric rise and acceptance owes much to its dynamic concept of life, and continuous action for fulfilment of a just and moral order. Here virtue is synonymous with strength - as implied in faith, character, and the will to succeed. Yet Islam enjoins on its followers the need to eschew arrogance of power and cultivate a temper of humility. These characteristics of Islam, therefore, lent a variety and colour to Indian life and have acted through the centuries as a desirable counterpoise to the Hindu conception of tranquility or repose. It is in this sense that Vivekanand, one of the noblest sons of India whose heart bled at the degeneration of his countrymen, advised Indians to have 'an Islamic body with a Vedantic heart', Indo-Islamic fusion, if viewed and promoted properly can become a mighty force in Asia and can match with the prevailing superiority of the West. Indeed, it may be in the interest of human mind itself to pursue a model combining intellectual adventure with moral restraint - verily, knowledge with reverence, as Tennyson said:

> "Let knowledge grow from more to more
> But more of reverence in us dwell."

The unbridled growth of knowledge about nature and the way she works has led to technological advancement and growing mechanization of life. However, this has bred not only an insatiable greed for gratification of senses, but also the arrogance of a rationalist and agnostic conscience. Without a feeling of submission to and humility towards the universal law which science unfolds - but which it cannot substitute - the stately cannot be a substitute-peace that comes of enlightenment has generally eluded the western world. "Learning conquers or mitigates the fear of death and adverse fortune" said Bacon, quoting Virgil's lines:

"Happy the man who has learned the causes of things and put under his feet all fears, and inexorable fate, and noisy strife of the hell of greed".

By "learning" Becon meant learning the secrets of nature by scientific method of which he was a pioneer in the western world. But his prophecy was not fulfilled largely because of the absence of moral temper in a social order built entirely on the might of scientific development. In spite of a loud commitment to social justice, the world remains sharply divided into two rival camps: privileged and unprivileged, the former ever piling the load of injustices on the latter.

It is in these respects, namely, the establishment of an omnipresent moral order and of compelling social justice, that Islam can continue to make a valuable contribution. But it must speak in a connotative idiom of vide acceptance. Viewed in this light, this is what the Islamic tradition of India has to offer and to show to the world. The Indian Muslims, about one third of the total Muslim population of the world, live in India intermingled with peoples of another ancient vintage, the intermingling producing a single stream of consciousness. We have tried to show in these pages the basic unity of the two, and their common approach to life and its problems, overriding geographical frontiers and artificial barriers. No force can dim the glow of Islam in India, lighted and spread by Muslim divines and Sufi saints. Even though religious fundamentalism is on the rise, there is enough room for optimism. It is important to remember that, in their basic philosophies, both Hinduism and Islam give primacy to the individual - the organization comes later. By a strange coincidence, this eternal truth, preached by Hindu seers and derived through Islamic Revelations, is now being discovered so very painfully in the West. Greater the sophistication in technology, greater the importance of man at the machine, rather than of the machine itself. The fetters binding down the individual are now loosening. Western thinkers are veering round to the oriental view that state, instead of being an obstreperous giant commanding unquestioned obedience must act now as trustee and servant in the interest of individual men and women and hold the universe, in the words of Chesterton, "as an adventure rather than a scheme", a view as continually held in the orient. We should no longer, as Emerson advised, allow "things to be in saddle and ride mankind", but soar our spirit to a life sublime. A proper understanding of our past is the surest way to build confidence for the future. This can provide a sense of strength despite the recent trends which seem to tear apart the fabric of the Indian polity. We can then imbibe the Greek poet's view of life, still full .

Ten

Conclusion

In the current political scenario the sectarian and communal forces are damaging the socio-religious fabric of the Indian society. Religious tolerance, an old tradition of the country is dying away. In such a situation secularism has got enormous significance for maintaining peace and harmony as an antidote. Maulvi Khuda Bakhsh Khan, the Founder of the Library had been advocating national integration and communal harmony throughout his life. The Library has also played a vital role in bridging the communal gap through its activities and rich collection presenting a secular outlook. In view of the communally charged atmosphere and the enlightened approach of the Founder it was decided to promote the cause of pluralistic society of India. With this intention we held a series of lectures on Secularism in India to discuss its various dimensions and to air a message of love. A coterie of intellectuals was invited from within and outside the State of Bihar. Five could turn up to share their views on the topic.

The word 'Secularism' has been used frequently after partition. It gets further momentum whenever there is a communal tension. What does it mean? What is the concept of secularism?

There is no agreed definition of secularism in the literature of law and social sciences. It has different connotations in different countries at different times. Let us see how it has been explained in various reference sources.

Secularism is described in *Webster's Third International Dictionary* "as a view of life of any particular matter based on the premise that religion and religious considerations should be ignored or purposely excluded or as a system of social ethics based upon a doctrine that ethical standards and conduct should be determined exclusively without reference to religion." The Compact Edition of the *Oxford English Dictionary* defines secularism as "the doctrine that morality should be based solely on regard to the wellbeing of mankind in the present life, to the exclusion of all considerations drawn from belief in God or in a future state." *The Encyclopaedia Britannica* explains secular as "non-spiritual, having no concern with religious or spiritual matters." It is used in the wider sense of "anything which is distinct, opposed to or not connected with religion or ecclesiastical things, temporal as opposed to spiritual or ecclesiastical." It has been described in *Encyclopaedia of Religion and Ethics* "as a movement, intentionally ethical, negatively religious, with political and philosophical antecedents." All these definitions and explanation lay stress on temporal, worldly or materialist approach of life and ignore the spiritual or religious postulates.

This is a western concept of secularism, which separates religion from the State. There is a complete segregation between the two. This concept of secularism was developed in Europe out of the conflict between the Church and the State so as to curb the authority of the former. It owes its name and in large measure its existence to the life and labours of George Jacob Holyoake born in Birmingham in 1817. He coined the term secularism in 1851 after some hesitation as to the merits of 'netheism' and 'limitationism' as alternatives, as best indicating that province of duty which belongs to the life.' (*Encyclopaedia of Religion and Ethics*). This was in fact a protest movement against religion. This interpretation of secularism does not find any place in Indian social order. Although it was derived from the west it never intended to be anti-religious, agnostic or irreligious. India is basically a multi-religious, multi-racial and multi-linguistic state. Religion has been a dominant factor in the life of an Indian from birth to death and even after death. Anti-religious concept of secularism is out of place in the Indian context. It is explained in Indian framework as *'Sarva-*

dharma Samabhava' i.e. equal respect to all religions. Is this interpretation of secularism practicable? Can this be executed? A believer will always attach more importance and respect to his own faith. Dr. Bindeshwar Pathak, Founder of Sulabh Movement, rightly comments in his article 'Secularism - Precept and Practice' in the book *Secularism: Concept and Practice*, edited by A.K. Lal, that 'it is quite natural for a Hindu to respect his religion more than others. This is true of the practitioners of other religions also. Therefore, to say that state leaders will have equal respect to all is farce.' Respect to all religions (but not equal respect) is a viable explanation of the term. The first part of Quranic Ayah 109 of Surah Al-Anam also teaches not to condemn other's religion. It states "And abuse not those whom they call upon besides Allah lest exceeding the limits, they abuse Allah through ignorance."

India is a coexistent society and the people were living cordially since the time immemorial. The pluralism has been a special feature of the country. It was during the British Raj that seed of hatred and animosity was sown in the hearts of Hindus and Muslims to achieve their ulterior motive. They subjugated the Indian nation following their 'divide and rule' policy. The two nation theory was an outcome of the then prevalent situation which resulted in the partition of the country. The framers of Indian Constitution having full cognizance of the political scenario and also the infrastructure of Indian polity and ethos made in the constitution provisions of Justice, social, economic and political: Liberty of thought, expression, belief, faith and worship: Equality of status and of opportunity. The word secularism did not appear initially in the constitution yet its character was secular to meet the diversity of the country. Almost 27 years after the promulgation of the Constitution on 26th Jan. 1950 the word 'Secular' was for the first time incorporated in 1976 during emergency as 42nd amendment in the preamble of the Constitution. This was simply a political motive to appease Muslims rather to befool them to win their votes. Objectively speaking, it could not bear any fruit, the situation remained the same rather it went to worst. The time witnessed that Hindu orthodoxy and religious fanaticism razed the 500 years old historical Babri Masjid down to the ground in the presence of the guardians of law. The whole episode has not shaken only Indian Muslims from their roots but the Muslims at large. A majority of sensible Hindus treated it as the complete failure of Indian democracy. This was sheer disrespect to our Constitution. Christians are now the target of Hindutva. Both of them have developed a fear psyche and lost confidence in their so-called leaders. Their religion, worshipping places and personal laws all are in danger.

Muslims are the second majority. Those who aspire for one religion, one rule are living in the fool's paradise. India is a pluralistic society. Diversity in unity is its speciality and beauty and it will continue till the doomsday. The people should be very careful as the constitution is under revision. The malicious intentions should be defeated by all means. Its secular nature is to be retained.

Secularism is a vague word having various interpretations and explanations. But one thing is very clear that there will be no religion of the state. It should be impartial to all the religions and even to the religion of the head of the state. It is essential for the progress of the country and a friendly environment that all the communities should prosper as per their constitutional rights.

Secularism is understood as antithesis of communalism. But it has lost its real value to curb sectarianism and promote communal harmony. The malady is, in fact, not in secularism, it is more in its implementation. All the rights guaranteed in the constitution should not be infringed by anyone. The constitutional provisions should be put into practice. Nevertheless, the dishonest and corrupt politicians with selfish motive, who are running the country, are one of the root causes of most of the evils. Judiciary must have the supremacy. But the reform is not possible on only legal plane. Social orientation of masses is also important to make them aware of their legal rights, moral values and religious toleration. No religion ever teaches hatred or animosity. It always communicates love, cordiality and fraternity. It is the politics of hatred which divides people on any pretext for power, lust and fame. A careful vigil and conscience can solve the problem.

Bibliography

Allman, G. J. *Greek Geometry from Thales to Euclid*, Dublin, 1889.

Al-Tabri: *Tarikhul Rasool wa-al-Mulk*

Arnold, T. W. *Preaching of Islam*, 2nd edit., London, 1913.

Bacon: *True Greatness of Kingdom*.

Bakr, A. B. M., *Islam's Influence on Indian Subcontinent*, Adam Publications, Srinagar, 2002.

Bar Hebraeus. *Chronicon Ecclesiasticum*, ed. J. B. Abbeloos et T. J. Lamy, Louvain, 1872-7.

Bevan, E. R. *House of Seleucus*, London, 1902.

Bhatt Bana: *Harshacharita*.

Book of Prayers: xxxvii.

Bouyges, A. M. *Sur le de Scientiis d'Alfarabi*, Beyrouth, 1924.

Brihidaranyak Upanishad.

Brooks, E. W. *Vitae Virorum Apud Monophysitas Celeberrimorurn*, Paris, 1907.

Catholic Emancipation Act, 1829.

Caetani, L. *Annali dell' Islam*, Milano, 1905-7.

Cambridge History of India, Cambridge, 1922.

Carra De Vaux. *Penseurs d' Islam*, Paris, 1921-8.

Christensen, *L'empire des Sasanids* in Jour. Assoc. Iran.

Crum, W. E. *Severe d'Antioche an Egypte*, in *Rev. Orient. Chert*.

Cumont. L., *Egypte des Astrologues*, Bruxelles, 1937

Denha, *Histoire de Marouta*, Diehi, Justinien, Paris, 1901.

Dewy: *Reconstruction*.

Doughty, C.M. *Travels in Arabia Deserta*, London, 1923.

Droysen, J. G. *Gesch. de Hellenismus*, Gotha, 1877-9.

Dulsem, P. *La Systeme du Monde*, Paris, 1915.

Durant Will: *Story of Philosophy*.

El-Beladhuri. *Kitab futuh al-buldan, Liber expugnationis regionum*, ed. J. de Goeje, Leiden, 1868.

Elias of Nisibis, Opus Chronologicum, Paris, 1909-11.

Fay, C.R.: *Great Britain from Adam Smith to the Present Day*.

Genesis: 1:25.

Goodspefd, *Athanasius (of Antioch), Conflict of Severus, PO*.

Harnack, A., *Lehrbuch der Dogmengeschichte*, Freiburg, 1894.

Hauser, *Ueber das Kitab al-hijar*, Erlangen, 1922.

Havell: EB *Indian Architecture*.

Hffele, C, J., *History of the Christian Church Councils*, English, Edinburgh, 1871-83.

Hirschberg, J., *Geschichte d. Augenheilkunde*, Leipzig, 1899-1918.

Hogarth, D. G., *The Nearer East*, London, 1905.

Holy Quran: Eng. Trs. by Abdullah Yousuf Ali.

Huart, C., *Histoire des Arabes*, Paris, 1911-12.

Inostranzev. *Iranian influences on Moslem literature*, Bombay, 1918.

James William: *Pragmatism*.

Janus, "*Zeitschrift fur Geschichte und Litt. des Medizin*," Leiden, 1924.

John, D., In *Migne Patrologia Graeca*.

Joshua The Stylite. *The Chronicle of Joshua the Stylite*, ed. W. Wright, Cambridge, 1882.

Jras., *Journal of the Royal Asiatic Society*, periodical, London.

Kant: *Eternal Peace & Other Essays*.

King, L.W., and Thompson, H.R. *Sculptures and Inscriptions of Darius the Great on the Rock of Behistan*, London, 1907.

Kularnava Tantra: Chapter XVII.

Labourt, J., *Le Christianisme dans l'Empire Perse*, Paris, 1904.

Land, J.P.N., *Anecdota Syriaca*, Leiden, 1862.

Leclerc, L. *Histoire de la Medicine Arabe*, Paris, 1876.

Loew, *Aramaische Pflanzennamen*, 1881.

MacDonald, D.B., *Development of Muslim Theology*, London, 1903.

Majumdar, Raychaudhari & Dutt, *An Advanced History of India*.

Maneckji Nusservanji D., *Zoroastrian Civilization*, New York, 1922.

Mas'udi. *Muruj adh-Dhab*, text trs. B. de Maynard et P. de Courteille, Paris 1861-71.

Meyer, E. Von. *Gesch. der Botanik*,Leipzig, 1856.

Mieli, A., *Pagine di Storia Della Chimica*, Roma, 1922.

Moti Chand, *History of Benaras*

Muir, Sir William, *The Caliphate, its Rise, Decline, and Fall*. London, 1891.

Muller, M., *Die Quaestiones Naturales des Abelardus von Bath*, Munster, 1934.

Nau, F., *Documents pour servir a l'histoire de l'Eglise Nestorienne*, in *PO*., xiii, fasc. 2, Paris.

Nicholson, R.A. *Literary History of the Arabs*, 4th Ed., London, 1922.

Ordeal of Richard Feverl.

Pagel, Einfuhrung in *die Gesch. der Medizin*, Berlin, 1898.

Politics, 1.13.

Procopius. Ed. *Dindorf, Corpus Script. Hist. Byzant*., Bonn, 1833-8.

Purgiter, *Ancient Indian Historical Tradition*, 1922.

Raymond, A. *Histoire des Sciences Exactes et Naturelles*, Paris, 1924.

Romain Rolland, *The Hellenic-Christian Mysticism*.

Romances. 309.

Sarkar, J.N., *Fall of the Moghal Empire.*

Sedillot, *Prolegomenes des Tables Astronomiques d'Oloug-Beg*, Paris, 1853.

Siddique, *Life of Muhammad.*

Smith, D. E., *History of Mathematics*, New York, 1923-25.

Socrates, *Ecclesiatica Historia*, ed. Oxford, 1844.

Spengler, *Decline of the West.*

St. Luke: 14:23.

Stapleton & Azo-Hussain, *Chemistry in Iraq and Persia in the Tenth Century*, Calcutta, 1927.

Steines, H. *Die Mu'taziliten oder die Freidenker in Islam*, Leipzig, 1865.

Strzygowski, J. *Der Ursprung des Christlichen Kirchenkunst*, 1919. Eng. trs. Dalton, Origin of Christian Church Art, 1923.

Swetashwatar Upanishad, VI. 5.

Tannery, P. *Recherches sur l'Histoire de l'Astronomie Ancienne*, Paris, 1893.

Tarachand: *Society and State in the Mughal Period.*

Thapar Romila: *The Past and Prejudice*, Publications Division, New Delhi.

Thomas, J. *Selections illustrating the History of Greek Mathematics*, Loeb Classical Library, 1941.

Trevelyan: *English Social History.*

Uttapalacharya: *Sivashtrotam*

Warmington, E. H. *The Commerce between the Roman Empire and India*, 1928.

Wiberg, J. *The Anatomy of the Brain in the Works of Galen and 'Ali' Abbas*, in *Janus*, 1914.

Wieleitner, H. *Gesch. der Malhematik*, Berlin, 1921.

William James: *Varieties of Religious Experiences.*

Index

A

Abbasid Caliphs (Abbasid Khalifas), 8, 89, 198
Abbasid·, 76
Abbasid Rulers, 8
Abdali, Ahmad Shah, 124, 139
Abu Bakr, 129
Abul Fazal, 187
Afghanistan, 191, 294, 300
Afghans, 122
Africa, 173, 191
Agra, 212
Ahmedabad Mill Workers' Satyagraha, 214
Aibak, Qutubuddin, 80, 193, 204
Akbar, 22, 78, 79, 81, 108, 205, 207-209, 212, 228
Alberuni, 72, 139, 143
Alamgir, 56
Allahabad, 51
Ambedkar, BR, 279, 280, 282-284
Ameer Ali, 68
Arab Merchants, 101
Arabia, 7, 23, 102, 112, 115, 127, 132, 133, 152, 153, 169, 191
Arabian Culture, 194
Arabs, 1, 7, 9, 20, 127, 151, 155, 194, 249
Arjun, King, 12
Arya Samaj, 146, 299
Aryan Law, 2
Aryans, 16, 173-175, 273, 274
Asia, 306
Assam, 52, 60
Asoka, 18, 228
Asoka's Rule, 18
Aurangzeb, 22, 54, 59-65, 79, 81 82, 123, 209, 210
Aurelius, Marcus, 71
Azad, Maulana Abdul Kalam, 298

B

Babar, 81, 184, 186, 205, 208, 211
Babri Masjid, 311
Baghdad, 8, 70, 82, 194, 198, 255
Bahadur Shah, 148
Bahmani Kingdom, 84, 156
Bahmani Kings, 208
Balban, 50, 51, 204, 208
Baluchistan, 191, 300
Benaras, 11, 79, 80, 156
Battle of Kerbala, 7
Bengal, 52, 102, 105, 244, 263, 286, 289-291
Bhakti Movement, 275
Bhakti Saints, 163
Bihar, 11, 23, 52, 244, 309
Bijapur, 123, 156
Bill of Rights, 90
Brahminical Law, 2

Brahmins, 7, 74, 91, 151, 156, 175, 178, 274
Britain, 110
British Rule, 276
Buddha, Lord, 19, 46, 79, 80, 157, 174, 178, 227, 247, 248
Buddhism, 4, 18, 19, 79, 155, 157, 179,195, 196, 227, 247, 275, 281
Buddhist Kingdoms, 15
Buddhist Revolution, 1, 2, 4, 6
Buddhist Monks, 11
Buddhists, 21, 35
Bud Shah, 157
Bukhari, Syed Jalal, 270
Burma, 108
Byzantine Empire, 115, 229

C

Calcutta, 52
Cambodia, 179
Caracalla, 258
Central Asia, 5, 7, 10, 108, 153, 179, 211, 248
Central Asian Barbarians, 114
Central Minorities Commission, 36
Ceylon, 108, 243, 295
Chaitanya, 6, 145, 149, 200, 252, 253, 271
Chalukyas, 122
Champaran Satyagraha, 214
Chandalas, 177
Chandragupta, 46
Chaturvarnaya, 73
Chaudhary, Asutosh, Sir, 52, 53
Chauhans, 11, 262
China, 8, 100-103, 106, 108, 109, 112, 130, 137, 141, 179, 243, 266
Chinese Technology of making Steel, 108
Chirag Ali, 68
Chirag, Shaikh Nasiral Din, 261
Chisti, Abdul Rehman, 209
Chisti Shaikh Salim, 261
Chisti, Khwaja of Ajmer, 270
Chelmsford Lord, 278
Cholas, 10, 11, 102, 115, 122
Christian Council, 24
Christian Countries, 1, 113
Christian Missionaries, 34, 276, 277
Christian Monasticism, 4
Christianity, 33, 34, 87, 129, 137, 143, 234, 247, 254, 302
Christians, 8, 21, 35, 39, 87, 89, 129, 191, 228, 229, 279, 290, 312
Code of Civil or Common Law, 69
Columbus, 102, 114

D

Dadu, 149
Dalits, 272, 273, 276, 277, 281-284
Dar-ul-Islam, 149
Deccan, 162, 208, 212
Delhi Sultanate, 83, 169, 173
Dravidian Culture, 18

E

East India Company's Charter, 289
East Indies Malaysia, 102

Egypt, 12, 129, 130, 139, 173, 176, 258, 259, 267
Eknath, 200, 253
England, 15, 39, 102, 103, 105, 110, 112, 119, 122, 124, 125, 288, 290, 294, 296
Europe, 6, 21, 70, 100, 101, 105, 106, 108, 110, 111, 150, 197, 288, 303, 304

F

Farid Baba, 165, 256, 270
Fatimid Khalifas of Egypt, 89
First World War, 298
France, 98, 118, 305
French Revolution, 299
Fundamental Rights, 30

G

Gaekwad of Baroda, 278
Gandhi, Mahatma, 17, 28, 53, 214-216, 223
Gangey, 11, 80
Germany, 127
Ghaus, Mohammad, 270
Ghazanavis (Ghaznavides), 11, 159, 192, 203
Ghazni, Muhammad, 139
Ghazni's Invasion, 4
Ghori, Mohammad, 12, 193, 200
Gokhale, Gopal Krishna, 213, 214
Golkunda, 123, 156
Govt. of India Act, 1935; 280
Greece, 136
Greeks, 74
Gujarat, 10, 12, 20, 102, 105, 108, 154, 169, 188
Gujarati Saints, 169
Gulbadan, 186
Gupta Rulers, 84
Gurdwaras, 55
Guru Angad, 257
Guru Arjun Dev, 257, 295
Guru Granth Saheb, 257
Guru Nank, 6, 144, 149, 200, 255-57, 271
Guru Ram Dass, 257

H

Hadith, 260, 265
Haj, 38
Haridas, Thakur, 201
Harshvardhana, King, 19, 128
Hastings, Warren, 81, 293
Havell, 3, 6
Henery VIII, 15
Hindu Civilization, 142, 143
Hindu India, 173
Hindu Rulers (Hindu Rajas), 60, 73
Hinduism, 16-19, 34, 37, 46, 65, 77, 79, 137, 142, 154-57, 217, 243, 270, 275, 281-84, 307
Hindus, 2, 13, 18, 21, 24, 26, 27, 56, 57, 61, 71, 72, 81, 89, 90, 93, 94, 139, 142, 143, 148, 151, 154, 158-60, 168, 169, 173, 195, 200, 211, 219, 228, 246, 263, 270, 271, 293, 294, 296
Hieum Tsang, 7, 19
Human Rights & Minority Rights Declaration & Conventions of UN, 43
Humayun, 205, 208, 211
Hussain Shah, 79, 295
Hyder Ali, 285

I

Iltutmish, 50, 77, 204, 205, 208
Imperial Library, 52, 209
Imperial Pratiharas, 122
Indian Constitution (Constitution of India), 29, 30, 42, 211, 212, 218-227, 230-240, 279-283
Indian Democracy, 312
Indian Economic System, 286
Indian Goods, 7
Indian Muslims, 139, 142, 153, 298, 309
Indian National Congress, 25, 26
Indian Polity, 308, 311
Indian Statutory Commission, 278
Indonesia, 39, 102
Industrial Revolution, 290
Iran, 9, 23, 50, 112, 173
Ireland, 238
Islam, 1, 2, 3, 5, 6, 8, 10, 12, 13, 16, 19, 21, 27, 28, 33, 37, 51, 66, 68, 69, 76, 77, 83, 90, 133, 137-43, 145, 149, 154, 155, 157, 183, 190, 194, 195, 229, 245, 258, 270, 275, 305, 307
Islamic Civilization, 8, 156
Islamic Conquest of Persia, 7
Islamic Law (Muslim Law), 21, 50, 206
Islamic Sufism, 46

J

Jagjeevan Ram, Babu, 276
Jahangir, 81, 186, 207, 209, 211, 212
Jai Singh, Raja, 22
Jain Tirthankars, 74
Jainism, 18, 155, 178, 179
Jains, 178
Jalel, Shah, 270
Jama Masjid (Delhi), 65, 212
Jama Masjid (Golkunda), 64
Japan, 243
Java, 10, 141, 179
Jayasi Malik Muhammad, 185
Jehad, 70, 255
Jinnah, MA, 27, 214, 223
Jizia, 206
Judaism, 254
Junagadh, 63

K

Kabir, 6, 23, 144, 149, 200, 249, 250, 252, 271
Kabul, 9
Kaki, Khwaja Bakhtiyar, 170
Kaki, Qutbal Din Bakhtiar, 261
Kanauj, 10. 137
Kanishka, 9
Kashmir, 100, 157, 158, 160, 161, 300
Kasim, Mir, 285
Khadija, 134, 135
Khan, Changiz, 70
Khan, Khana, 184
Khan, Mauli Khuda Bakhsh, 309
Khan, Muhammad Liyakat Ali, 133
Khilafat Movement, 299
Khan, Sir Sayyid Ahmad, 28
Khilji, Alauddin, 21, 50, 51, 71, 77, 82, 84, 204, 208
Khorasan (Khurasan), 7, 196

Khuda Bakhsh, S., 64
Khusro Parvez, 50
Khusru, Amir, 165-67, 171, 184
Kirtivarman, 180
Krishna Bhakti Movement, 168
Kshatriyas, 74, 75, 82, 85, 91, 176, 178, 180, 246, 262, 274

L

Library of Queen Victoria, 52
Lodi, Ibrahim, 79
Lodi, Sikandar, 80

M

Madhya Pradesh, 52, 53
Magadh, 11
Mahakaleshwar Temple (Ujjain), 61
Maharana Pratap, 22
Maharani of Kutch, 64
Mahavir, Lord, 46, 178, 179
Mahayan Buddhism, 247
Mahmud of Ghazni, 10-12, 202
Malaya, 108, 155
Malechha, 177
Malukdas, 144
Malviya, Madan Mohan, 214
Monsabdari System, 91
Man singh, 22
Maratha Army, 109
Marathas, 123, 124
Mathura, 10
Mauryans, 112
Mecca, 12, 129, 255
Medina, 12, 129
Mehta, Phiroz Shah, 213
Mesopotamia, 8, 191, 259
Mexico, 116
Minorities Commission (National Minority Commission), 35, 36
Minority Educational Institutions, 41, 42
Mithila, 11, 263
Moghul Conquerors of India, 6
Moghul Court, 187, 210
Moghul Princes, 185
Mongols, 71, 107
Mughal Empire, 21
Mughal Rulers (Mughal Emperors), 105, 210, 212
Mughals, 46, 108, 151, 184
Muhammad Sa'dullah, 61
Muslim Conquest of India, 5
Muslim Educational Conference, 133
Muslim League, 25, 26, 214
Muslim Marriages, 207
Muslim Personal Law, 68
Muslim rule, 20, 21, 50, 51, 77, 83, 107
Muslim Ruelrs (Muslim Monarchs in India/Muslim Kings), 21, 22, 50, 51, 70, 73, 77, 89, 153, 204, 207, 253, 298
Muslim Saints, 163
Muslim States, 15, 77
Muslim Women in India, 40
Muslims (Muhammedans/Musalmans), 2, 3, 5, 7, 13, 20, 24, 27, 35, 38, 39, 40, 42, 67, 77, 81, 82, 93, 94, 98, 103, 104, 122, 140, 142, 146, 148-150, 152-154, 158, 168, 169, 184, 196, 197, 206, 229, 244, 245, 253, 264, 270, 271, 293, 294, 296-99, 305, 311, 312

Mysore, 53

N

Nadir Shah, 124
Nagar Seth, 62, 106
Namdev, 23, 144, 200
Nasir Shah, Sultan, 169
Nasiruddin, Sultan, 169
National Commission for SC & ST, 36
National Educational Policy, 40
Nehru, Jawaharlal, 26
Nehru Report (Motilal Nehru Committee's Report), 230, 231
Nepal, 11
Nirgun Bhakti, 167
Nizamu-ul-Mulk, 285
Nizamuddin Aulia, 160, 161, 270
Non-Aryans (non Aryan Peoples), 273, 275
Non-Cooperation Movement, 214
Northern India, 156
Nund, Rishi, 1, 5, 9, 16

O

Orissa, 10, 52, 106

P

Pakistan, 25, 27, 28
Palestine, 115
Palas, 10, 11
Pan-Islamic Movement of Jamaluddin Afghani, 67
Papal Supremacy, 113
Parmhans, Ram Krishna, 65
Parsis, 35, 39
Pataliputra, 10
Pathans, 122, 151
Persia, 1, 7, 10, 23, 119, 123, 130, 136, 141, 169, 191, 211, 258, 259
Persian Empire, 102
Persian Poetry, 171
Peru, 116
Pluralism, 29, 32, 272, 300, 311
Prithviraj (Chauhan King), 12
Punjab, 10, 11, 270, 300

Q

Quasim, Mohammad Bin, 20, 151, 153, 173, 191, 192, 202
Quit India Movement, 24
Quran, 2, 5, 17, 19, 23, 38, 50, 68, 76, 78, 86, 150, 187, 204, 260, 265
Quranic Injuctions, 76, 78, 259, 270
Quranic Law, 78
Qutub Minar, 139
Qutubuddin, Mubarak, 82

R

Rabidas, 252
Radha Krishnan, Dr., 225
Rajasthan, 52
Rajgopalachari C, 217
Rajputs, 74, 81, 203
Ramananda, 23, 249, 252
Ramanuja, 248
Ramdas, 200, 253
Ranade, Gobind Mahadev, 65
Rashtrakutas, 10
Red Fort in Delhi, 212
Reign of Sikandar, 158

Roman Bandits, 113
Roman Empire, 111, 129
Romans, 246
Rome, 111, 113, 136
Roy, Rammohan, 65
Rulers of Travancore & Cochin, 238
Russia, 119,124

S

Safdar Jung of Oudh, 285
Sagun Bhakti, 167
Saifuddulah, 285
Saivism, 158
Sakas, 74
Sankaracharya, 52, 180
Sapru, Tej Bahadur, Sir, 54, 55
Satnami Movement, 277
Sayyids, 151
Secularism, 38, 224, 226, 229, 309-312
Shah Alam, 285
Shah Husain, 169
Shahaiyas, 10, 151, 156
Shahjahan, 81. 123. 209. 211
Shershah, 79, 208
Shikoh, Dara, 209, 294
Shivaji, 22
Shudras, 175-77, 247, 274
Sikandra, 212
Sikkim, 143, 200, 281
Sikhs, 35, 39
Simon Commission, 278, 279
Sindh, 1, 20, 164, 173, 300
Sindhia, Mahadji, 207
Sir Syed, 66, 67
Som Nath, 12
South India, 154
Spain, 100, 141, 191, 266
Srichand, 257
State Minorites Commission, 36, 37
Suddhi Movement, 299
Sufi Philosophy, 163
Sufi Saints, 81, 167, 168, 249, 267
Sufis, 265, 266, 270
Sufism, 168, 185
Suhrawardi, Sheikh Shaftabuddin, 162
Sulabh Movement, 311
Sultan Baba, 165
Sultan Husain, Shargui, 172
Sumatra, 141, 179
Sundar Dass, 253
Surdas, 22
Switzerland, 304
Syed Burhanuddin, 169
Syria, 12, 115, 130, 259

T

Tagore, Rabindranath, 224
Taj Mahal, 212
Tamil Nadu, 247
Temple of Multa, 4
Temple of Someshwar Nath Mahadev, 54
Temple of Somnath, 4
Temple of Thaneswar, 4
Temples of Bhubaneswar, 46
Temples of Khajuraho, 46
Tibet, 243

Tilak, Bal Gangadhar, 213, 214
Timur, 153
Tipu Sultan, 51-54, 140, 285
Transoxania, 191, 196
Travancore Dewaswon Fund, 238
Tudor, Mary, 15
Tughlaq, Firoz, 140
Tughlaq Mohammad, 50, 77, 204, 208
Tukaram, 6, 149, 200, 253
Tulsidas, 22, 253, 254, 271
Turkey, 299
Turkish Empire, 101, 102, 104, 106, 115, 124
Turkish Khilafat, 298
Turkistan, 152
Turko-Afghan Rule, 71
Turko-Afghan Rulers, 72,73, 91, 176
Turko-Afghans, 70, 173
Turks, 46

U

UK, 31
UP, 52, 53
USA, 31, 110
USSR, 31
Ujjain, 61
Ulema, 66, 77, 138, 205
Ummaiyyads, 9
University Grants Commission, 42
Urban Textile Manufacturing Centres, 104

V

Vaishnavism, 79, 179, 252
Vaisyas (Vaishyas), 175-177, 274
Varanasi, 64
Vijaynagar Empire, 84
Vivekananda, Swami, 19, 21, 65, 141, 241

W

Wahabi Movement, 298
West Asia, 20
Western-Eastern Bengal, 10
Western Europe, 103

Y

Yathrib, 190

Z

Zain-ul-Abedin, 79, 157, 160, 207
Zakat, 38
Zamindars, 287, 289
Zamorin, 155
Zorastrianism, 175
Zoroastrians, 7

□□□